T0333812

Systematic Trading

Robert Carver is an independent investor, trader and writer. He spent over a decade working in the City of London before retiring from the industry in 2013. Robert initially traded exotic derivative products for Barclays Investment Bank and then worked as a portfolio manager for AHL – one of the world's largest hedge funds – before, during and after the global financial meltdown of 2008. He was responsible for the creation of AHL's fundamental global macro strategy, and then managed the fund's multi-billion dollar fixed income portfolio.

Robert has Bachelors and Masters degrees in Economics, and is a visiting lecturer at Queen Mary, University of London. He was written three books: *Systematic Trading: A unique new method for designing trading and investing systems* was published by Harriman House in 2015, *Smart Portfolios: A practical guide to building and maintaining intelligent investment portfolios* came out in 2017, and *Leveraged Trading: A professional approach to trading FX, stocks on margin, CFDs, spread bets and futures for all traders* came out in 2019.

He manages his own portfolio of equities, funds and futures using the methods you can find in his books.

Every owner of a physical copy of this version of

Systematic Trading

can download the eBook for free direct from us at Harriman House, in a format that can be read on any eReader, tablet or smartphone.

Simply head to:
ebooks.harriman-house.com/systematictrading
to get your free eBook now.

Systematic Trading

A unique new method for designing trading and investing systems

Robert Carver

Hh

HARRIMAN HOUSE LTD

18 College Street

Petersfield

Hampshire

GU31 4AD

GREAT BRITAIN

Tel: +44 (0)1730 233870

Email: contact@harriman-house.com

Website: www.harriman-house.com

First published in Great Britain in 2015

Copyright © Robert Carver

The right of Robert Carver to be identified as the Author has been asserted in accordance with the Copyright, Designs and Patents Act 1988.

Hardback ISBN: 9780857194459

eBook ISBN: 9780857195005

British Library Cataloguing in Publication Data

A CIP catalogue record for this book can be obtained from the British Library.

Page number cross references refer to the print edition.

"In every case the accuracy of experts was matched or exceeded by a simple algorithm... Why are experts inferior to algorithms? One reason... is that experts try to be clever, think outside the box, and consider complex combinations of features in making their predictions. Complexity may work in the odd case but more often than not it reduces validity."

Daniel Kahneman, *Thinking, Fast and Slow*

Reviews of Systematic Trading by Robert Carver

"A remarkable look inside systematic trading never seen before, spanning the range from small to institutional traders. Reading this will benefit all traders."

Perry Kaufman, author of *Trading Systems and Methods*

"Rob goes into a level of depth which most trading book authors either deliberately avoid or simply lack knowledge of. Rob's background in the industry is beyond reproach and the informational contents of his book shows his experience and depth of knowledge. If you want to enter the professional systematic trading field, Rob's book is a must."

Andreas Clenow, CIO Acies Asset Management
and author of *Following The Trend*

"Being a hedge fund manager myself and having personally read almost all major investment and trading books, this is by far one of the best books I have read in over 15 years on a tough subject for most."

Josh Hawes, Hedge fund manager

"Robert has had very valuable experience working for many years in a large quant hedge fund, which makes the book doubly worth reading.... Well worth a read for anyone who trades, in particular for systematic traders (whether you're a novice or more experienced)!"

Saeed Amen, FX trader and author of *Trading Thalesians*

Preface

Systematic trading and investing

I am very bad at making financial decisions. Like most people I find it difficult to manage my investments without becoming emotional and behaving irrationally. This is deeply irritating as I consider myself to be very knowledgeable about finance. I've voraciously read the academic literature, done my own detailed research, spent 20 years investing my own money and nearly a decade managing funds for large institutions.

So in theory I know what I'm doing. In practice when faced with a decision to buy or sell a stock things go wrong. Fear and greed wash through my mind, clouding my judgment. Even if I've spent weeks researching a company it's still hard to click the trade button on my broker's website. I have to stop myself buying or selling on a whim, based on nothing more than random newspaper articles or an anonymous blogger's opinion. But then, like you, I'm only human.

Fortunately there is a solution. The answer is to fully, or partly, systematise your financial decision making. Creating a trading system removes the emotion and makes it easier to commit to a consistent strategy.

I spent many years managing a large portfolio of trading strategies for a systematic hedge fund. Unfortunately I didn't have the opportunity to develop and trade systems to look after my personal portfolio. But after leaving the industry I've been able to make my own trading process entirely systematic, resulting in significantly better performance.

There are many authors and websites offering trading systems. But many of these 'systems' require subjective interpretation, so they are not actually systematic. Some are even downright dangerous, trading too quickly and expensively, and in excessive size. They present you with a single 'one size fits all' system which won't suit everybody. I will explain how to develop your own trading system, for your own needs, and which should not be excessively dangerous or costly to operate.

I've found systematic investing to be more profitable, and to require less time and effort. This book should help you to reap similar benefits.

Who should read this book

This book is intended for everyone who wishes to systematise their financial decision making, either completely or to some degree.

Most people would describe themselves as traders or investors, although there are no consistently accepted definitions of either group. What I have to say is applicable to both kinds of readers so I use the terms trading and investing interchangeably; the use of one usually implies the other is included.

This book will be useful to amateurs – individual investors trading their own money – and to market professionals who invest on behalf of others. The term 'amateur' is not intended to be patronising. It means only that you are not getting paid to manage money and is no reflection on your level of skill.

This is not intended to be a parochial book solely for UK or US investors and I use examples from a range of countries. Many books are written specifically for particular asset markets. My aim is to provide a general framework that will suit traders of every asset. I use specific examples from the equity, bond, foreign exchange and commodity markets. These are traded with spread bets, **exchange traded funds**[1] and futures. But I do not explain the mechanics of trading in detail. If you are not familiar with a particular market you should consult other books or websites before designing your trading system.

It might surprise you, but this book will also be useful for those who are sceptical of computers entirely replacing human judgment. This is because there are several parts to a complete trading system. **Trading rules** provide a prediction on whether something will go up or down in price. These can be purely systematic, or based on human discretion. But it is equally important to have a good **framework** of position and risk management. I believe that a systematic framework should be used by all traders and investors for position and risk management, even if the adoption of fully systematic rules is not desirable.

If you can beat simple rules when it comes to predicting prices, I show you how to use your opinions in a systematic framework to make the best use of your talents. Alternatively you might feel it is unlikely that anyone, man or machine, can predict the markets. In this case, the same framework can be used to construct the best portfolio consistent with that pessimistic view.

Three examples

Throughout this book I focus on three typical groups of systematic traders and investors. Don't panic if you don't fit neatly into any of these categories. I've chosen them because between them they illustrate the most important issues which face all potential systematic traders and investors.

---

1. All terms in **bold** are defined in the glossary.

In the final part of the book I discuss how to create a system tailored for each of these audiences. Before then, each time you see one or more of these heading boxes it indicates that the material in that section of the book is aimed mainly at the relevant group and is optional for others.

Asset allocating investor

An **asset allocating investor** allocates funds amongst, and within, different **asset classes**. Asset allocators can use systematic methods to avoid the short-term chasing of fads and fashions that they know will reduce their returns. They might be lazy and wise amateur investors, or managing institutional portfolios with long horizons such as pension funds.

Asset allocators are sceptical about those who claim to get extra returns from frequent trading. For this reason the basic asset allocation example assumes you can't forecast how asset prices will perform. However some investors might want to incorporate their views, or the views of others. I show you how to achieve this without overtrading or ending up with an extreme portfolio.

Unlike the other examples asset allocators usually don't use leverage. I illustrate the investment process with the use of unleveraged passive **exchange traded funds (ETFs)**. But the methods I show apply equally well to investors in **collective funds** of both the active and passive varieties, and to those investing in portfolios of individual securities.

My own portfolio includes a basket of ETFs which I manage using the principles of the asset allocating investor.

Semi-automatic trader

Semi-automatic traders live in a world of opportunistic bets[2] taken on a fluid set of assets. Semi-automatic traders think they are superior to simple rules when it comes to forecasting by how much prices will go up or down; instead they make their own educated guesses. However they would like to place those bets inside a systematic **framework** which will ensure their positions and risk are properly managed. This frees them up to spend more time making the right call on the market.

In my example the semi-automatic trader is comfortable with **leverage** and investing with **derivatives**. They are both buyers and sellers, betting for or against asset prices. My semi-automatic trader is active in equity index and commodity spread bet markets, but the example is widely applicable elsewhere.

---

2. I am not using the gambling term 'bet' here in a pejorative sense. In my opinion the distinction some people draw between financial gambling, trading and investing is completely meaningless: they all involve taking financial risk on uncertain outcomes. Indeed professional gamblers usually have a better understanding of risk management than many people working in the investment industry.

I trade a portfolio of UK equities using the framework I've outlined here for semi-automatic traders.

Staunch systems trader

The **staunch systems trader** is a true believer in the benefits of fully systematic trading. Unlike the **semi-automatic trader** and the **asset allocating investor**, they embrace the use of systematic **trading rules** to forecast price changes, but within the same common **framework** for position risk management.

Many systems traders think they can find trading rules that give them extra profits, or **alpha**. Others are unconvinced they have any special skill but believe there are additional returns available which can't be captured just by 'buy and hold' investing. They can use very simple rules to capture these sources of **alternative beta**.

Systems traders may have access to **back-testing** software, either in off-the-shelf packages, spreadsheets or bespoke software. It isn't absolutely necessary to have such programs as I will be providing a flexible pre-configured trading system which doesn't need back-testing. However if you want to develop your own new ideas I will show you how to use these powerful software tools safely.

Like semi-automatic traders, staunch systems traders are comfortable with **derivatives** and **leverage**. Although the examples I give are for futures trading, they are equally valid for trading similar assets.

I trade over 40 futures contracts with my own money using a fully systematic set of eight trading rules.

The technical stuff

Inevitably this is a subject which requires some specialised terminology. Although I try and keep jargon to a minimum it's usually easier to use a well-known shorthand term rather than spelling everything out. Words and phrases highlighted in **bold** are briefly defined in the glossary.

As well as standard finance vocabulary I use my own invented terms. So phrases like **instrument block** are also in bold type, and appear in the glossary with a short explanation. Certain important concepts require deeper understanding and I will include more detail when I first use them, as in the box below.

All detailed explanations in the text are signposted from the glossary, to help you refer to them later in the book.

CONCEPT: EXAMPLE

These concept boxes give detailed explanations of key concepts in the book.

What is coming

Running a systematic strategy is just like following any list of instructions, such as a recipe. Many books on trading are like fast food outlets which give you something quick and convenient to eat from a limited menu. However I am going to help you create your own strategies; this is more than just a cookbook, it's a guide to writing recipes from scratch. Inventing your own system requires extra work upfront, but it is more satisfying and profitable in the long run.

To create your own recipes requires an understanding of the science of food chemistry and of different kinds of dishes. Similarly, part one of this book – 'Theory' – provides a theoretical basis for why you should run systematic strategies and gives an overview of the trading styles that are available.

Part two – 'Toolbox' – provides you with two key methods used in the creation of systematic strategies: **back-testing** and **portfolio optimisation**. Like sharp kitchen knives these are powerful tools, but also potentially dangerous. When misused large trading losses can be made despite apparently promising ideas. I will show you how to use them properly – and when you don't need them.

Part three – 'Framework' – provides a complete and extendable **framework** for the creation of systematic strategies. Finally in part four – 'Practice' – I show three different uses of the framework in action. I illustrate how it can be adapted for each of the **semi-automatic trader**, **asset allocating investor** and **staunch systems trader**.

This book couldn't possibly be a comprehensive guide to the entire subject of trading. Appendix A contains some books I would recommend for further reading and others I've referred to in the text. There is also advice on where you can get data and access to suitable brokers to begin investing systematically.

I've avoided putting mathematical formulas and detailed algorithms into the main text. Instead appendix B contains detailed specifications for the trading rules, appendix C covers portfolio optimisation, and appendix D includes further details on implementing the framework. The website for this book – www.systematicmoney.org/systematic-trading – includes additional material.

This is not a book about automating trading strategies. It's possible to trade systematically using an entirely manual process with just a spreadsheet to speed up calculations, so automation is not necessary. Nevertheless automation is desirable when running fast and complex strategies. My website also includes some details on my own automated system and guidance to help you develop your own.

Contents

Introduction

January 2009

IT WAS 23 JANUARY 2009 AND I WAS IN MY LONDON OFFICE. ALTHOUGH I had a desk overlooking the Thames I was usually too busy to appreciate the view. My day job was managing a portfolio of systematic trading strategies for a large hedge fund. But right now I was focusing on my own bank balance.

Data was about to be released indicating how the UK economy had performed in the last three months of 2008. It would be bad news – the official confirmation that we were in recession – but nobody knew how bad. This didn't mean extra work for me however, since a bank of computers would adjust our clients' portfolios automatically when the news arrived. So I decided to devote some rare free time to trade my own money.

With a stressful full-time job I was not a particularly active trader but very occasionally an opportunity came up that was too good to miss. This was one of them. In my research I found that historically when people's fears were confirmed by terrible economic numbers was often the best time to buy; and this was potentially the worst news I'd seen in my lifetime.

Careful analysis showed that the banks, hardest hit by the financial crisis, should rebound the most if things improved. I was particularly attracted to Barclays. I had traded for their investment bank a few years before and their balance sheet was in relatively good condition. But I also looked at investing in the other major UK banks. In all I was prepared to risk 10% of my portfolio on four banking stocks.

Then the figures came out. They were worse than expected with GDP falling by 1.5%. Barclays dropped 15% almost immediately, taking it to the lowest level I had ever seen. I waited for the market to stabilise and prepared to trade. Then I hesitated. Everything had happened as expected – I should go ahead and buy. But what if this went wrong? What if the financial industry really was imploding, as everyone else seemed to think?

Panicking, I quickly changed my orders, knocking a zero off each so that only 1% of my portfolio was at risk. It was one of the biggest mistakes of my investing career.

FIGURE 1: GOOD TIMING, TINY POSITION, WHEN TRADING BARCLAYS SHARES IN 2009. BARCLAYS SHARE PRICE.

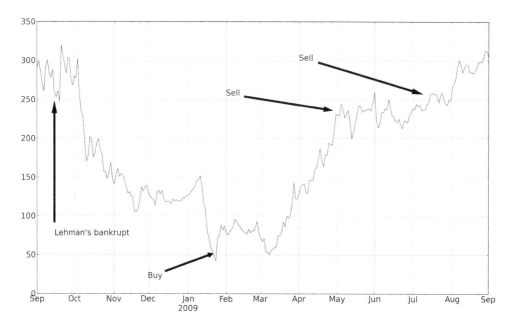

Source: Authors records.

As figure 1 shows, that day I bought Barclays for 53p a share, and just a few months later I sold my shares for an average of £2.50 each. Although Barclays was the top performer, my other bank shares also multiplied in value. I had made a decent profit but my own panic prevented me from making much, much more.

I had planned carefully and meticulously, done everything right, and then at the last moment let my emotions get the better of me.

September 2008

Just a few months earlier I had been sitting in the same office and at the same desk. But on this particular day I had no time to think about my own money. The US government were variously trying to rescue, or had given up on, investment bank Lehman Brothers, insurer AIG, and mortgage agencies Freddie Mac and Fannie Mae. Our computer trading systems continued to run smoothly whilst the markets were in the middle of the most savage moves of a generation. But we had other things to worry about.

Although we were profitable could we trust the banks and brokers with whom we had deposited our cash? What if our clients redeemed their investments to cover holes elsewhere in their portfolio – could we pay them? What if the whole global financial system completely seized up? We were terrified. Perhaps we should just liquidate everything, put our money into gold bars, and wait for the storm to pass. At the very least we considered reducing the risk our computers wanted to take, perhaps by half. One of our main competitors had already done exactly that.

After yet another crisis meeting, where we decided to take no action for now, I left the meeting room and returned to my desk. As I sat down a colleague came over and started typing on my keyboard.

"You'll definitely want to see this," he said. He pressed return, and a live estimate of today's profitability appeared on my screen. For the first time in our firm's history it showed a ten digit number. We had made over a billion dollars in a single day. Our computer system had stuck to its preprogrammed set of trading rules and mechanically exploited the market moves almost to perfection, whilst terrified humans had discussed closing it down.

Humans are better than computers at complex intellectual tasks. But as these two stories show, our emotions prevent us from fully utilising this intelligence. The solution is to use systems to make trading decisions.

Why you should start system trading now

Many people have been using systems to trade in one form or another for decades, but they are still a small minority. Although there are several relatively large systematic hedge funds, including the fund I used to work for, significantly less than 10% of actively managed global assets is fully systematically traded. But the investment world is changing and now is a better time than ever before to consider trading or investing with systems.

Firstly, institutional investors like pension funds have moved away from expensive **active management,** including hedge funds, to cheaper **passive management**. With passive management there is no 'skill' to pay for, less trading and so lower costs. In a low inflation environment active management fees of 1% or more are an intolerable drag on performance, even without the extra 20% of performance charged by hedge funds.

Passive indexing, buying shares or bonds in fixed weights, is effectively a form of systematic trading, albeit a very simple one. I'll show how this concept can be extended and improved in the **asset allocating investor** example.

The returns from hedge funds can be separated into **beta** – what you can get by tracking the market, **alpha** – the skill the hedge fund manager has, and **alternative beta**. An example of alternative beta is the additional return you can get from buying stocks with low price-to-earnings (PE) ratios, and selling those with high PE ratios – the **equity value** premium.

Alternative beta doesn't need skill, but it can't be earned just by buying and holding shares. However it can be produced by following relatively simple rules. Some **collective funds** have been created to allow investors to get access to alternative beta, but they are still relatively expensive. Institutions should seriously consider using systematic rule-based trading to create in-house cheap alternative beta portfolios. The **staunch systems trader** example shows how this can be achieved.

It's also easier than ever for amateurs to invest in a systematic way. Technology has revolutionised the financial industry. In the past amateur investors had to rely on yesterday's newspapers for share prices and news. Now it's possible to download historical price data for free from numerous websites.

Computing power has continued to fall in price and you can run quite sophisticated strategies on $30 Raspberry Pi micro computers. Instead of using expensive full service stockbrokers to place trades, cheap retail brokers allow you to trade at commission levels which are a fraction of what was possible 20 years ago.

There has been an explosion in the availability of numerous retail **passive funds**. In particular a vast array of dirt cheap **exchange traded funds** has appeared, allowing the passive tracking of almost every conceivable financial index. It's much easier to buy and sell securities covering a wider variety of **asset classes** and countries than in the past.

But there have been other developments that are a mixed blessing. Derivatives like contracts for difference and spread bets allow amateurs and professionals to use **leverage** more easily. But unless you are careful these can quickly send your account value to zero, or even below. In the **semi-automatic trader** example I show how discretionary traders can trade in a relatively safe and controlled way by using a systematic **framework** to manage their risk.

The offering of retail stockbrokers has been radically improved. They give you access to websites and apps that make trading as easy as ordering from Amazon. You can find brokers that allow you to submit orders automatically from software, making fully automated trading a possibility. A more recent development is the appearance of online platforms which allow you to easily implement automated strategies.[3]

These are great tools, but they are offered solely to encourage more buying and selling. You should never forget that your broker makes more money when you trade frequently, whilst you lose out unless the extra trades are sufficiently profitable. I'll show in this book how costly overtrading is, and how you to avoid it.

---

3. I'm less keen on the appearance of 'social trading' websites where you 'follow' someone else's trading strategy. It makes no sense to let an unregulated, unqualified and probably inexperienced stranger manage your money; with minimal, statistically insignificant, evidence that they are capable of doing so.

There are now many **back-testing** software packages available. These allow you to test potential strategies to see which made the most hypothetical money in the past. As I will explain in later chapters if you're not careful this will often lead to losing actual money in the present.

Finally, there are many books and websites containing trading systems, advice and guidance for trading, of which more in a moment. So there is no shortage of tools and advice to begin investing systematically, although you do need to be careful as they are lethal if not used safely.

It's dangerous out there

Imagine for a moment you have just walked into a car dealership. Whilst admiring the vehicle on display you are approached by a slick suited salesman.

"This looks great, but it's a bit small for me. What other models do you have?" you ask.

"Actually this is the only model we make," he replies.

"Okay... Would you recommend the convertible, or is the fuel consumption too high?"

"We don't have a convertible."

"Right. How much extra would it cost to get alloy wheels and air conditioning?"

"Nothing. We don't do them."

"Does it come in red?"

"No. Just black."

You'd be pretty surprised. In reality a new car buyer is offered so many options that the possible permutations usually run into millions! Car dealers can do this because cars are *modular* – made up of individual components which can be easily changed. When buying a new car we can specify different engines or add options like a fancy stereo. Later on we can still change certain parts like the tyres.

Now consider the large number of books and websites describing various trading systems. Many are too vague to be considered systematic but others include quite detailed rules. Nearly all of these publicly available trading systems are not modular, and can't be easily adapted. You don't have the opportunity to ask the author questions like:

"I notice you used a 20-day moving average here. When would it make sense to use a 30-day moving average? You say we should put 2.5% of our capital into each trade. Why? What will happen if I put 5% in? I like your trading rules, but how would I use those in my own position management framework? How can I use this to trade gasoline futures?"

I will answer these questions, and many more, later in the book. Now let's return to the imaginary conversation with our hypothetical car dealer.

"How fast does it go?"

"It does exactly 150.6 miles an hour."

"Wow! I bet it drinks fuel at that speed. What's the fuel economy like at 55?"

"No you weren't listening. It always does precisely 150.6. No faster or slower."

"Isn't that a little… dangerous?"

"Well it was fine on the manufacturer's test track."

Once again consider the many publicly available trading systems. Many advocate trading extremely quickly, holding positions for only a few days, minutes or even seconds. In many markets traded by amateur investors that will lead to extremely high trading costs. Frighteningly the majority of trading systems also suggest holding sizable positions which are far too risky unless you know in advance you will be a brilliant trader who is also very lucky. Using these systems is like driving at 200mph and hoping you won't crash or run out of fuel.

To take an example, one expert on spread betting proposes putting at most 10%, but usually 5%, of your capital into each trade. Sensibly he suggests you diversify, holding several positions in different markets at once. He then proposes using a particular type of trading rule which means positions would be held on average for about a week.[4]

This sounds safe, but should actually come with a significant health warning. To overcome the trading costs this would generate on an index spread bet and break even you would need to make a return of 83% a year.[5] Worse still, to avoid a high chance of losing most of your entire investment you'd need to average 256% a year after costs; implying an annualised pre-cost return of 339%![6]

Thinking that you can overcome these odds is a sign of serious overconfidence, the main weakness of all traders and investors. I will explain why these systems are dangerous, and how to make your trading safer.

Why you should read this book

I don't believe there is any magic system that will automatically make you huge profits, and you should be wary of anyone who says otherwise, especially if they want to sell it to you. Instead success in systematic trading is mostly down to avoiding common mistakes such as over complicating your system, being too optimistic about likely returns,

---

4. This is a real system, but I will not identify the author. It is by no means the worst system I have seen.
5. If you are interested I explain why on page 192.
6. The calculation for this is on page 151.

taking excessive risks, and trading too often. I will help you avoid these errors. This won't guarantee vast returns, but it will make failure less likely.

My main aim isn't just to give you a single predefined system for trading, but to provide you with a modular **framework** which can be adapted to meet your needs. Part three describes the framework in detail. Just like you can choose different engines and tyres on a car, my framework includes options for different **trading rules** and position sizing calculations.

I haven't just pulled a bunch of components out of a parts bin. Each element of the framework has been carefully designed with months of careful research, built on many years of experience. I'll explain the available options, which I prefer, and why.

Just like cars can be modified I will show you how to incorporate your own trading rules and change other parts of the framework. I will warn you of the dangers of being too aggressive, which will result in your bank account blowing up like an over-tuned engine. I'll discuss the correct amount to bet on a particular trade, and how long to hold positions for.

In part four I show how to create trading strategies for each of the three example groups I mentioned in the preface. Sticking with the car analogy you can create a sturdy family car for **asset allocating investing**, an experimental kit car for **semi-automatic trading**, or a sporty two seater convertible of a trading system if you are a **staunch systems trader**. But before you get your fingers greasy you need to do some preparation. So the first part of the book which follows is all about *theory*, and in the second part I explain how to use your *tools* safely.

PART ONE.

Theory

Chapter One. The Flawed Human Brain

HUMAN MINDS CAN DO WONDERFUL THINGS, BUT ARE DEEPLY flawed when making financial decisions. In this chapter I explore economic theories about human behaviour, and why systematic trading and investing makes sense. I also show how our irrationality can interfere with the design of systematic strategies.

Chapter overview

Humans should be great traders, but...	The research that tells us why humans make bad decisions.
Simple trading rules	The dumb systems that are better at investing and trading than clever humans.
Sticking to the plan	Why you must be committed to your systems for them to work.
Good system design	Avoiding the human failings which can still be dangerous when designing systematic trading strategies.

Humans should be great traders, but...

Why do we need to trade or invest in a systematic fashion? What is wrong with using our own intuition to trade in a discretionary way? After all our brains have an astonishing ability to absorb and react to complex data, like those we see in financial markets. In my own Barclays trade described in the introduction I did analysis that would be virtually impossible to replicate with a systematic rule. But a simple rule would have been more successful than I was.[7]

---

7. If in 2009 I had developed the idea of **semi-automatic trading** then I could have taken more advantage of my uncharacteristically brilliant analysis, by putting the trade on in a **framework** which controlled my risk properly.

Unfortunately there have been many other times when a systematic strategy would have made better decisions than I did. For example in 2004 I bought some shares in UK oil company BP. They quickly rose about 5% and I sold them for a small profit. They subsequently rallied to a much higher level. I resolved never to sell too quickly again.

Then in late 2009 I decided to recycle some of my Barclays profits into buying BP. Initially they went from £5 to over £6. But in April 2010 one of BP's drilling rigs exploded in devastating fashion, killing 11 people. The shares started to fall, and a month later they were back at £5. Scarred by my earlier experience I hung on, convinced they would rebound. I finally sold at £3, which turned out to be the bottom.

I got it wrong both times. Was this just bad luck – a BP jinx? Am I a particularly poor trader, or is this evidence of a deeper problem with human psychology?

In fact despite their awesome complexity human brains like mine, and yours, are fundamentally flawed. In the jargon they are subject to **cognitive biases** which result in irrational behaviour. These instincts are so strong they mostly overwhelm any natural advantage that humans should have over simple decision-making rules. To see why this happens we need to understand how economists have tried to model and understand human behaviour.

The death of rational economic man

When the ideas of classical finance were developed in the 1950s economists assumed that people behaved in a purely rational way, resulting in perfectly efficient markets. Over time many apparent anomalies in this theory were discovered. But these were easily dismissed by the academic establishment as irrelevant, statistically insignificant or explainable through some combination of risk factors. Crucially nobody was able to come up with an alternative model that was as self-consistent and elegant as the efficient markets hypothesis.

From the 1980s onwards the field was penetrated by researchers from the discipline of psychology. For these experts in the human mind, the economist's framework of pure rationalism must have been highly amusing. A key insight these academic interlopers brought was that our brains are loaded with baggage from the distant past.

Parts of our grey matter are still hardwired for survival in a hostile environment where quick thinking was better than slow thoughtful consideration. As a result we have deep-rooted instincts that make it extremely difficult to behave in the rational way that classical finance expects. The new field that the interlopers created was behavioural finance, and it did have its own unifying model: prospect theory.

Why we run losses and stop out profits

Prospect theory explains why investors get it wrong when confronted with certain trading decisions, such as whether to sell out of a position which is now showing a loss. Most people show the greatest reluctance to take losses, as I did in 2010 with BP.[8]

This has been catchily described as "get-evenitis" by Hersh Shefrin.[9] This aversion to taking losses is a very powerful instinct. Humans do not seem to view a paper loss as real until it has been crystallised, so we can postpone the painful feeling of losing money. We are also reluctant to admit that we made a mistake with our initial purchase. Selling is an admission of failure.

Conversely, if a position has risen in value we are happy to take profits and sell quickly, as in my 2004 BP trade. The main motivation behind selling positions at a small profit appears to be to minimise regret. If the stock fell back after reaching a new high we would castigate ourselves for not taking profits earlier. Selling also confirms that our initial buy decision was correct. We hunger to get that confirmation as quickly as possible.

Both of these effects are at odds with classical financial theory, which says that people's actions and preferences for risk are unrelated to whether they have made paper profits or losses. In contrast prospect theory says we take *more* risks in a losing position to get even, but we want *less* risk when winning, preferring a quick and certain gain to a chance of losing our profits.

Unfortunately taking small profits and letting losses run is almost always a bad idea. I can show you this by back-testing a **trading system** which mimics someone taking profits on small rises, but allowing losses to grow larger before cutting – an 'early profit taker'.[10] A back-test shows how profitable this rule would have been if it had been run in the past.

Figure 2 shows part of the back-test and illustrates how the rule would have traded treasury futures during summer 2011, when the USA's sovereign debt rating was downgraded causing a counter intuitive rally. It sells and goes short in early June on a small profit and then misses the subsequent rise in prices.

---

8. For more academic detail see for example Terence Odean, 'Are Investors Reluctant To Realize Their Losses?', *Journal of Finance* 1998.

9. Shefrin 2007, *Beyond Greed and Fear*. I highly recommend this book for a clear overview of behavioural finance, despite its age. In academic circles this is the 'disposition effect' described in Shefrin and Statmen, 'The disposition to sell winners too early and ride losers too long: theory and evidence', *Journal of Finance* 1985.

10. This is based on the 'A and B' system defined in appendix B with parameters A = 5 and B = 20.

FIGURE 2: EARLY PROFIT TAKER MISSES THE 2011 RALLY IN US 10 YEAR TREASURY BONDS

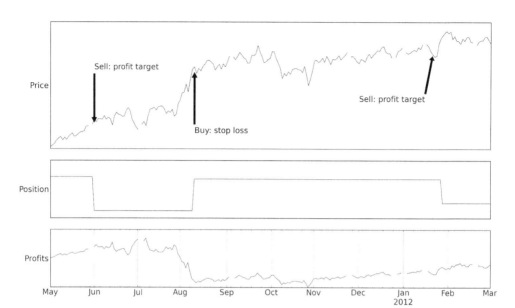

I compared this to the results from employing the opposite strategy – 'an early loss taker'.[11] Figure 3 shows this rule did much better during the same time period.

CONCEPT: BACK-TEST

To run a **back-test** you take historic data and calculate how a trading strategy would have behaved, and the profits or losses it could have made, had you been using it in the past.

Suppose you thought that buying the pound/dollar FX rate at 1.5 and selling it at 1.8 was a profitable strategy. You could take the history of the FX rate and then see what trades, and any profits, you would have made historically if you really had bought and sold according to this rule.

Back-testing is an invaluable tool for creating new trading rules. But when misused it can be dangerous, as we'll discover in chapter three, 'Fitting'.

---

11. This is also based on the 'A and B' system in appendix B with A = 20 and B = 5.

FIGURE 3: EARLY LOSS TAKER STAYS IN THE 2011 US BOND RALLY UNTIL BEING STOPPED OUT

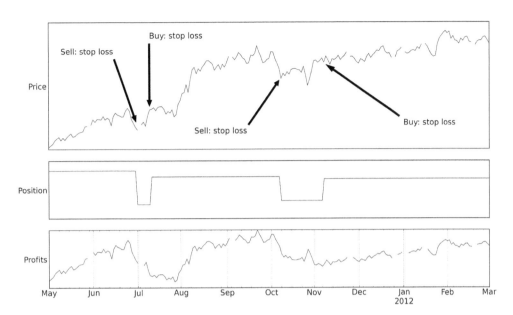

When I **back-tested** these two rules on 31 futures contracts I found that the early loss taker beat the early profit taker in 27 of them. Tests done on similar rules, across a wide variety of **asset classes**, confirm this finding. The early profit taker rule, which mimics our natural instincts, does worse than a rule which does the opposite.

Gamblers anonymous

Some of my relatives equate trading to high stakes gambling; an attitude I am usually quick to dismiss. But there may be some truth to it, at least in certain situations. To understand why it's worth knowing that certain types of gambling are more addictive than others, probably due to certain factors which reinforce the stimulation the brain receives during play.

There appear to be three main factors associated with the most addictive games. Firstly there should be an illusion of control, which encourages the perception of skill. Lottery players often prefer to pick their own numbers. Secondly, the game should include apparent near misses; frequent chances of *almost* winning the biggest prize. These are especially potent if you also receive lower value prizes, as in lotteries and slot machines. Finally, the game should be rapid and continuous to give a constant flow of stimulation. Buying a lottery ticket is not as addictive as an instant lottery or scratch card where the result is known immediately.

The illusion of control is present with all forms of active investing. Ironically the feeling of control is almost absent when investing systematically, which is one reason why many people find it difficult to utilise this trading method.

But the near miss and rapidity factors are clearly more likely to be associated with very frequent 'day trading'. As we'll discover later in the book it is extremely difficult to make profits when trading quickly, and only a small percentage of day traders manage to cover their costs, and make both a reasonable income and decent return on capital. Yet many amateurs feel compelled to try, and to continue trying, to beat the odds. Their frantic churning of trades is not so very different from the addict spending hours in front of a slot machine.

This particular brain deficiency leads to financial decisions that aren't just poor, but potentially life destroying.

Simple trading rules

Given there are flaws in the human brain which seriously affect our decision-making ability, what can we do about it? Easy: we should use systematic **trading rules** to make our decisions. These can help mitigate our own serious flaws, but they can also allow us to exploit the weaknesses that other human traders still have; their **cognitive biases** which result in behavioural anomalies in the market.

For example the early loss taker rule I mentioned above isn't just correcting our human instinct to take profits early and hang on to losses. It earns extra returns when other people persist in doing the opposite.

Personally I find it very reassuring to have explanations based on cognitive biases of why certain trading rules are consistently profitable. This gives me confidence that what I am seeing isn't just a statistical blip in a **back-test**. It means that the relevant rules should continue to work unless human behaviour changes radically. I'll return to this theme in chapter two – 'Systematic Trading Rules'.

Sticking to the plan

There is no point running a systematic trading strategy unless you can stick to it. Suppose you make a New Year's resolution to follow the early loss taker rule. Like most such resolutions it will probably prove hard to keep. When a long position in gold futures hits the 5 cent stop loss the early loss taker rule has set you will probably start making excuses:

> "The fundamentals are good. They haven't changed. I will just hold on a bit longer. Just this once. If it goes down 10 cents – which it won't – then I will definitely sell."

You might not even close at a 10 cent loss, kicking yourself for not selling earlier, and continue to hang on for the rebound that never comes, until the pain is unbearable and you close out. A small profit would also prove irresistible, with its own litany of excuses why you should deviate from the rule, just this once.

I call this process of interference by our internal monologue *meddling*. Meddling is due to the biggest **cognitive bias** of all: overconfidence. We think we are cleverer than the trading system and we are. We think we know more than the trading system and we do; the system focuses on a narrow set of quantifiable inputs, whilst we can analyse many kinds of complex information. We think being clever and knowing more implies we will make better decisions – but we usually don't, thanks to cognitive biases.

To stop meddling with our trading systems we require what economists call a **commitment mechanism**. The idea of a commitment mechanism is several thousand years old. One of its earliest appearances is in the story of Odysseus. The mythical Greek wanted to hear the songs of the Sirens without endangering himself or his vessel. So he ordered his crew to stuff their ears with beeswax, tie him to the mast and dutifully ignore his inevitable cries to steer the ship on to the rocks.

A modern example of this is given in Victor Niederhoffer's book *Education of a Speculator*. At this point in the story hedge fund manager Victor has a large long position in silver futures. We join him in early 1980 when the Hunt brothers, who had been squeezing the market upwards, are about to capitulate, which will cause the price to drop:

> "I decided to set my loss limit at 50% of my winnings... The model story on this point is Odysseus... I locked myself inside a racquetball court instead of tying myself to a ship's mast. I issued instructions to my assistant and future wife, Susan.
>
> 'Do not listen to my entreaties if I wish to double further. If the losses reach 50% of the winnings, reduce my positions by one-half. If I beg to be released, sell everything out.' ...
>
> Some rumors about liquidation by the Hunts had hit the fan... I immediately placed a call to Susan 'Untie me. Disregard everything I said before' ... My faithful companion followed my original directions."

Susan closed the entire position and Victor lived to fight another day. But how can we ensure we stick to our strategies without the use of ropes or future wives?[12]

Trading systems must be objective

To be committed you must have an *objective* trading system. Many systems aren't objective and require some discretion to apply. A highly subjective rule would be something like 'Sell for small losses, and hold on to large profit making positions'. This is similar in spirit to the early loss taker rule defined earlier, but it's much too vague.

---

12. This comment isn't intended to imply that all investors and traders are unmarried heterosexual men. However, if your partner is a man rather than a woman you should be wary of using them as a commitment mechanism, as they may make things worse; research shows that women generally make better investment decisions.

At the first sign of a loss it's likely you will start to redefine what constitutes 'small' to justify not selling. Few systems are that poorly defined, but many have 'rules' in them which allow for a significant degree of subjective interpretation. Technical analysts rarely agree on which patterns exist in a particular chart, and what should be done with them.

Creating a purely objective system is a powerful commitment mechanism. If you have a subjective system and your instinct goes against it, then you'll soon be bending the rules. But if everything is clearly defined it creates a line in the sand beyond which any deviation is obvious. You cannot fool yourself that you are following a system if you blatantly ignore objective rules.

Furthermore we can only produce **back-tests** for purely objective systems. You will see why this is important later in the chapter.

Automation – the use of dogs in finance and engineering

Another advantage of objective systems is that they can be automated, and automation is a good commitment mechanism. You can't automate subjective systems because computers cannot eyeball trend lines on charts; they need firm statements like 'Buy if the 20 day moving average is above the 40 day'. They cannot interpret commandments like 'Sell once the pattern is triggered unless there is a firm sign of bullish volume' without a clear definition of both the pattern and the meaning of bullish volume.

So an objective system is one which a computer *can* run. But it does not mean a computer *must* run it. You can run many trading strategies using pencil and paper, or relatively simple spreadsheets, to calculate trades which you then execute manually. Certain kinds of systems involving complex rules, faster trading frequencies or trading in large numbers of **instruments**[13] would be very time-consuming, or impossible, to run without automation. But for simpler systems automation isn't necessary. Full automation is also problematic for discretionary **semi-automatic traders**, although they could automate their position and risk management **framework** once they've made their trading decisions manually.

Furthermore automation doesn't stop meddling. Firstly, consider the degree of automation. Having a system which requires a human to do the actual execution of automatically generated trades is still prone to meddling. If the process is completely automated from end to end then interference is harder. There is an old joke that the best systematic trading setup consists of a computer, a man and a dog. The computer runs a fully automated strategy, the man feeds the dog, and the dog bites the man if he touches the computer.[14]

---

13. **Instrument** is my term for something that you trade or invest in. So a share of BP is an instrument, as is a corn future, and so is a spread bet on the yen/dollar exchange rate.
14. This joke evolved from earlier jokes involving various kinds of hardware rather than trading systems. It is generally attributed either to management theorist Warren Bennis, or to employees of Bell labs.

Secondly, any good automated software would have ways to override it in an emergency. If you desperately want to meddle then there will be frequent 'emergencies'. Automation is of little help unless you have faith in your trading rules. A system which is fully automated but not completely trusted is potentially lethal.[15] Any sane person would be tempted to shut it down at the first sign of trouble. So automation aids commitment, but it must be done with a well designed system in which you have full confidence.

Good system design

So what is a well designed system? How can you make something which you can trust, commit to and won't meddle with, regardless of whether it is automated or not?

It is much easier to trust a system which is objective. Firstly, because it is transparent: you know given some particular data exactly what the positions should be. Secondly, you can **back-test** an objective system over history. This will give you an indication of what its past behaviour was, and how it should trade in the future. For example suppose a system typically lost around 5% on one of every ten trading days in the simulated past of your back-test. You shouldn't worry if in real trading you lose 5% every couple of weeks.[16]

As well as requiring systems to be objective I also prefer those that are relatively simple, transparent and based on underlying ideas,[17] such as my previous hypothesis that prospect theory explains the success of the early loss taking rule. Transparency is important for gaining trust in trading systems, just as it is in politics. In the next chapter I'll explain in more detail why I prefer systems whose performance and behaviour can be explained.

In addition to these positive attributes there are also three significant pitfalls to avoid when designing trading systems: over-fitting, overtrading and over-betting.

Over-fitting

A new trading system does not arrive out of the ether. It has to be designed and developed by an actual, probably overconfident,[18] person. It is all too easy for that person to make design mistakes due to those same **cognitive biases** they are trying to escape from by trading systematically.

---

15. The HAL computer in Arthur C. Clarke's *2001: A Space Odyssey* is a good example of what happens when you take automation too far and then don't trust the system.

16. In fact by using my **framework** you can make predictions about likely losses even in situations when you can't **back-test**, such as when you're a **semi-automatic trader** not using systematic trading rules.

17. Compared to say a system which has been built purely by **back-testing** a large number of trading rules and picking the best regardless of whether it can be explained, a process sometimes called **data mining**. I'll return to this distinction in the next chapter.

18. It's not just trading system designers who are overconfident. There is a significant amount of academic research showing examples of overconfidence in discretionary finance, for example amongst equity analysts and macroeconomic forecasters.

Firstly 'narrative fallacy': our brains are great at seeing patterns where there are none. Whilst developing trading rules there is often a **fitting** process during which the best rules are selected by looking at **back-test** results. If we're not careful the rules selected will fit the data too well. They will be highly tuned to one set of market conditions and perform worse in actual trading than a simpler rule would. The system will be **over-fitted**. Narrative fallacy means we have a tendency to see more predictability in historic asset prices than really existed and so we're naturally drawn to over-fitted trading rules. I'll return to this problem in chapter three, 'Fitting'.

Second bias, and perhaps the most serious of all: overconfidence. This manifests itself in a lack of diversification. Surveys of individual portfolios find that most amateur investors have relatively few securities in their portfolio, with a bias towards their home country, and also lack diversification across **asset classes**.

You might think that experts, with access to sophisticated quantitative tools, wouldn't make these mistakes. Unfortunately they often do. This happens when they don't consider the considerable uncertainty in expected asset returns. The most commonly used optimisation models assume they know the pattern of returns precisely. Small changes to the model inputs will produce extreme portfolios with all their eggs in one or two baskets. The result can be just as bad or worse than the portfolios of mere amateurs.

In practice many experts fiddle with the raw output of optimisations until they end up reflecting their own expectations of what the result should have been! I will discuss this further in chapter four, 'Portfolio Allocation'.

Overtrading

People are highly overconfident about their own abilities relative to others. This is another **cognitive bias**: illusory superiority. For example nearly all drivers consider themselves above average, a theoretical impossibility and also highly unlikely given the number of deaths annually from road accidents.

Both amateur investors and professional managers have a tendency to trade too frequently.[19] There are extra costs involved in trading more often. Overtrading suggests overconfidence in your own relative ability to overcome the higher hurdle of bigger costs. As I pointed out above, frequent trading can also be addictive and lead to behaviour which is indistinguishable from problem gambling.

When designing trading systems if you **over-fit** you will end up with systems that perform unrealistically well in **back-tests**, and wrongly assume that returns will easily be high enough to overcome trading costs.

---

19. For academic research on this see Odean and Barber, 'The common stock investment performance of individual investors', 1998 working paper.

Over betting

It will be extremely difficult to refrain from meddling if you're worried about wiping out your capital. Take the system I mentioned above with a one-in-ten chance of a 5% daily loss. If that was ten times **leveraged** you would have a 10% chance of losing *half* your capital on any given day. Most sane people would panic after losing 50% on one day, and start meddling like crazy.

Unfortunately over betting is endemic amongst amateur investors with easy access to leverage through derivatives like spread bets. If your confidence is unbounded you can bet the maximum that your broker allows you to. Potentially this could be a ten-fold leverage on an individual equity bet, equating to an annual **standard deviation** of returns of around 200%. This is nuts.[20]

CONCEPT: STANDARD DEVIATION

The **standard deviation** is a measure of how dispersed some data is around its average; it's a measure of risk. The precise formula is in the glossary, but in most cases you'll use a spreadsheet formula or software to calculate it.

Standard deviations are often used to describe the dispersion of the returns of an asset, or profits from a trading system. I use the term **volatility** as a shorthand for standard deviation of returns. One unit of standard deviation is also sometimes called a **sigma**.

In this book we'll usually be dealing with daily returns and using daily volatilities, but it's often useful to think about the annualised standard deviation – how much deviation we expect to see over a year.

Standard deviation doesn't increase linearly, but with the square root of time. Over the roughly 256 business days in a year you'd expect annual standard deviation to be larger by the square root of 256, or 16.[21] So you multiply daily standard deviations by 16 to get the annualised version, or divide by 16 to go from annualised to daily. In contrast to go from *average* daily returns to annualised average returns you just multiply by the number of days in a year, or 256. Then to go from annualised to daily you divide by 256.

Equities have an annualised standard deviation of about 20% a year. Bonds tend to be safer, depending on their maturity. A typical two year bond has an annualised sigma of around 1.5% a year, and a ten year bond would be more like 8%.

---

20. At the time of writing some UK providers of FX spread bets offer leverage of up to 500 times. That isn't nuts, it's clinically insane.
21. I'm making an assumption here that adjacent returns don't influence each other, or in the jargon of statistics they have zero autocorrelation.

We often assume our returns have a particular type of *distribution*. A distribution is just a way of describing the pattern of your data. A common distribution I use is the **Gaussian normal distribution**. If returns are Gaussian normal, then the mean and standard deviation alone are sufficient to say how likely certain returns will be.

If your daily returns are Gaussian normal then you will see movements one sigma or less around the average about 68% of the time, and returns two sigma or less about 95% of the time. In 2.5% of days you'd see a change more than two sigma above the average. You'd also see a return which is two sigma worse than the average 2.5% of the time. The Gaussian normal distribution is symmetric.

Let's consider the 200% annualised standard deviation mentioned above. 200% a year translates into 12.5% a day if you divide by the square root of time, 16. For the average daily return even if you're making an optimistic 200% a year, after you've divided by 256 you earn just 0.8% per day. A plus one sigma return would be 12.5% above the average of 0.8%, or 13.3%. A one sigma loss would be 12.5% below the average, or -11.7%.

FIGURE 4: SCARILY YOU CAN EXPECT TO LOSE 40% IN ONE DAY, EVERY THREE YEARS, FOR A TRADING SYSTEM WITH 200% ANNUALISED STANDARD DEVIATION OF RETURNS, AND AVERAGE RETURNS OF 200% PER YEAR

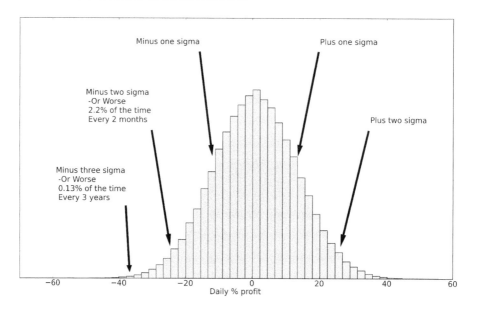

You'll see returns between -11.7% and +13.3% a day around 68% of the time, and between -24.2% and +25.8% a day 95% of the time. Around 2.5% of the time you'd see losses of more than 24.2% a day. That's quite a hefty daily loss which

you'd get every couple of months. And as figure 4 shows about once every three years you'd lose three **sigma** or 37.2% in one day!

Scarily that's probably still optimistic because the normal distribution tends to underestimate the chance of really bad returns. According to the normal distribution we should get daily falls of more than 4 sigma about once a century. But from 1914 to 2014 the US Dow Jones index fell by more than 4 sigma around 30 times!

You or your investors need to be comfortable with the losses you're likely to make. The size of your positions must reflect the amount of risk you can handle. I'll explain this in more detail in chapter nine, 'Volatility Targeting'.

Chapter Two. Systematic Trading Rules

A TRADING RULE IS A SYSTEMATIC WAY OF PREDICTING PRICE movements. Trading rules are a core component of any trading system, so how can you find trading rules that will work? Why do they work? What styles of trading are available? Finally, how successful should you expect trading rules to be?

Chapter overview

What makes a good trading rule	Some key elements that make a trading rule more likely to be successful.
When trading rules don't work	Reasons why a trading rule which worked in back-test may not work in practice when actually traded.
Why are certain rules profitable?	Explanations for why profit making rules exist, to help you work out if that profitability is likely to be repeatable.
Classifying trading styles	The main ways in which you can classify rules into trading styles, and the important characteristics each style has.
Achievable Sharpe ratios	What are realistic Sharpe ratios to expect?

What makes a good trading rule

Staunch systems trader

This section mostly relates to how **trading rules** are fitted. This is less applicable to **asset allocating investors** and **semi-automatic traders**, and they can skip to 'Why are certain rules profitable?'

It is carefully built from ideas or data

Systematic trading assumes the future will be like the past. Hence you should create rules that would have worked historically, and hope that they will continue to work.

But there are at least two different ways to find rules that made money in the past. One common method, which I call **data first,** is to analyse some data, find some profitable patterns and create some trading rules to exploit them. This is sometimes called **data mining**. The alternative, **ideas first**, is to come up with an idea, then create a rule, which is then tested on data to see if it works.[22] Here is Leda Braga, head of hedge fund Systematica, describing ideas first in an interview with Bloomberg in February 2015:

> "There's a creative moment when you think of a hypothesis, maybe it's that interest rate data derives currency rates. So we think about that first before mining the data. We don't mine the data to come up with ideas."

Designing an ideas first system is like saying: "I want to design a system that captures this source of return. I hope this source is still around in the future."

Whereas for a data first system: "Here is a system that was profitable in the past given the patterns in the market (which I won't try and explain or understand). I hope these patterns persist in the future."

---

22. There is a third method which is to use an idea which you cannot or will not test on historical data. Strictly speaking, this wouldn't be systematic trading.

Advantages of ideas first	Advantages of data first
If an idea works no further potentially dangerous **fitting** is required.	There will be a bias with ideas first to testing things that you know will work, either because of 'market lore' or academic studies. This is a form of implicit **over-fitting**.
Any fitting will probably be done in a small subset of alternatives.	With ideas first it is tempting to try a large number of ideas to find the ones that work. This is definitely over-fitting.
You tend to get simpler and more intuitive trading rules with ideas first.	In data first all the fitting is explicit, so the degree of over-fitting can be controlled.
You can construct rules that make intuitive sense, with a story behind them.	A compelling theory or story does not guarantee that the source of returns is repeatable, and could give a false sense of security. This is the narrative fallacy I mentioned in Chapter 1.
It's easier to classify the trading rule and work out where its profits are coming from.	Clever data analysis might unearth novel strategies that were previously unknown.

In my experience consistently profitable trading comes out of careful research, done by thoughtful and knowledgeable people, who seek to understand where their profits come from. The loss making systematic trading I've seen has often been the result of haphazard data mining, done without any consideration of the reasons why a rule might have appeared profitable in the past or might not be in the future.

That experience, combined with my preference for things I can trust and understand, means I favour the ideas first method. This usually results in intuitive, simpler and more transparent rules. As long as a small number of ideas are tested **over-fitting** is less likely. In the next chapter, 'Fitting', I focus on ideas first testing because it is simpler and does not require sophisticated techniques to implement safely.

But in some situations the data first process could be better; for example in high frequency trading where there is plenty of data, rules can be refitted regularly and novel ideas are more likely to be found as market structure evolves.

You should be aware of the strengths and weaknesses of your preferred method and use it appropriately.

Explainable profits

Understanding why trading rules make money is very important. If you know why something was profitable in the past you can also have some idea of whether profits will continue, or if and when the rule might fail.

With an **ideas first** approach you can easily explain why a strategy was profitable, since the explanation is inherent in the original idea. For example you might have tested a **trend following** rule, which you think makes money because of **cognitive biases** explained by prospect theory.

With **data first** any explanation has to follow the fitting process. You first examine how a rule behaves and then infer what might be causing the effect. The more complex a data driven trading rule is the harder it will be to explain.

There is however a danger in seeking out explanations. Remember the narrative fallacy, another cognitive bias: humans like stories. We're more likely to believe in rules which have convincing explanations, even if their performance doesn't stand up to statistical scrutiny. To trust a trading rule I like to have both a good story and a rigorous **back-test**.

Intuitively understandable behaviour

A strategy that is intuitive is much easier to trust. If in advance of an earnings announcement you see Unilever's equity price rising a **trend following** system ought to be buying. If the strategy sold instead that might be a cause for concern and you would check for bad data or software bugs. Usually though you'd see what was expected and be able to relax.

A complicated system might buy or sell when prices moved higher, depending on the exact pattern. This would make its behaviour less obvious and more unpredictable.

As simple as possible

It is much easier to explain the profitability and behaviour of simple trading rules, those with few moving parts and no weird interactions. **Ideas first** rules should be simple unless you begin with a very convoluted idea, or over complicate it to get a more profitable **back-test**, neither of which is recommended.

Data first rules can be very simple or extremely complicated, depending on how many parameters are fitted. A data first rule with more parameters will be less explainable, and more vulnerable to **over-fitting**. But a complex data first rule can also exploit a novel trading pattern that simpler rules will miss.

Can be systematised

Ideas need to translated into systematised rules. Not all styles of trading are entirely suitable for this, because they are inherently subjective or because of data limitations. They can still however be wrapped up inside a systematic position management **framework**, as I show in the **semi-automatic trader** example.

Too subjective

Many methods of trading cannot be systematised because it's impossible to write down a set of relatively simple, objective and generic rules. For more esoteric forms of technical analysis turning a strangely named candlestick pattern into a precise rule is difficult. Another example would be **merger arbitrage** where you have to assess the likelihood of a deal going through based on analysis of a number of hard to quantify factors.

Data limitations

Even if a strategy is objective the necessary data might be unavailable. Even if you could write trading rules for **merger arbitrage** the necessary information about legal and regulatory issues cannot easily be converted into an algorithm friendly format.

There might also be a shortage of data. As you will see in the next chapter, 'Fitting', many years of data are needed to properly test a strategy. Some hedge funds have recently used data such as Google search popularity and Twitter trending to forecast markets. These ideas make good press releases, but there won't be enough data to properly evaluate them for many years.

You might also struggle to compare data between **instruments**. For example accounting measures aren't consistent across countries because of different rules and standards. This means inter country **equity value** strategies are difficult to implement.

When trading rules don't work

Staunch systems trader

This section mostly relates to how **trading rules** are fitted. This is less applicable to **asset allocating investors** and **semi-automatic traders**. They can skip to 'Why are certain rules profitable?'

There are various reasons why a rule that was successful in back-test might fail in reality.

It never really worked

First there are rules which apparently work in a **back-test**, but wouldn't have actually made money in the past. The rules might be **over-fitted**, which I will discuss at length in the next chapter. Alternatively they could rely on forward looking data that was published with a delay not present in the back-test. There may be also **survivorship bias** in the instruments you are considering. You might have underestimated trading costs or missed out an important element of the market structure at the time, such as constraints on **short selling** of equities. Finally your history could be too brief and miss out on a crucial period when the strategy would have blown up.[23]

The world changes

You want strategies that worked in the past and will continue to do so. But what if the behaviour or market pattern you are trying to exploit vanishes?

For example what if systematic traders, using the same rules, dominate a market? Won't the relevant strategies all stop working? This is most problematic for **relative value** strategies which try and buy when assets become cheap and sell when they are expensive. With a large population of similar systems any slight mis-pricing will be immediately corrected and returns will vanish.

Conversely **trend followers** might be happy to see price trends reinforced when they collectively dominate a market, however when prices reverse they could get caught in a synchronised rush for the exit.

When computers have a significant advantage, as in ultra high frequency trading, they have squeezed out people almost entirely. These are no longer taking advantage of human weaknesses or market structure, but are engaged in an arms race where success comes from pure speed and anticipating your opponent's reaction. This area falls entirely outside the domain of this book.

Why certain rules are profitable

This section is relevant to all readers

Whether you are using systematic rules or making discretionary forecasts it's important to understand where your returns are coming from and what your 'edge' is – if any. This section briefly covers the theory around this subject.[24] It presents some possible reasons why certain assets, portfolios of assets, or **dynamic** trading rules make profits.

---

23. This is the aptly named 'Peso problem' and is particularly problematic for **negative skew** strategies which I define later in this chapter.

24. An exhaustive treatment of this topic can be found in *Expected Returns* by Antti Ilmanen.

Risk premia

When you buy insurance you pay a premium. Premia are set at a level where insurers expect to have occasional large payouts, but to be profitable on average. The insurance buyer is guaranteed to lose over the long run, but in return is covered against rare significant losses. These two different profiles of returns are also seen in the financial markets, so the analogy of buying and selling insurance is very useful.

Anyone wanting to buy 'financial insurance' will happily suffer below average market returns, whilst those willing to sell would get higher returns through earning a **risk premium**, analogous to the insurer's profits. Certain assets are more heavily exposed to certain kinds of risks; buying these assets brings additional returns from various risk premia.

Persistent risk premium

Some risk premia persist for long periods, like the extra return you'd expect from investing in equities versus safer assets like bonds. A range of other risk factors such as book-to-market ratios and firm size are used in **equity value** strategies. In other assets there are different premia. For example longer maturity bonds earn a premium over those which mature earlier since investors like to be compensated for lending over longer periods.

Timing varying risk premium

Buying cheap credit default swap insurance on risky mortgages in 2006 subsequently made hedge fund manager John Paulson billions of dollars when the market melted down a year later.[25] Conversely when there is blood on the streets you can buy risky assets for peanuts, as in early 2009 when I bought my insufficiently aggressive stake in Barclays.

Clearly risk premia are not constant. People's appetite for risk varies over time as they veer between the relative euphoria of years like 2006 and the panic of 2009. You can make profits buying cheap premia and selling expensive ones. This is a form of **mean reversion** trading, where you assume premia, and hence prices, will revert to some long-term equilibrium.

In practice it's impossible to say exactly what the 'correct' value of a premium should be and infer if you should be buying or selling. The market can also move away from its correct value for long periods of time. Nevertheless this is another useful source of return.

Skew and unlikely events premium

The rational investor of classical financial theory only cares about an asset's **Sharpe ratio (SR)** – it's average returns adjusted for their **standard deviation**. This only makes sense if all assets have symmetrically distributed returns. But in practice assets with the same SR

---

25. See *The Greatest Trade Ever* by Gregory Zuckerman.

could make steady losses with occasional large returns (like an insurance buyer), or steady gains with occasional large losses (as a seller of insurance does). This implies that the **skew** of each asset's returns is different.

CONCEPT: SHARPE RATIO (SR)

The Sharpe ratio (SR) measures how profitable a trading strategy or holding an asset has been, or is expected to be. To calculate it you take returns and adjust them for their risk.

Strictly speaking you should take the 'excess' return over and above a risk free interest rate,[26] although this isn't relevant for a trader using derivatives,[27] nor as important in the post 2009 low interest rate era as it was before.

Formally it is the mean return for a particular time period divided by the **standard deviation** of returns for the same time period. So the daily SR would be the average daily return, divided by the standard deviation of daily returns. However I normally use the annualised Sharpe ratio – annualised returns divided by annualised standard deviation. Assuming there are 256 business days in a year the annualised SR is roughly 16 times the daily.[28]

The Sharpe ratio is not a perfect measure. In particular its assumption of symmetric gains and losses is unrealistic. It is useless for comparing assets where infrequent large losses occur with others that have rare large gains; for this you need to consider **skew**.

CONCEPT: SKEW

In chapter one when discussing standard deviation I said that a large loss was as likely as a large gain for the symmetric **Gaussian normal distribution**. A two **sigma** move up in price would occur around 2.5% of the time, with the same chance of a two sigma move down.

But many assets don't have a symmetric distribution – their returns are *skewed* to one side or the other. In many cases large losses are more likely than large gains.

---

26. The US Fed funds rate, UK Bank of England base rate, or whatever is relevant elsewhere.
27. For derivative traders the cost of funding is embedded in their returns. This ignores the interest received on any margin posted or excess funds.
28. This is because you multiply the average daily return by the number of trading days in a year, or 256, to annualise it, but you multiply the daily standard deviation of returns by the 'square root of time', and the square root of 256 is 16. See page 21. Technical note: This is an approximation which is only exact for returns with **Gaussian normal distributions** and no autocorrelation.

Global stock markets fell 20% on a single day in October 1987 – about 20 **sigma** – but they have never rallied as rapidly.

Where an asset has a higher chance of a large down move than an equivalent up move, it is said to have a *negative* **skew.** If large up moves are more likely then it has *positive* skew.

Assuming they have the same **Sharpe ratio**, the returns from a positively skewed asset will contain more losing days than for those of a negatively skewed asset. But the losing days will be relatively small in magnitude. A negatively skewed asset will have fewer down days, but the losses on those days will be larger.

Returning to my earlier analogy, buying insurance is a positive skew strategy. You will experience frequent small losses (paying out premia) with occasional large gains (receiving payouts). If you sell insurance then you'll get frequent small gains and occasional large losses – negative skew.

Figure 5 and table 1 show the return distribution and statistics of two assets with different skews but the same Sharpe ratio.

FIGURE 5: TWO ASSETS, SAME SHARPE RATIO, DIFFERENT SKEWS

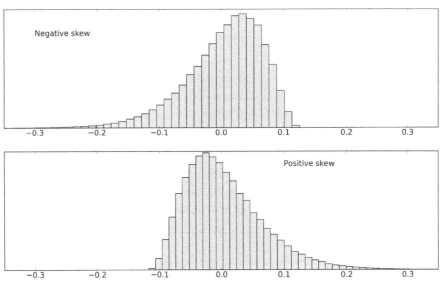

Which is better, positive or negative skew? It depends...

TABLE 1: CHARACTERISTICS OF NEGATIVE VERSUS POSITIVE SKEW

	Negative skew	Positive skew
Mean of daily returns	0.4%	0.4%
Sigma of daily returns	6.3%	6.3%
Annualised Sharpe ratio	1.0	1.0
Skew of daily returns	-1.0	1.0
Median daily return	1.4%	-0.6%
Average Gain:Average Loss	0.8	1.4
Hit rate (% of positive returns)	59%	46%
Expected annual worst daily loss	-22%	-10%
Expected annual best daily gain	10%	22%

Equities normally have mildly negative skew. 'Safe haven' assets like gold and Swiss francs tend to have positive skew. However the skew of these assets is relatively mild compared to owning options.

One group of option-like assets are the **equity volatility indices**: the VIX index on the US S&P 500, and the V2TX index on the European Euro Stoxx 50. Both of these can be traded with very liquid futures.

Buying the VIX and V2TX futures gives you highly positive skew, but as you are effectively purchasing insurance against unexpectedly high equity volatility it also tends to have a negative Sharpe ratio (SR). Similarly selling the futures gives a positive SR, but with an extremely negative skew. Each of these futures has skew around four times higher than their underlying index.

Many people have a strong dislike for the occasional large losses of negative skew which is why they buy home insurance. **Relative value** strategies tend to exhibit this behaviour, so investors should demand a skew premium for investing in them.

Conversely positive skew is attractive, which partly explains why even highly numerate and rational people like me buy lottery tickets. A related effect is that most of us overestimate very rare probabilities. This means we will overpay for disaster insurance, such as deep out of the money put options that will only pay off if stocks drop 20%.

People also like to have a small chance of winning large amounts; they buy out of the money call options, favour 200-1 horses whose real chance of winning is 1,000 to 1, and once again they buy lottery tickets. They will happily give up return premia to those who are willing to take the other side of these gambles.

These various illogical preferences can be explained by **cognitive biases**.

Leverage

Do you borrow to invest? Classical financial theory assumes people will borrow freely, but many investors cannot or will not do so. Borrowing to buy stocks on margin is still unusual behaviour for amateur traders. Although the availability of **derivatives** like futures and contracts for difference has increased substantially they are still a tool for the brave minority. Many institutional funds do not borrow either, whilst for others there are limits imposed by regulators and brokers.

This means that high **Sharpe ratio (SR)** assets with low returns, but even lower **volatility**, will remain unloved by those who require high returns and can't borrow to invest. They would rather buy high return assets with higher risk, even if the additional risk is not fully compensated for and the SR is lower.

As a result undiversified portfolios are common, with equities contributing nearly all the volatility. People prefer riskier stocks, epitomised by the technology bubble in 1999. This effect also explains why short maturity bonds have historically had higher SR than longer maturity bonds. The lucky investors who can use leverage should outperform others over the long run. But beware: in a crisis a death spiral can easily develop in portfolios built on debt. Prices fall, brokers ask for more margin or restrict borrowing entirely, investors have to sell, and prices fall further. These forced sales at the worst possible price can eliminate years of profits.

I'll discuss the safe use of leverage in chapter nine, 'Volatility targeting'.

Liquidity and size

The degree of **liquidity** in an asset is how easily we can buy or sell without unduly affecting the price. Larger institutional investors have to buy in large size and liquidate quickly on client redemptions, so they prefer liquid assets, which then get their prices bid up relative to less liquid alternatives. Thus we get the well known effect of smaller companies offering better returns. Liquidity premia also explain the attractiveness of 'alternative' assets like land and venture capital. Investors happy to hold less liquid portfolios for longer periods have greater opportunities for higher returns.

The premia for liquidity, size and leverage can vary over time, presenting opportunities for well timed buying and selling. For example **derivatives** related to mortgage backed assets were liquid and attracted premium prices at the end of 2006; a year later they were almost untradeable and willing buyers could get significant discounts even on heavily depressed official quotes.

When others have to trade

Not everyone trades because they are trying to make money. Some are forced to. For example central banks wishing to keep their currency weak – such as Switzerland or Japan – can do so indefinitely if they are comfortable with the ensuing costs.[29]

A **foreign exchange carry** trading rule that borrows in low interest rate currencies like Switzerland and invests in high interest rate currencies will be consistently profitable as a result, at least until the currency policy is abandoned (as it was for Switzerland in January 2015). This can lead to sudden losses, making carry a decidedly negative **skew** strategy.

Here are some other examples from different **asset classes**. End of year trading to minimise taxation or 'window dress' balance sheets creates seasonal effects in equity prices. Insurance companies might have to buy rare long maturity bonds to hedge liabilities, pushing up their price. As long as the position size of those forced to trade is greater than those who exploit them these opportunities will persist.

Another set of money making opportunities is available to those willing to act as liquidity *providers*. Note this is different from earning a liquidity premium by holding illiquid assets for long periods. Liquidity providers behave as market markets, trying to capture the spread that less patient traders don't mind paying. This is definitely negative **skew** territory as unforeseen price spikes can quickly wipe out large quantities of patiently accumulated small gains.

Barriers to entry, returns to effort and cost

Some trading rules have barriers to entry in the form of costs or investments that need to be made to realise profits from them. High frequency strategies require renting expensive servers located physically within exchange buildings, as well as developing specialised software. The returns of such systems need to be high enough to compensate for the investment needed, as well as their much higher costs.

If an opportunity requires a lot of work to exploit, then it may be passed up by most investors and additional returns would be available. An example would be investing in private firms, where lengthy due diligence and legal work is required. It's important to understand that just because something takes time, and may require specialist knowledge, doesn't mean the profits are a payment for *skill*. The extra returns available are just fair compensation for the time and effort needed.

---

29. Conversely, governments cannot maintain strong currencies indefinitely against market pressure as their foreign reserves will eventually run out. This happened in 1992 when the UK government tried to support the pound to keep its value within the European Exchange Rate Mechanism. Hedge fund manager George Soros bet against the Bank of England and made a billion pounds or so when they capitulated.

Behavioural effects

A classical financial economist would be comfortable with most of the above explanations. But you can also create rules which extract returns from other people's behavioural weaknesses. These effects persist because of market inefficiencies such as bans on **short selling**, and the sheer weight of money influenced by these biases.

The early loss taker trading rule of chapter one is a simple **trend following** rule which I believe is profitable because of prospect theory biases. People don't want to keep recent winners, they prefer hanging on to losers, and they will give up excess returns for the nice warm feeling they get from behaving like this. Prospect theory can also explain preferences people have around return **skew** and overweighting unlikely events, which I've already touched on. There are a large number of other behavioural biases, and strategies that could be built on them.

Self-fulfilling prophecy

Many weird **technical** trading systems such as Fibonacci numbers and the like have absolutely no justification, except perhaps some tenuous link to behavioural theories. But because a lot of people use these ideas we do get persistent price movements around key levels, and they may end up working. It is hard to say if they will continue to work in the future.

Pure alpha and skill

Warren Buffett, John Templeton, Peter Lynch: there are a small number of investors who seem to be able to persistently generate extraordinary profits that none of the above theories can easily explain. It is possible they are just very lucky, the one in a billion monkey who has by sheer fluke successfully written a sonnet. But they may possess the rare elixir of **alpha**; genuine skill in making investment decisions.

It is unlikely that what these outliers do can be written down and reproduced systematically. Those who exhibit pure skill can adapt to changing market opportunities in a way that a systematic rule never could. If you think you are part of this elite group then the **semi-automatic trader** example is for you.

Classifying trading styles

This section is relevant to all readers.

This section is useful for all three example groups. I believe even **semi-automatic traders** would benefit from having a good understanding of the likely risks of their style of trading.

Static versus dynamic

A trading strategy could be **static** – where you invest your portfolio and then do nothing. The returns from **static** strategies inherit the characteristics of the underlying assets. Alternatively it could be **dynamic** – where you actively trade. In this case you will earn additional types of return from buying and selling, and the characteristics of those returns will depend on your trading style.

There are various degrees of static strategies. The most vanilla flavour is a simple buy and hold portfolio. Let's pretend that Apple and Microsoft have the same price per share. If you can't decide between them then you'd buy equal numbers of shares in Apple and Microsoft today.

Next week Apple brings out a new iGadget and doubles in price, whilst sclerotic Microsoft halves after releasing a new Windows that everyone hates. As a buy and hold investor you would do nothing. Your portfolio is now seriously unbalanced; 80% in Apple and only 20% in Microsoft.

The second degree static strategy is to re-balance your portfolio so you keep the same cash value in each company. You'd need to sell your Apple shares to the point where you only had 50% of your portfolio in the designer of swanky white gadgets, whilst simultaneously buying shares in the semi-monopolistic software house.

Now suppose you wanted not just an equal cash value for the two companies but equal *risk*. This is often called **risk parity** investing. We'll assume risk is equal to the recent **standard deviation** of the daily percentage changes in price for each firm.

CONCEPT: RISK

Risk is a slippery concept which is difficult to pin down. I like to divide the world of risk into **predictable risks**, or what Donald Rumsfeld[30] would call Known Unknowns, and **unpredictable risks** (Unknown Unknowns).

It's very hard to forecast what the return will be each day over the next few weeks for an asset or portfolio. But you can model and estimate what the variation in returns is likely to be. Estimates based entirely on assuming that recent levels of variation will persist tend to be relatively good.[31] The element of risk that is encapsulated by a model of variation is the *predictable* part.

However there is always the danger that you haven't correctly estimated the underlying variation, or that the level of variation will change, or that your model of where market returns come from is wrong or incomplete (perhaps because of **skew** and other nuances since returns aren't usually exactly **Gaussian normal**).[32] These are all sources of *unpredictable* risks.

I define predictable risk as being equal to the recent historic level of the **standard deviation** of percentage daily changes in price. This is a useful simplification but one which ignores the unpredictable elements of risk. The dangers of this assumption should always be at the front of your mind.

Again suppose for simplicity each technology stock starts life with the same standard deviation of returns, so for a third degree portfolio you would put 50% of your cash in each stock.

Now Apple has to recall its latest iPhone due to a technical fault, so the price crashes. The next day it rebounds to its prior level on news that Apple is to buy *coolstartup.com*. Although the price is unchanged the expected risk of thrilling Apple shares (defined as the recent standard deviation of returns) has doubled relative to dull Microsoft. If you did nothing, two-thirds of your estimated portfolio risk would be coming from AAPL, and just one-third from MSFT.

In a fourth degree static portfolio you rebalance to get a *constant* expected risk allocation. Once again you'd need to sell Apple and buy Microsoft to bring things back into line. My example **asset allocating investor** will be running a fourth degree static portfolio. Although they will not use any dynamic trading rules, they will use the systematic **framework** to ensure that their portfolio risk remains as desired.

---

30. In a speech in 2002 US Secretary of State Donald Rumsfeld identified three kinds of knowledge: known knowns, known unknowns and unknown unknowns.
31. I'll discuss exactly how you measure recent levels of standard deviation in chapter ten, 'Position sizing'. If you can't wait, it's on page 155.
32. This essentially is the problem that Nassim Taleb discusses in his book *The Black Swan*.

CONCEPT: VOLATILITY STANDARDISATION

One of the most powerful techniques I use in my trading system **framework** is **volatility standardisation**. This is adjusting the returns of different assets so that they have the same expected risk. As I discussed above, my standard definition of expected risk is to use an estimate of recent **standard deviation**.

This has a number of benefits. It allows you to have portfolios where each component contributes an equal amount of risk. Furthermore, as you'll see later in the book it means that you can apply the same trading rule to different assets, if the trading rule is applied to volatility standardised returns.

It also means that you can easily combine different **trading rules**, and run portfolios of rules for multiple **instruments**.

Skew again

The most overlooked characteristic of a strategy is the expected **skew** of its returns, i.e. how symmetrical they are.

As you shall see in chapter nine, 'Volatility targeting', the different characteristics of positive and negative skew trading determine how much risk you should take. If you are using a systematic **trading rule** and have access to **back-testing** technology you can measure your skew. Otherwise you will need to make a judgment on what it is likely to be based on your trading style.

Be aware that if you are making steady profits nearly every day, and most of your trades are winners, then there is a good chance you are engaged in negative skew trading. It's just that you haven't yet seen any rare large losses.

Positive skew	Negative skew
Frequent small losses and infrequent large gains.	Frequent small gains and infrequent large losses.
Like buying an insurance policy.	Like selling an insurance policy.
Similar to buying options, you benefit from prices moving more than expected.	Similar to selling options, you benefit from prices moving less than expected.
Because losses tend to be small and frequent, risk management is easier.	Because losses are large and infrequent, risk management is harder.
Leverage required depends on **asset class**, but is lower than for negative skew.	Often requires leverage to achieve decent absolute returns in normal times; so gets killed in bad times.

Positive skew	Negative skew
Examples:	Examples:
• Trend following strategies.	• FX **carry**
• Bets done by buying options, e.g. if you think the stock market will weaken then buying put options.	• Fixed income relative value as practised by Long Term Capital Management (LTCM), a large hedge fund that blew up in 1998.[**]
• John Paulson in 2006 buying cheap credit default swap insurance on securities backed by mortgages.[*]	• Market making.
• Tail protect hedge funds that try and provide cheap insurance against large market moves, as practised by Nassim Taleb amongst others.	• Short option strategies, e.g. selling equity option 'straddles' (pairs of call and put options). Such as Nick Leeson of Barings who lost around $1 billion selling straddles in January 1995.[***]

[*] See *The Greatest Trade Ever* by Gregory Zuckerman.
[**] See *When Genius Failed* by Roger Lowenstein.
[***] See *Rogue Trader* by none other than Nick Leeson.

Trading speed: Fast vs Slow

Very slow (average holding period: several months to many years)

Very slow systems look almost like **static** portfolios, with additional gradual changes in position coming from their trading rules. Rules often involve **mean reversion** to very long run equilibrium such as **relative value** equity portfolios that buy past losers, and sell recent winners.

Returns from **dynamic** trading get worse the less frequently you trade because of the **law of active management**; at these slow speeds they will be very poor. These lower profits can't be statistically distinguished from noise, so you should avoid using these kinds of rules in systematic strategies.

CONCEPT: LAW OF ACTIVE MANAGEMENT

The **law of active management**, first articulated by Richard Kahn in 1989, states that the **Sharpe ratio**[33] of a trading strategy will be proportional to the square root of the number of independent bets made per year.

This law gives us some idea of how profits should vary with trading speed. Suppose you're holding one asset at a time, and making one 'bet' per year (buying, holding for 12 months before selling, then repeating), and that you expect an SR of 0.15 from this activity.

Now if you decide to make four 'bets' a year, holding the asset for three months, then because 2 is the square root of 4 you should expect an SR of 2 × 0.15 = 0.30. If you begin betting every single business day, then with around 256 business days in a year the SR will be 16 times larger than 0.15, or 2.4. This is a very decent Sharpe ratio indeed.

Unfortunately this result is theoretical and has its flaws. Firstly it assumes that the 'skill' of the trader is constant across holding periods. However the skills required to day trade are very different from those a long-term investor needs, as I'm sure Warren Buffett would agree. This is particularly true for systematic trading rules which tend to have a 'sweet spot' holding period. For example at medium frequencies of weeks to months most assets exhibit **momentum**; but at shorter and longer horizons they behave differently.

More importantly the law ignores transaction costs. As you'll see later in the book these can seriously damage the returns of fast traders, except perhaps in very cheap markets.

Nevertheless this result seems to hold reasonably well for longer periods where costs are not an issue. Most trading rules see their Sharpe ratios declining once they have holding periods exceeding several months. If due to high costs you need to trade this slowly you are probably better trying not to forecast asset prices at all, like an **asset allocating investor**.

The other important implication of the law is that diversification across assets can substantially improve returns. If you can find four assets which have zero **correlation** then you can double your Sharpe ratio. Whilst this might seem unrealistic a trading strategy with a large number of **instruments**, covering a group of half a dozen **asset classes**, the returns of which will be relatively uncorrelated, can have returns which are two to three times those for a single asset.

---

33. Actually it's the information ratio, which is identical to the Sharpe ratio except that the numerator is the return relative to a benchmark rather than the risk free rate. For our purpose however the distinction isn't important.

Medium (average holding period: a few hours or days, to several months)

Again because of the **law of active management** you get more attractive returns as you reduce your holding period to a few months or less. Profits from trading rules become statistically significant and they can be **back-tested**.

Although trading rules can't attain the large **Sharpe ratios** of high frequency trading they are readily accessible to a wider population of traders. A manual system, run part-time, working on daily data and trading through an ordinary broker works well enough. As a result more people's effort and research goes into investigating this particular realm, so it's perhaps less likely that there are any highly profitable and novel trading rules that have not yet been discovered.

Trading costs need to be accurately measured to decide whether an **instrument** should be traded at a faster or slower speed within this region. Large institutional traders also need to determine if a market has the capacity to absorb their trading. I cover these subjects in chapter twelve, 'Speed and Size'.

Fast (holding period: microseconds to one day)

The final part of the spectrum goes from day trading down to millisecond level high frequency trading and market making. Typical raw Sharpe ratios could be very high due to the number of trades made, but costs will chew up a big chunk of profits. Special execution algorithms are needed to reduce costs below normal levels. **Back-testing** requires sophisticated models of the evolution of the order book.

There are higher barriers to entry than at slower speeds; co-located servers and fully automated software is needed. Also faster strategies are likely to have limited capacity. Capital requirements are small as positions are not held overnight, but there is always the danger of extreme losses due to markets gapping, or systems going rogue. It is impossible for humans to monitor trading activity in real time so you need very tight controls and good monitoring systems.

All this means that realising the very high theoretical Sharpe ratio from super fast strategies is no picnic. The domain of high frequency trading mostly falls outside the scope of this book.

Technical vs fundamental

Strategies vary in the **source of data** they use, either using technical or fundamental information, or both. Purely **technical** rules only use price data. Non price, **fundamental** data, comes in two main flavours: micro and macro. Micro data is about a specific asset, for example the yield of a particular bond or the PE ratio of a company. Macro data such as inflation and GDP growth covers entire economies.

I have worked extensively with both fundamental and technical data. Technical systems are easier to build and run, but in another example of barriers to entry the additional effort required for including fundamental rules is usually rewarded with higher returns. The examples in this book are all technical, but only because they are simpler to explain.

Portfolio size

There are successful traders who only ever trade one futures contract. At the other extreme large equity index funds could have thousands of holdings. Remember that the **law of active management** shows that diversification is the best source of additional risk adjusted returns. Both traders and investors should hold more positions when they can; ideally across several **asset classes** to get the greatest possible benefit. With larger portfolios you're also less exposed to **instrument** specific problems such as bad data or temporary **liquidity** issues.

However smaller portfolios make sense for **semi-automatic traders** or for those running entirely manual systems. As I'll discuss in chapter twelve, 'Speed and Size', those with relatively small accounts also have to limit the number of positions they take.

To make them tractable the examples in this book have relatively small numbers of instruments. But I trade over 40 futures contracts across multiple asset classes in my own fully automated system since I firmly believe in diversification.

Leverage: more risk and yet more skew

Leverage is borrowing to invest or trade. The borrowing can be explicit as when trading equities on margin, or implicit as with **derivatives** like futures. You need leverage when the natural return and risk of an asset is less than desired. If you want a 10% return on average, and your asset is a bond with an expected **Sharpe ratio** of 0.5, but only a 5% annualised **standard deviation,** then you need to lever up four times.[34]

Is leverage dangerous? Not always. Leverage alone is a poor measure of risk, as varying amounts make sense for different assets. What makes it deadly is the potential for large unexpected losses.

Suppose you'd put on a **relative value** trade in 2007 between two highly **correlated** bonds, buying four year and selling five year bonds, both issued by the Greek government.[35] This would have earned you a fairly steady return of much less than 1% a year but with almost zero volatility. Because of the low natural risk you would probably have used leverage to increase your chances of getting a reasonable return like 5% or 10% a year.

---

34. With no leverage your expected return will be the Sharpe ratio of 0.5 multiplied by the standard deviation of 5%, e.g. 2.5%. To get a return of 10% you need to leverage your portfolio four times since 2.5% × 4 = 10%.

35. For finance geeks reading this it's implicit here that I am doing this trade on a duration neutral basis.

In early 2010 the close relationship between these two bonds collapsed due to the huge uncertainty about the likelihood and timing of a European bailout of Greece. You would have seen significantly higher losses on your four year bond than profits on the five year, and a huge loss overall.

To rub salt into the wound even though you could cover the initial losses your brokers then demanded yet more margin. You ended up forced to sell out at the worst possible price. Because you used leverage to do the trade you would have had no choice but to liquidate the position, even though it would be profitable when the bonds finally matured.

Notice that this relative value trade is a classic example of negative **skew**, small consistent gains until the trade goes terribly wrong. These steady gains tricked you into thinking that the position was low risk, and lured you into using leverage to improve your returns. But you have the **unpredictable risk** that the volatility or **correlations** will change, and for negative skew positions it will usually surprise with large losses rather than gains.

So beware of gearing up on apparently low risk with an asset or with a style of trading which is likely to have negative skew, even if you haven't yet seen any evidence of the large downside. As we'll see later in the book I'm firmly against trading instruments with very low volatility, and leveraging up negative skew trading rules too highly.

Contrarians, market followers and crowded trades

Mean reversion and **relative value** traders act as *contrarians* – they seek to take advantage of mis-pricing which means buying low after falls and selling when the price has risen. Other styles of trading involve *following* the market; notably the various forms of **trend following**. Contrarian traders like to catch falling knives and buy more as prices fall. **Trend followers** will close positions that have started to lose money, like the early loss taker trading rule. Market followers tend to see positive **skew** from taking small losses as the trend moves against them, with an occasional large profit from a significant move in their favour. Conversely contrarians see negative skew, with many small profits as each mis-pricing is corrected, then occasional large losses when prices jump away from their equilibrium.

Crowded trades are deadly. They happen when the majority of market participants have the same bet on, which could be from behaving as contrarians or market followers. As the story goes when the shoeshine boy or the taxi driver is in the market, it's time to get out. Crowded trades are most lethal when a leveraged strategy has started to go wrong and positions have to be liquidated to meet margin requirements.

Relative value strategies which need high leverage are particularly vulnerable to crowds. Often after a long stable period of rising markets these trades get swamped by people seeking extra returns. This results in the available profits being reduced, the apparent risk falling, and required leverage increasing further. Then the music stops and their negative skew becomes horribly apparent.

Two classic examples are the meltdown of fixed income relative value hedge fund manager Long Term Capital Management in mid-1998[36] and the Quant Quake – sharp losses seen over just two days by equity relative value systematic funds in August 2007.

Achievable Sharpe ratios

This section is relevant to all readers

It's important to have a realistic sense of what level of **Sharpe ratios (SR)** are achievable. As I said in the previous chapter, inflated expectations can lead to over betting (which we'll discuss more in chapter nine, 'Volatility Targeting') and overtrading (see chapter twelve, 'Speed and Size'), both of which will seriously damage your chances of trading profitably.

Let's begin with one of the simplest possible risky investments, a long only equity position in one company. Although they have been higher in the past, excess equity returns on single equities will probably average around 3% a year in the future. This is because the main cause of higher returns was the significant fall in inflation from the mid 1970's; something that won't be repeated. With annualised **standard deviation** of around 20% this implies an SR of 3% ÷ 20% = 0.15 is realistic.

Using the results implied by the **law of active management**, investing in a portfolio of equities will do slightly better. A group of at least 20 equities trading in the same country but diversified across different industries should have an SR of around 0.20. This is also what I'd expect from holding an equity index, like the S&P 500. If you invest globally across multiple countries you can probably get to a Sharpe ratio of around 0.25.

To do much better you'd need to allocate across multiple **asset classes**: equities, bonds, commodities and so on. Because **correlations** between asset classes are usually low a portfolio covering several of these types of assets can probably expect to reach a Sharpe ratio of around 0.40. Notice this is slightly more than double what you get from investing in an equity index. This is a realistic maximum figure for **static** strategies, like those used by **asset allocating investors**.

It's much harder to say what the returns should be for **dynamic trading rules**, like those used by **staunch systems traders**. My own experience is that with a reasonably diversified set of rules the average SR on a single **instrument**, such as a commodity future or FX spread bet, is around 0.40.[37] Again if you trade across multiple asset classes then you can get around double this.

---

36. See *When Genius Failed* by Roger Lowenstein.

37. This result comes from using trading rules with holding periods of a few days up to several months. My own highly diversified futures trading system has a **back-tested** SR of 1.0, and in part four I create a simplified version of this with an SR of just over 0.50. Both back tests are done following the advice in part two, so the SR are realistic and not **over-fitted**.

But many traders have highly unrealistic expectations of **back-tested** Sharpe ratios of 2.0, 3.0 or even higher; just on single instruments! These values are far too optimistic and are caused by **over-fitting**, which I'll discuss more in part two. In reality SR consistently greater than 1.0 are rarely achieved, even by sophisticated institutional investors. Analysis of returns from a group of systematic hedge funds shows that none could sustain a Sharpe ratio above 1.0 for more than a few years.[38]

What sort of SR should discretionary **semi-automatic traders** expect? This is a more difficult question to answer. It is generally accepted that only a minority of traders are profitable. Most likely to be losers are day traders and those in relatively expensive markets such as retail FX spread betting.

I'm inclined to be optimistic and assume that a competent trader following the advice in this book would get an average SR betting on a single instrument at a time of around 0.25. This is obviously lower than the trader using a systematic trading rule. Such traders tend not to diversify across asset classes. However if they did this would imply a total portfolio SR of no more than 0.50.

There is a good chance the Sharpe ratios I've given here probably won't meet your needs or expectations. There are two apparently easy ways to try and increase them, both of which are incredibly dangerous.

Firstly you could trade negative **skew** strategies. Very high SR is often a result of hidden negative skew. Take an imaginary strategy which returns 100% in year one, 65% in year two, 100% in year three, 65% in year four and so on. After 20 years the SR is an astonishing 4.6. Unfortunately in year 21 you make minus 100% and lose your entire investment. It turns out this system had seriously negative skew.

Although this might seem like a bad result the Sharpe ratio after 21 years is still an excellent 1.7, even once the skew has revealed itself. Clearly this is not a genuine example, but less extreme instances of this have actually occurred. For example the SR of Long Term Capital Management, the hedge fund which blew up in 1998 and which I mentioned earlier in the chapter, was also around 4.6.

The second path to the mirage of higher Sharpe is to trade more quickly. The **law of active management** implies that if you can realise a Sharpe ratio of 0.40 on a single instrument when trading with a holding period of a month, then betting once a day could boost that to an SR of 1.8. If you held your positions for just an hour and bet eight times a day you'd get to an SR of 5.2! As I said earlier, this assumes that profitable opportunities can be found at such timescales, and also ignores trading costs.

---

38. The analysis was done on a large set of Commodity Trading Advisors, a type of fund that is dominated by systematic **trend followers**. These returns are post fees (so the gross returns would be higher), but also include interest received on margin funds. These two effects roughly balance out. A small number of other types of systematic hedge fund are able to consistently return Sharpe ratios above 1.0. However, as I'll discuss below, this is often due to negative **skew**.

Table 2 assumes that you can achieve these theoretical pre-cost SR, but then takes costs into account.[39] It looks like trading every day, or every couple of days, could theoretically give you an SR above 1.0 on a single asset. However this is only true if you use futures, which are very cheap to trade. Most amateur investors use more expensive derivatives; for example spread bets in the UK. It's impossible, even in theory, to trade these quickly and profitably.

TABLE 2: CAN YOU REALLY MAKE MORE MONEY TRADING FASTER? IN THEORY IF YOU TRADE FUTURES, WHICH ARE CHEAP. WITH EXPENSIVE ASSETS LIKE SPREAD BETTING, NO CHANCE

Holding period	Theoretical SR pre-cost	After cost SR, average future	After cost SR, average spread bet
1 month	0.40	0.37	0.28
1 week	0.83	0.71	0.27
1 day	1.8	1.2	-0.75
Half a day	2.6	1.4	-2.5
One hour	5.2	0.28	-16.4

The table shows the theoretical Sharpe ratio (SR) for a given holding period (rows), assuming the one month SR is 0.40. SR are also shown after costs have been deducted, for a typical futures contract and spread bet respectively.

Conclusion

You may assume that I have a strong dislike for certain investing styles and **instruments**, in particular those with negative **skew**. Nothing could be further from the truth and about a third of my own trading system is in this category.

Instead I think that a balanced combination of **trading rules**, with different styles that work in different environments, is better than any single alternative. It's important that you understand and can cope with the risks of your trading system. You, and your client if you're a professional money manager, must be comfortable with the likely behaviour of your strategy.

I also believe finding the best trading rules is less important than designing your **trading system** in the correct way. In particular you need to avoid the serious crime of **overfitting**. This will be the subject of the next chapter as we move on to part two – the tools of systematic trading.

---

39. In chapter twelve, 'Speed and Size', I'll calculate how much it costs to trade different instruments. Those costs are used here.

PART TWO.

Toolbox

Chapter Three. Fitting

Staunch Systems Trader

This entire chapter is about using data to create the **trading rules** used by **staunch systematic traders**. It is not necessary reading if you are going to use my **framework** to make discretionary forecasts as a **semi-automatic trader** or without any rules at all as an **asset allocating investor**.

A DECISION TO RUN A SYSTEMATIC TRADING SYSTEM MEANS YOU have to select one or more **trading rules** and discard others as being unworthy. This process is often called **fitting**. Given our human tendency to be overconfident this procedure is fraught with danger. You need to beware of **over-fitting**:[40] selecting a set of trading rules that fit past data too well and which are unlikely to make money in the future.

Chapter overview

The perils of over-fitting	The dangers of trying to selectively choose and fit rules based on past data.
Effective fitting	Steps you must follow if you insist on fitting your trading rules.
How I choose my rules	The process I use to avoid fitting almost entirely.

---

40. Another common term for this is **curve fitting**.

The perils of over-fitting

The 50 model kid

Shortly after leaving the hedge fund industry, I began discussions about consulting, and managing some capital, for Aqueduct Capital,[41] a local proprietary trading firm. The office contained the usual mixture of grizzled ex-LIFFE traders and naïve youths, all day trading a handful of futures contracts. But the boss was particularly proud of his quantitative team which consisted of a couple of 20-somethings toting PCs running an off-the-shelf **back-testing** software package.

"This is Joe. He's only been here a month and he's already come up with 50 new trading rules that are profitable in back-tests!" exclaimed the boss.

"Yes, this software is amazing. It can automatically test hundreds of rules a day," added Joe.

I managed to keep a straight face and replied as diplomatically as I could, "Well I am sure some of them will work."

Inevitably the joint venture discussions then broke down, which was fortunate as the firm was liquidated a few months later. The discovery of apparently profitable rules sifted from thousands of possibilities is an incredibly dangerous approach, for reasons that will become apparent in the rest of the chapter.

Ideas first testing for rules and variations

Before understanding why Joe was on the wrong path you need to be clear on what **fitting** actually involves. I'm going to restrict my attention in this chapter to the **ideas first** method that I introduced in chapter two. You already know that I prefer the ideas first approach, but the reason I use it here is because it's much easier to explain and understand how to avoid over-fitting, than with the alternative of **data first**.

The fitting process is going to involve selecting one or more **trading rules** from a list of candidates, each based on a brilliant idea. Let's look at a contrived example, but beware this is not a rule I would recommend using. The basic hypothesis is that the British pound/US dollar currency rate seems to move in ranges as figure 6 shows. You might think that buying pounds if they're 5% below their average over the last year, and selling at 5% above, is a good strategy. This is an example of a **mean reversion** rule.

You would now test this initial rule on historical data and look at how it performs and behaves. At this stage if the rule is unpromising you can drop it and move on to the next idea. If you like it enough you can proceed to the next stage which I call **calibration**, although it's possible and often desirable to just stick with the initial version.

---

41. All names have been changed to protect the ignorant.

FIGURE 6: GBP VS USD EXCHANGE RATE

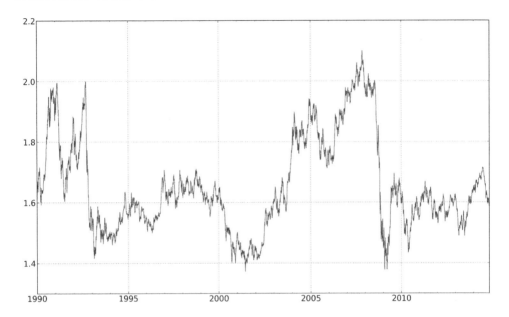

During calibration you examine some **variations** on the basic trading rule. In the simple example you could test the original range of plus or minus 5% against alternatives such as 3%, 6% or 10%; or you can compare the current price against the average price over the last year, or week, or two years and so on. Usually you would choose the most *profitable* rule using a performance measure like the **Sharpe ratio**. Calibration can also be used – as I will show later in the book – to find rules which *behave* in a given way, such as trading at a given speed. You can then decide which variation, or variations, to keep.

Once you have chosen a portfolio of trading rules and variations you need to decide how to allocate your capital amongst them. Portfolio allocation decisions like this are the subject of the next chapter. For the moment it's worth noting that a poor variation can be rejected out of hand, or given a relatively small allocation in the overall system.

What if you want to use data first methods? Then you will need to be sufficiently expert to apply the principles in this chapter with your own preferred tools.[42] You should not use a data first method for which you don't have any deep understanding. I strongly suggest that you do not use a method blindly, just because it came packaged with some **back-testing** software.

---

42. The main danger of the data first process is that you allow too many degrees of freedom. (I will not be defining this term since anyone using a data first approach ought to understand it already. If you don't you're in trouble!) Whereas the danger of ideas first is that you test too many ideas, or variations of ideas, until you find one (or 50!) that work. Either approach can result in over-fitted trading rules which look great in **back-test** but underperform once actually trading.

Before we continue here's a final note of caution about ideas first testing. Any worthy trading systems designer will know their history, have read all the right textbooks and be aware of what other people trade. You could end up testing only ideas that you already know will work, which is a form of implicit **over-fitting**. As a result no matter how careful you are with the subsequent fitting process your back-tested **Sharpe ratios** will probably still be overstated – beware overconfidence!

Cheating with a time machine

Let's consider the first common mistake when fitting, which is pretending that you had access to a time machine.

When fitting there are always two distinct time periods. First there is the period used to *fit* the model, and secondly the time period used to *test* it. To illustrate this consider again the example of trying to fit a GBPUSD trading rule, and assume you're trying to find the best single variation. Suppose you've got ten years of daily price data available to fit on.[43]

The easiest and probably most common method is to use the whole ten years as your fitting period, and find the single most profitable variation over that decade. You then go back and test how this single variation did over each of the same ten years. For each year that you are testing in, you use the same model, based on the entire ten years of data.

Figure 7 shows this for an example model running between 1990 and 2000. Each stage of the fitting occupies a row. So the first row shows that you would use all the data from the years 1990-2000 to fit the model which you test in 1990. In stage two you use the same fitted model to test performance in 1991, and so on.

The performance of this **back-test** will be amazing; too good to be true. Since no time machine was really available you didn't actually have the whole ten years of data in 1990 and you wouldn't necessarily have chosen the right variation. This is known as an **in sample** back-test because you are using the same data to fit and test performance. In sample testing should be avoided as it will produce extremely optimistic back-test results, and favour more complex rules that fit the data better but won't do as well in real trading.

There are better alternatives. A common one is to split the sample into two historical periods as in figure 8. You take all the data from the first half, 1990 to 1994, and fit the best variation over that period. Then you use that single variation to test your performance on the second **out of sample** period, which in this case is each year from 1995 to 2000.

---

43. Throughout this book I'm going to assume that you are using daily data. This often means you can get longer histories of prices and it is appropriate for the kinds of trading rules I'll be discussing. Having data at a higher frequency is only necessary if you're testing very fast trading rules, such as those that expect to hold positions for less than a week.

The problem with this is that you waste half your data, and end up with only six years of performance to look at.[44] You also don't account for any potential changes in market structure in the second half of the data.

FIGURE 7: IN SAMPLE BACK-TESTING: EFFICIENT BUT DISHONEST

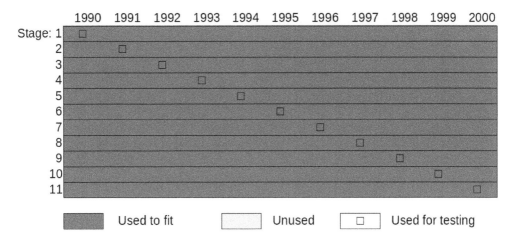

In sample testing. You use all the data to fit and then test performance from the start. In each stage (row) you test data for a different year, but use data from all years to fit.

FIGURE 8: HALF OUT OF SAMPLE TESTING: HONEST, BUT WASTEFUL

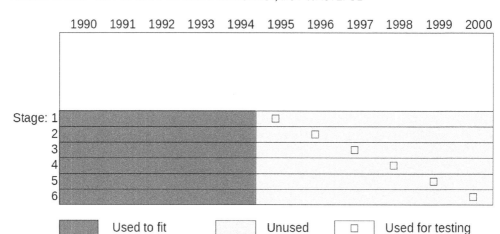

You fit your trading rules on the first half, and then test performance on the second half. In each stage (row) you test a different year, but always using the first half of the data to fit. No testing is done in the first half of the data. The second half of the data isn't used for fitting.

My preferred solution is to use an **expanding** window, as in figure 9.[45] Suppose you think you need at least a year to fit your system. In the next stage you fit on the first year of data for 1990, and then test the resulting variation in the second year, 1991. Then in stage three of figure 9 you test in 1992 using the variation fitted with data from the years 1990 and 1991. To test 1993 you use the best variation fitted using 1990, 1991 and 1992.

This continues until 2000 when you're using the previous ten years of data to select the best variation. Because you only fit using the past you're not cheating. You also use as much of the past as you 'legally' can, so nothing is wasted.

The only problem with this method is that if the world changes you'll still be using potentially irrelevant past data. To avoid this you could fit on the last five or ten years of data, once you have enough history to do so, and discard earlier years. This is a **rolling window**.[46] As figure 10 shows a five-year rolling window is identical to the expanding window until 1996. At this point you would discard 1990, and use only the years 1991 to 1995 to fit the best variation.

The length of the window needs to be short enough to pick up changes in market structure, but long enough to give statistically significant results. As you'll see later you often require multiple decades of data to fit models, which makes the use of rolling windows problematic.

---

45. This is sometimes called *anchored fitting*.
46. Another widely used term for this is *walk forward fitting*.

FIGURE 9: EXPANDING OUT OF SAMPLE IS BOTH EFFICIENT AND HONEST

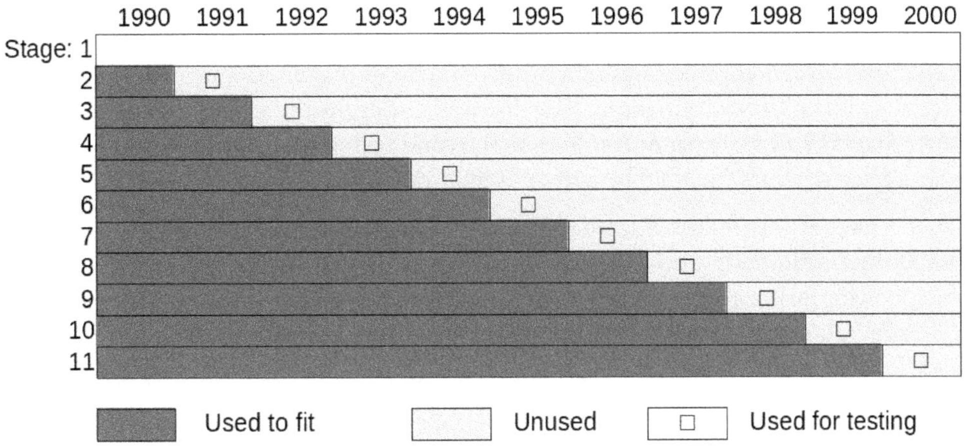

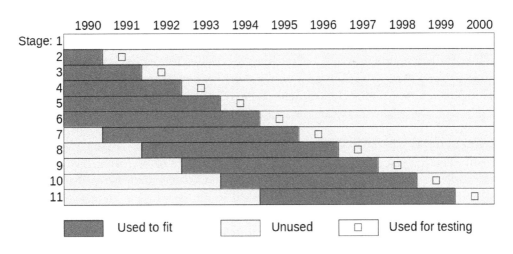

Every year you fit the data only on the past. Each row shows the fitting and testing done for a particular year.

FIGURE 10: ROLLING OUT OF SAMPLE ADAPTS TO CHANGING CONDITIONS, BUT MAKE SURE YOU HAVE ENOUGH DATA FOR STATISTICAL SIGNIFICANCE

Every year you use the past data to fit; up to five years' worth. Each row shows the fitting and testing done for a particular year.

When fitting goes bad

Now let's examine a concrete example of poor fitting practice. I'm going to select the best **variation** of the early loss taker **trading rule** I introduced in chapter one to run over the CME gold futures contract, out of a possible menu of 90 variations.[47] This might seem excessive, but it's fewer variations than Joe was testing in my earlier anecdote. Bear in mind that if I had a five parameter trading rule, and I allowed each parameter to take one of ten discrete values, then I'd be testing 10,000 variations!

Once I have at least one year of data I find the highest performing variation based on the **Sharpe ratio (SR)** from the previous 12 months. I then test the performance for the following year, again using the last 12 months of data. This process is then repeated annually. You should recognise this as a one year **rolling window back-test**.

Which of the following alternatives do you think will give me the best performance?

1. Picking the *best* variation: Each year I use the best performing variation from the previous year.

2. Picking a *random* variation: Ignoring my fitting, each year I choose one variation at random. Because the randomness of each choice will influence the results I run this experiment a number of times, and take the average performance.

3. Keeping *all* the variations: Again ignoring my fitting, I keep all 90 variations, and use an equally weighted average of their forecasts.

If you're a big fan of fitting the results are disappointing. Choosing the best rule each year from the previous year gives me a rather poor SR of 0.07. If I go for the second option and just choose a random rule annually each January 1st, then on average I get a Sharpe of 0.2. The best option is to forget about selecting trading rule variations entirely and run an equal blend of them all. This gives an SR of 0.33, which is pretty good for one kind of trading rule run on a single **instrument**. These results could be a fluke but I get similar results on many different instruments and trading rules.

Why does fitting do so badly?

Firstly choosing just one variation to run at a time smacks of overconfidence. As you'll see shortly we rarely have enough evidence that one rule is definitely better than another. Secondly one year of data is wholly insufficient to decide which trading rule is best. I make this problem worse by fitting on the history of a single instrument, gold futures. Finally, like Joe, I am testing far too many variations.

---

47. For those who are interested this is based on the 'A and B' system defined in appendix B. Values for B (the stop loss value) will be the integers from 1 to 10; to capture different trend lengths. Because I only want to look at trend following rules (early loss takers) I iterate only over values of A (the profit target) that are equal to or larger than B: A = 1 × B, 1.5 × B, 2 × B, … 5 × B. This gives 90 possible variations in all.

The hazards of rule selection

The multiple testing problem – even some random rules will look good

Why is it so dangerous to test large numbers of **trading rules** and **variations**? Apart from the effort involved it's very likely that you will end up picking a poor rule just by chance.

To see why here is an experiment. Let's suppose I am trying to achieve alchemy and find profitable rules where there are none to be had. I have a pool of a certain number of possible trading rules, all of which have true expected average returns of zero, although in a real scenario I wouldn't know this beforehand! The rules are entirely arbitrary and their returns are generated from random data.[48]

For each test I get one year of return data for each rule in my pool, as in the gold futures example above, and select all the rules whose **Sharpe ratio (SR)** in that year is higher than a given minimum level. If no rule has an SR above the threshold then I won't choose any. All the rules that pass the test will be kept (even if there are 50!).

Because the underlying data is random I need to generate new data multiple times and then repeat the test to get meaningful results. I then measure the average number of rules accepted given a specific minimum level and the size of the pool available. As table 3 shows, even if I'm strict and set an extremely high minimum SR of 2.0 I'll still pick up a couple of bad rules if I test enough of them.

TABLE 3: IF YOU TEST ENOUGH RULES, SOME BAD ONES WILL ALWAYS SLIP THROUGH

Number of rules tested in pool	Minimum Sharpe ratio		
	0.5	1.0	2.0
1	<1	<1	<1
5	1.4	<1	<1
10	3	1.5	<1
50	16	8	1.2
100	30	16	2.3

The table shows the average number of rules accepted from pools of arbitrary unprofitable rules, given different pool sizes (rows), which were tested to see if their Sharpe ratio exceeded a minimum cutoff (columns).

48. Many of the examples in this chapter will use imaginary daily returns of various arbitrary trading rule variations. These fake returns are randomly generated with the kind of characteristics I want: expected mean, standard deviation (from which we get the Sharpe ratio), and where relevant **correlation** with other variations. I then run these tests many times and report the average result, so the answer is not influenced by how each series of random numbers come out.

Practically then what SR cutoff should I use? As none of the imaginary rules are truly profitable ideally I wouldn't accept any. But in real fitting situations we can't set the bar too high or even good rules will be discarded; after all a realistic SR for a real trading rule, tested on one **instrument,** is only likely to be around 0.30. Let's suppose I would be happy with a 5% chance of picking out at least one rule that was truly unprofitable. Also in the real world I'd usually have more than one year of data, so let's see what effect additional history has on my findings.

Table 4 has all the results. As you might have suspected the length of the return series is very important here. More history means less chance of a zero SR rule getting a lucky streak, so I can set the cutoff lower. However, even with 30 years of data I can't risk testing more than a handful of rules, and even then the cutoff is far too high when many perfectly good variations will only have true Sharpe ratios of 0.3.

TABLE 4: WITH MORE HISTORY YOU CAN SET A LOWER SHARPE RATIO THRESHOLD TO AVOID PICKING A BAD RULE FROM A LARGER POOL

Number of rules tested	Years of data			
	1	5	10	30
1	1.5	0.7	0.5	0.4
5	2.3	1.1	0.8	0.5
10	2.8	1.2	0.8	0.6
50	3.4	1.5	1.0	0.6
100	3.4	1.5	1.1	0.7

The table shows the Sharpe ratio cutoff needed when testing a given size pool (rows) of trading rules, with a certain amount of years of historical data (columns) to ensure you only have a 5% chance of picking out one or more truly bad rules.

How much history do you need to decide if a rule is good?

You've now seen that a common mistake is to use insufficient historical data to select or calibrate a rule. How much data do you need? How long do you need to decide if a rule has a positive **Sharpe ratio (SR)** and is worth keeping?

To answer this I generated more random trading rule daily returns, this time assuming an underlying positive Sharpe ratio, which again I wouldn't know in advance. As more trading history is generated I can estimate the SR each year and the average so far. At the same time I look at the distribution of those annual Sharpe ratios.[49] This allows me to get

---

49. For a more technical discussion of this issue, see Andrew Lo's paper 'The Statistics of Sharpe ratios' in *Financial Analysts Journal* 58:4, July/August 2002.

a feel for how statistically significant my measured average SR is; was I just lucky or is this really a good system?

A classic test for statistical significance is the T-Test. In this example it determines whether an estimated Sharpe ratio is likely to be positive given the estimate of its mean and **standard deviation**. The further away the mean is from zero, as measured in units of **sigma**, the more likely the unknown SR is actually positive.

This test is commonly used with a threshold of two **sigma**. If an estimated average SR is more than two standard deviations above zero there would only be a 2.5% chance of this happening if the true SR was actually negative.

Figure 11 shows the evolution of the average measured SR for an arbitrary trading rule, and around it the upper and lower 'confidence intervals'. Each confidence interval is two **sigma** away from the average, so when the lower interval pushes above zero I know there is only a 2.5% chance the trading system is really a loss making rule in disguise.

FIGURE 11: WITH A TRUE SHARPE RATIO (SR) OF 0.5, IT TAKES MORE THAN TEN YEARS TO PASS THE T-TEST AND CONCLUDE THE SR IS PROBABLY POSITIVE

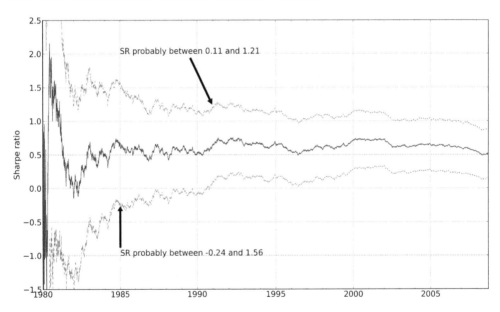

In the figure you can see the average SR converging quickly on the true value of 0.5 SR. But it takes over ten years before the lower confidence interval goes above zero and the T-Test is finally passed. Only then can we be reasonably certain this is not a loss making system.

If I repeat this for a rule with a true SR of 1.0 I get figure 12. The time to pass the test here is just a few years. On average it will always take less time for higher SR strategies to prove their profitability.

FIGURE 12: WITH A TRUE SHARPE RATIO OF 1.0 WE PASS THE T-TEST IN A FEW YEARS

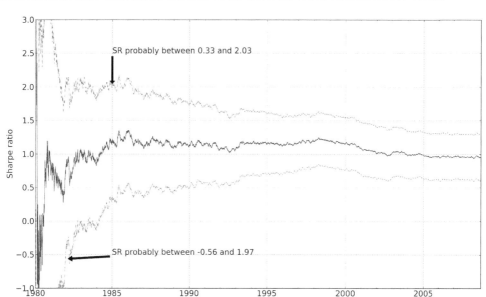

Let's find the average time to pass the test for a given true Sharpe ratio. After running the necessary experiments I get table 5. Except for very good rules you need at least ten years, and usually more, to be sure a strategy makes money.[50] The average trading rule for one **instrument** has a realistic SR of around 0.3; so you'd need nearly 40 years of history!

TABLE 5: IT TAKES DECADES OF DATA TO SEE IF MOST STRATEGIES ARE LIKELY TO BE PROFITABLE

True Sharpe ratio	0.2	0.3	0.4	0.5	0.7	1.0	1.5	2.0
Average years to pass profit T-Test	45	37	33	20	10	6	3	1.4

The table shows average time in years to pass the T-Test for profitability given the true Sharpe ratio of the trading rule.

---

50. These results also depend on the **skew** of returns. For example, with a true SR of 1.0 I needed about three years' more data for a typical negative skew volatility selling strategy to pass the T-Test, compared to a positive skew **trend following** strategy.

How much history do you need to decide if one rule is better than another?

Now what if you have some alternative rules and want to find the best. Let's suppose I again have two random rules, one with a true **Sharpe ratio** (SR) of 0.30, and the other an SR of 0.80. Initially I'm going to assume these are quite different rules with no **correlation** between their returns. This time to perform the T-Test I need to estimate the difference in the two Sharpe ratios, and measure the average and standard deviation of that difference.

FIGURE 13: IT TAKES THREE DECADES TO DISCOVER THAT THIS SR 0.8 STRATEGY IS PROBABLY BETTER THAN AN UNCORRELATED STRATEGY WITH SR 0.3

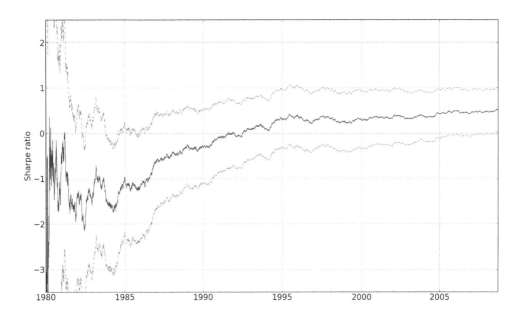

In figure 13 is the average difference in SR and the relevant confidence intervals for this difference. Once the lower confidence interval goes above zero then we can be reasonably certain that one rule is better, as again there is only a 2.5% probability of this happening by chance. You can see from figure 13 that the time to certainty is around 30 years!

Table 6 shows the average time taken to pass the T-Test when comparing an SR 0.30 rule with one that truly has a higher SR. These results vary depending on the difference in SR and the correlation of the rules. More closely related rules will be easier and quicker to distinguish for a given SR difference.[51] In practice distinguishing rules requires

---

51. More subtly the overall level of the Sharpes involved will also influence the results, as Andrew Lo's paper discusses. The skew of the rules is also important, even when comparing rules with similar skew.

considerable historical data except for the rare cases of variations which are both highly correlated, and also perform very differently.

TABLE 6: CAN YOU DISTINGUISH TRADING RULES GIVEN A FEW YEARS OF DATA? ONLY IF THEY ARE HIGHLY CORRELATED AND ONE HEAVILY OUTPERFORMS THE OTHER

Sharpe ratio advantage	Correlation between rules				
	-1.0	0.0	0.5	0.8	0.95
0.1	47	47	46	44	37
0.25	46	45	40	32	10
0.5	41	37	25	10	3
1.0	23	11	8	2.5	0.5

The table shows the number of years needed for us to be reasonably certain that one rule is better than another, given the SR advantage of the better rule (rows) and the correlation between the trading returns of the two rules (columns).

Should you fit one trading rule for all instruments?

In 2010 the large systematic hedge fund in which I worked was reorganised into **asset classes**. My team managed the fixed income portfolio, another ran equities and so on. Initially the trading strategies we ran were fairly similar. However over time, as we did more market specific research, we all became convinced that we needed to customise our systems differently.

In many cases we went further and also began to fit different parts of our portfolios separately. We might for example have fitted emerging and developed market bond futures with different trading rule variations.[52] Fitting separately is common, and many system traders take this to the extreme and fit every **instrument** separately. Almost all **back-testing** packages, such as the one Joe was using, default to fitting trading rules on a single instrument at a time. So you would have one **variation** of a rule for the British pound/dollar, another for euro/dollar and so on.

This is a classic example of the narrative fallacy, a **cognitive bias** we have seen before. To our human minds it makes sense to have different stories, and so different trading rules, for different instruments.

---

52. In reality we didn't do this. Or did we? Unfortunately I can't give real examples without breaking the terms of my non-disclosure agreement.

But is this the right thing to do? It depends on whether the behaviour of each variation over the various instruments is significantly different. If it isn't then you're likely to be **over-fitting** by individually tailoring each rule for every instrument. In practice there isn't usually a statistical difference between different instruments, particularly if they are closely related such as a group of equity index futures.[53]

In fact pooling your data and fitting multiple instruments together is an excellent way of getting more data history, which gives you a better shot at being able to distinguish profitable and loss making trading rules.

As an example I have two trading rules in my own portfolio which for a typical single instrument have **Sharpe ratios (SR)** averaging 0.05 and 0.30 respectively. Despite being perfectly uncorrelated, table 6 shows I'd need 45 years to distinguish them; almost impossible when even the earliest financial futures only began trading in 1972. However the same rules run on a portfolio of instruments have SR of 0.13 and 1.13.[54] The table shows I'd need just 11 years of data to distinguish these two Sharpe ratios from each other.

To make pooling easier you should design trading rules that are generic and can work with any instrument. I'll give some examples of generic rules in chapter seven, 'Forecasts'.

Some rules for effective fitting

If you haven't been warned off fitting, and insist on using data to select and calibrate trading rules, then following this advice should keep you out of serious trouble. Those who are now rightly terrified of fitting can skip ahead to the next section, where I show you how I avoid fitting almost completely.

Keep it simple

I am not a fan of complex fitting methods and I prefer not to use them. But if you do consider yourself an expert in a dark statistical art then naturally you would want to practise it. Just be aware; the more complex the method the harder it will be to realise when you are **over-fitting**.

---

53. There are some exceptions, notably when there are different trading costs for the instruments concerned, which I'll cover in chapter twelve, 'Speed and Size'.

54. Technical note: These are the returns you'd get if you traded an equally weighted portfolio of instruments using the same trading rule. The improvement in **Sharpe ratio (SR)** comes from the diversification effect across instruments. The alternative method is to stitch consecutive series of instrument returns together. This gives a very long history of returns, but the SR of the stitched series will be almost the same as the average across individual instruments (it is not identical to the average because of the effect of varying lengths of price series for different instruments).

Fewer alternatives

As table 4 shows reducing the pool of **trading rules** and **variations** considered is crucial unless you have many years of data.[55]

Ban time machines

You should always use **rolling** or **expanding out of sample** fitting. If using a **rolling** window don't make it too short; be aware of the number of years needed to distinguish rules from random noise, and each other (tables 4, 5 and 6).

Don't drop rules casually

Before picking one rule or variation and discarding others based on past performance, look carefully at table 6. It's unusual in reality to find highly **correlated** rules with radically different performance. More likely you will find very different rules with perhaps a **Sharpe ratio (SR)** difference of 0.5 but almost no correlation, or highly correlated rule variations which are very similar in SR. In both cases you need 30 years of data to differentiate them.

It's rare to have 30 years or more of price history, so it's difficult to justify picking one rule over another on performance alone.

Pool data across instruments

You're going to need all the data you can to make good fitting decisions. The easiest solution is to pool data from multiple **instruments**.

Only if there is a statistically significant difference in performance between various rules across instruments should you fit them individually. In practice this is rarely necessary.

Compare apples with apples

I've assumed throughout this chapter that you will use **Sharpe ratio (SR)** to compare rules. But comparing a positively **skewed** rule and a negatively skewed alternative purely on SR is highly misleading, as negative skew rules will tend to have flatteringly high SR.

When the future won't be like the past

Be careful of focusing on outright performance, rather than returns relative to benchmarks. This is very dangerous because many **asset classes**, like equities and bonds, have done extraordinarily well over the last 40 years or so. The easiest way to get extra **back-tested** profits is to use trading rules which are more highly **correlated** with the underlying asset class.

---

55. If you are using a more complex fitting technique then you need to keep your degrees of freedom appropriately small.

This is unlikely to work in the future as the main cause of these high returns was significant falls in inflation; something that won't be repeated.

How I choose my rules

There are many ways to navigate the fitting minefield. My own preference is to avoid it almost completely, by selecting trading rules and variations without looking at actual performance. I use the following process:

1. Come up with a small number of **trading rules** to exploit each idea I have about how the market behaves.

2. For each rule select a few **variations**. At this stage I am not looking at performance, but at behaviour such as trading speed and **correlation** with other variations.

3. Allocate **forecast weights** to each variation, taking uncertainty about **Sharpe ratios** into account. Poor rules will have lower weight, but are rarely entirely excluded.

This process means that I don't use performance to fit trading rules and variations. Instead returns data is reserved for finding forecast weights. These weights determine in what proportion each variation is used to predict each instrument's returns. The next chapter will explain how this portfolio allocation can reduce the weight on apparently poor variations without risking over-fitting.

Any variation that ends up with a negligible weight in the final portfolio can ultimately be dropped from your live trading system, reducing the complexity of implementation. This gives the same end result as excluding the rule earlier, but it means any **back-tested** performance incorporating the excluded rule will be more realistic.

Start with a small number of ideas

I prefer to come up with a relatively small number of ideas for trading rules. In my own portfolio I have eight rules drawn from five different themes, but if I was starting from scratch I'd begin with just a couple of rules: the **trend following** and **carry** rules that I will show you in chapter seven, 'Forecasts'.

You should have a *small* number of rules because:

1. Less risk of over-fitting: Fewer ideas means less chance of over-fitting, and a lower critical **Sharpe ratio** is required before accepting a rule (table 4).

2. Many ways to skin the feline: One kind of market behaviour can be picked up in multiple ways. For example we can capture trends with **momentum** oscillators, divergence and breakout systems to name but a few. There is little value in having dozens of similar rules for one kind of behaviour.

3. Keep it simple: With my process all the rules will survive the selection process so starting with too many rules will create complexity in the trading system. Complex systems are more difficult to trust and understand.

Far too much time and effort is spent by both amateur and professional trading system designers in looking for more, and better, trading rules. But the marginal value of adding additional rules is low, especially if they are of the same trading style. The average **correlation** between different rules trading a particular **instrument** is higher than between instruments trading the same rule. So diversification amongst instruments is preferable to rule diversification.

Adding new instruments is a tiresome task of uploading and checking data which is less fun than coming up with more trading rules, but in my experience is of far more benefit.

Keep the right number of variations

Although I prefer to have relatively few **trading rules** I wouldn't normally have just one variation of any rule which can be calibrated. But there is no need to use 90 or more possible combinations! For example if you're trying to capture price **momentum** then you will probably need a variation that captures relatively fast trends, one that captures very slow moves and perhaps two to three in between.

If two of your variations have more than a 95% **correlation** you can safely drop one of them since it will have almost no marginal benefit. You can also remove variations whose trading costs will be too high, or which trade extremely slowly and so are unlikely to give you significant returns. But do not drop variations purely because of their performance.

Don't look at returns - yet

My preference is to reserve actual historic performance data for deciding which **forecast weights** to give to **trading rules** and their **variations**. Done properly this can give you realistic **back-tested** performance and still down-weight poor trading rules. But if you've already used real data to pre-select only good rules then your back-test performance will be too optimistic, and you'll have **over-fitted**.

So at this stage it's only behaviour such as **correlation** and likely trading costs you should be looking at, not performance. You must avoid contaminating the back-test.

There isn't much detail about this process here but there will be examples of how it works later in the book. Whether you fit your trading rules, or use my hands off approach, the next problem is to decide how much of rule X and how much of Y – and how much of **instrument** A or B – to use in your trading system. This problem of **portfolio allocation** is covered in the next chapter.

Chapter Four. Portfolio Allocation

Staunch systems trader

Asset allocating investor

This chapter is about deciding how you share out your trading capital between different **instruments** or **trading rules**. Deciding the allocation between instruments is important for **asset allocating investors**, whilst **staunch systems traders** have to make both kinds of decision.

It isn't relevant if you're a **semi-automatic trader**, since you won't use systematic trading rules and will trade different instruments opportunistically. You can skip this chapter.

DECIDING HOW TO ALLOCATE WITHIN A PORTFOLIO OF ASSETS IS a problem every investor faces. How much in equities, bonds or cash? Should you split your equity allocation evenly between countries or just stick it all in the USA?

Allocation decisions are equally important for systematic investors and traders. If you're a **staunch systems trader** running more than **one trading rule**, including any **variations**, then you need to decide what **forecast weights** to use when you combine rules together to forecast the price of each instrument.

Both staunch systems traders and **asset allocating investors** also need to decide **instrument weights**; how much of your portfolio to put into the trading systems you have for each **instrument**. Because the tools in this chapter are for making both kinds of decision, I'll refer to portfolios of generic assets, which could be either instruments or trading rules. Later in the book I'll show you specific examples of each of the two types of allocation problem.

Just like trading rules, portfolio weights can be **over-fitted**. Optimising weights can give you a portfolio which does really well in **back-tests**, but which fails badly when traded in reality. Such portfolios are usually highly extreme; allocating to just a small subset of the assets available. In this chapter I'll show you how to avoid the pitfalls of these highly undiversified portfolios.

Chapter overview

Optimising gone bad	How classic portfolio optimisation can often result in over-fitted extreme portfolio weights.
Saving optimisation from itself	Some insights from an alternative technique, bootstrapping, which can help us understand what is going wrong.
Making weights by hand	How to use a simple method called handcrafting to get portfolio weights.
Incorporating Sharpe ratios	Using additional information about expected performance to improve handcrafted weights.

Optimising gone bad

Introducing optimisation

Portfolio optimisation will find the set of asset weights which give the best expected risk adjusted returns, usually measured by **Sharpe ratio**. The inputs to this are the expected average returns, **standard deviation** of returns, and their **correlation**. The standard method for doing this was first introduced by Harry Markowitz in the 1950s. It was a neat and elegant solution to a complex problem.

Unfortunately it's all too easy to be distracted by elegance, and forget the important assumptions underlying the maths. As you will see below, blind use of this method frequently results in ugly portfolios with extreme weights. Just because an equation is wonderful to behold doesn't mean you should slavishly use its results without thought of the consequences. As Einstein said, "If you are out to describe the truth, leave elegance to the tailor."

In the early part of my career I was fatally distracted by the lovely equations and ended up with some terrible portfolios, until I learned the error of my ways. Subsequently I often had to review the allocation decisions made by researchers who were less experienced, although undoubtedly cleverer and more academically qualified than myself.

When I asked one of these rocket scientists what they thought about the extreme portfolio weights they'd found I often got a shrug. "These are what the optimiser came up with." The unspoken assumption was that the equation *must* be right. Hopefully after reading this chapter you will be less accepting of attractive mathematics.

Some good news

Portfolio optimisation is hard. But there are a few difficulties that don't arise when you're using it to design trading strategies. This is because you aren't deciding directly how large your positions in various **instruments** should be. Instead you're deciding what weight should be given to different parts of your **trading system**. These can either be the **forecast weights** telling you in what proportion to use **trading rule variations** for a particular instrument, or the **instrument weights** determining how much of your capital to allocate for trading each instrument.

This gives you two advantages. Firstly, you can't have negative weights in your portfolio; you can't short trading rules, so the lowest possible weight is zero. If a trading rule is expected to lose money you shouldn't include it at all.[56] Secondly, using my **framework** will mean that profits from your trading rules have identical expected **standard deviation** of returns. This is because of the **volatility standardisation** I spoke about in chapter two, 'Systematic Trading Rules'. By using this technique you simplify the problem and only need to use expected **Sharpe ratios** and **correlations** to work out your weights.

Although you won't be optimising the underlying positions in individual assets like equities or bonds in your trading systems, I will be using portfolios of simple assets in this chapter to make the examples more straightforward. However to make it easier to interpret the results I will adjust asset returns before any calculations so that they have the same standard deviation as you'll have when you work with trading system returns.

The unstable world of portfolio weights

Let's take a simple example of allocating capital between three assets: the NASDAQ and S&P 500 US stock indices, and the US 20 year benchmark bond. I am using data from January 1999 to mid-2014 and all returns are **volatility standardised** to have the same expected standard deviation. Each year from January 2000 onwards I'm going to use returns from all previous years to calculate some optimal weights.[57] Because each optimisation uses all available data to create a single set of weights I call this a **single period optimisation**.

---

56. A rule with a significantly negative Sharpe ratio either has very high trading costs and should be omitted, or it is consistently wrong and so should be inverted with longs and shorts reversed before incorporating it into the portfolio (although you'll probably also want to consider the logic of your original idea before proceeding).

57. If you read the previous chapter you should recognise this as an **out of sample expanding window**.

The calculation is done using the classic Markowitz optimisation; I find the maximum risk adjusted return (e.g. **Sharpe ratio**) using the estimated means and **correlations**, and standard deviations (which are all identical because I've used **volatility standardisation**). I also don't allow weights to be negative and they have to sum up to exactly 100%.

Figure 14 shows the weights calculated for each year.[58] In the last throes of the late 1990s tech boom I naturally put all my money into the fast rising NASDAQ. This then implodes, and is permanently removed from the portfolio. For much of the remaining period I put my entire capital in bonds. At the end I only have 25% in equities, all of which is in the S&P 500. This is a very extreme portfolio, with very unstable weights.

FIGURE 14: SINGLE PERIOD OPTIMISATION USUALLY MEANS EXTREME WEIGHTS

The figure shows the portfolio weights produced by single period optimisation done each year on all previous data.

Not all statistical estimates are created equal

Faced with such nightmares a natural reaction is to discard any hope of optimising. Perhaps we should just allocate equally to all the assets we have. Many academic researchers have

---

58. Remember these are displayed as if all assets had the same standard deviation. So in practice roughly twice as much actual money would be allocated to bonds than shown here, due to their lower volatility.

also come to this conclusion and there is plenty of evidence that equal weights are hard to beat.[59]

When do equal weights make sense?[60]

1. Same volatility: If all assets had the same expected standard deviation of returns. This is always the case for the **volatility standardised** assets we're using.

2. Same Sharpe ratio: If all assets had the same expected **Sharpe ratio (SR)**.

3. Same **correlation**: If all assets had the same expected co-movement of returns.

If these assumptions aren't correct, then what should your portfolio look like?[61]

What kind of portfolio should we have with...

1. Same Sharpe ratio and correlation: Equal weights.

2. Significantly different Sharpe ratio (SR): Larger weights for assets that are expected to have higher SR, smaller for low SR.

3. Significantly different correlation: Larger weights for highly diversifying assets which have lower correlations to other assets, and smaller for less diversifying assets.

Let's see if these assumptions are true in the simple example. Figure 15 shows the distribution of Sharpe ratios for each of the three assets. Notice that the lines mostly overlap; this means we can't distinguish between the historic performance of each asset. Although bonds did have a higher average SR the advantage isn't statistically significant. If you read the previous chapter, and remember table 6, it is no surprise that the 15 years of data isn't enough to say with confidence which asset had the best SR.

---

59. For example see DeMiguel, Victor, Lorenzo Garlappi and Raman Uppal, 'Optimal versus naive diversification: How inefficient is the 1/N portfolio strategy?', *Review of Financial Studies* 2009.

60. To be pedantic there are some unusual portfolios where equal weights are optimal that don't fulfill these criteria, but they aren't relevant here.

61. The portfolios examined by academic researchers mostly consisted of equities from the same country, which tend to have similar standard deviation and correlations. In this situation equal weights will indeed be hard to beat.

FIGURE 15: HARDER TO DISTINGUISH SHARPE RATIOS THAN YOU THINK

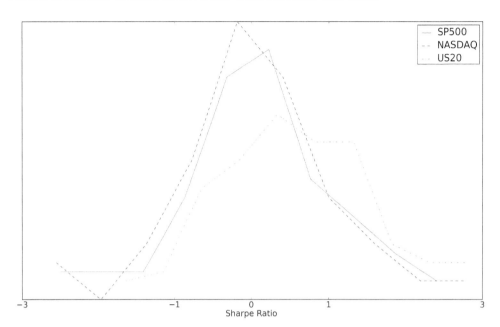

The figure shows the distribution of Sharpe ratios for the three assets in my example portfolio.

On the contrary, we can often distinguish different correlations. Figure 16 shows the distribution of correlations in my simple example. You should be able to easily pick apart the correlated equities and the diversifying bond asset.

So in the simple example I should be able to do better than equal weights, as there is significant data about correlations. A good portfolio would have more of the diversifying bond asset than the equities, but wouldn't take much account of the insignificantly different Sharpe ratios. However the classic optimiser doesn't work like this, because it can't see all the information in figures 15 and 16. It uses only the average SR and correlation, not knowing or caring how much uncertainty there is in each estimate.

FIGURE 16: EQUITIES CLEARLY CORRELATED WITH EACH OTHER, AND NEGATIVELY WITH BONDS

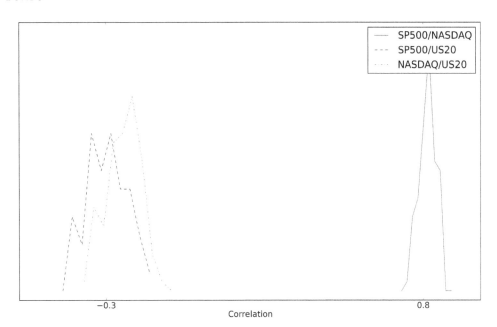

The figure shows the distribution of correlations for pairs of the three assets in my example portfolio.

Saving optimisation from itself

How can we fix this problem? I have two techniques that I use. The first, which is quite hard work, is called **bootstrapping**. This involves repeating my optimisation many times over different parts of the data, taking the resulting weights, and averaging them out. So the weights are the *average of many optimisations*, rather than *one optimisation on the average* of all data.

The justification for bootstrapping is simple. I believe that the past is a good guide to the future, but I don't know which part of the past will be repeated. To hedge my bets I assume there is an equal chance of seeing any particular historical period repeated. So it's logical to use an average of all the portfolios which did best in previous periods.

Bootstrapping has some nice advantages over classic optimisation. Most of the individual optimisations have extreme weights. However with enough of them it's unlikely the average will be extreme. If I have noisy data, and the past contains periods which were very different, then the optimal portfolios will be close to equal weights. But with significant differences in **Sharpe ratios** or **correlations** similar portfolios will crop up repeatedly, and the average will reflect that. The averaged weights naturally reflect the amount of uncertainty that the data has.

Let's see the results of running an **expanding window** bootstrap optimisation on our simple three asset portfolio. Figure 17 shows the results over time, whilst table 7 compares the final weights with a classic **single period optimisation** and equal weights.[62] After the first year the weights are relatively stable, and for all periods less extreme than for the single period method. However the diversifying allocation to bonds is greater than with equal weights, so this portfolio should do better.

FIGURE 17: BOOTSTRAPPED PORTFOLIO WEIGHTS: STABLE AND EVENLY SPREAD

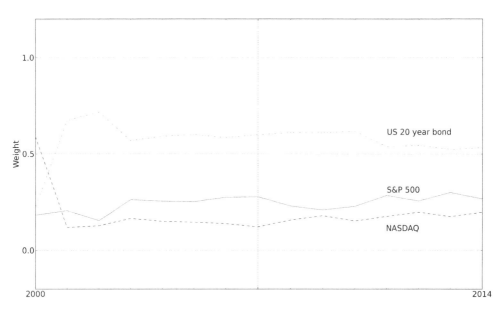

The figure shows the portfolio weights I get over time from using the bootstrap method on the example assets.

---

62. This is the result of using 100 bootstraps, each 1 year in length, with daily returns drawn randomly with replacement.

TABLE 7: BOOTSTRAPPED WEIGHTS ARE MORE EVEN THAN THE SINGLE PERIOD METHOD, BUT ACCOUNT FOR CORRELATIONS BETTER THAN EQUAL WEIGHTS

	Equal weight	Single period	Bootstrapped
US 20 year bond	33%	68%	53%
S&P 500 equities	33%	32%	27%
NASDAQ equities	33%	0%	20%

The table shows the final portfolio weights using equal weights and after optimising using both single period and bootstrapped methods with an expanding window.

Bootstrapping requires a suitable software package, the ability to write your own optimisation code, or a black belt in spread-sheeting. If you are interested in this technique there are more details in appendix C. Meanwhile I'm going to show you the second, much simpler, way I use to get robust portfolio weights.

Making weights by hand

Something weird happens if you ask an experienced and skilled expert in portfolio optimisation, but not one who uses **bootstrapping**, to do some work for you. Under your gaze they will pull out their optimisation software and diligently produce some weights. As we've seen these are inevitably awful, with many assets having zero weights and one or two having huge allocations. The artisan will then suggest you go for a coffee whilst they do their magic.

When you return the weights have suspiciously changed; they're now much nicer and less extreme. Upon interrogation the expert will admit they have tortured the software with all kinds of arcane tricks until it produced the right result. Experts know from glancing at the problem roughly what a good answer should look like, and their skill lies in extracting it from the computer.

I remember once being told "Optimisation is more of an art than a science." This never seemed particularly satisfying. I would have preferred a process that always produced exactly the same result for the same data set, regardless of who was operating the machinery.

After leaving the financial industry I set myself the task of creating my own trading system, which naturally meant doing some optimisation. As it would take time to write the necessary code for bootstrapping I thought I'd use the simpler single period method for my first attempt. I soon found myself with weights I didn't like, and true to form began fiddling to improve them. After toying with the optimiser for a few minutes, I quickly realised it would be better to cut out the artistic pseudo-optimisation stage entirely. Why not just write down the right weights to start with?

The only tool required would be a sharp pencil, and something like the back of an envelope or a beer mat to write on. A little harder was defining exactly what 'good' weights would look like for a given portfolio.

I started with small portfolios. For simple situations where equal weights were justified this was easy. To deal with more difficult groups I used the results from experiments on artificial data with the bootstrapping method.

To cope with larger portfolios I made the problem modular. So I first worked on subsets of the portfolio which I formed into groups, and then calculated the weight of each group relative to others. If necessary I used more than one level of grouping depending on how complicated the problem was.

The **handcrafting** method was born. Let's see how it works in more detail.

Handcrafting method

The procedure involves constructing the portfolio in a bottom-up fashion by first forming groups of similar assets. Within and across groups you set allocations using a table of optimal weights for similar portfolios. These weights come from my own experiments with **bootstrapping**.

As you would expect the method assumes that all assets have the same expected **standard deviation** of returns. I also assume, for now, that they also have the same **Sharpe ratio (SR)**. I'll relax that assumption later, but as you saw above and perhaps in the last chapter it's quite common to be unable to find statistically significant differences between the Sharpe ratios of assets.

So all you need is an idea of what **correlations** are likely to be. As you'll see these don't need to be precise, and you can either estimate them with historical data or take an educated guess given the nature of the assets in your portfolio. If you don't want to do your own guessing then tables 50 to 57 in appendix C show some rough correlations between the returns of different **instruments**, and sets of different **trading rules** for the same instrument.

Once you have your correlations you need to group the most highly correlated assets together. Except with unusual portfolios the groupings will normally be pretty obvious; so for example in a Nikkei stock portfolio you'd probably put all Japanese utility stocks together, all banks together and so on.

Groups should ideally contain only one, two or three assets, but more is okay if their correlations are similar enough. Within these small groups there are only a limited number of distinctive correlation patterns that really matter.

The correct weights for these patterns are shown in table 8. If the exact correlation value isn't shown then you should round to the closest relevant number.[63] Negative values should be floored at zero.[64] The three asset correlations shown are those between assets A and B, A and C, and B and C respectively. These give the weights shown for assets A, B and C respectively.

TABLE 8: GROUP WEIGHTS TO USE WHEN HANDCRAFTING PORTFOLIOS

Group of one asset	1	100% to that asset
Any group of two assets	2	50% to each asset
Any size group with identical correlations	3	Equal weights
Four or more assets *without* identical correlations	4	Split groups further or differently until they match another row
Three assets with correlations AB, AC, BC		**Weights for A, B, C**
3 assets correlation 0.0, 0.5, 0.0	5	Weights: 30%, 40%, 30%
3 assets correlation 0.0, 0.9, 0.0	6	Weights: 27%, 46%, 27%
3 assets correlation 0.5, 0.0, 0.5	7	Weights: 37%, 26%, 37%
3 assets correlation 0.0, 0.5, 0.9	8	Weights: 45%, 45%, 10%
3 assets correlation 0.9, 0.0, 0.9	9	Weights: 39%, 22%, 39%
3 assets correlation 0.5, 0.9, 0.5	10	Weights: 29%, 42%, 29%
3 assets correlation 0.9, 0.5, 0.9	11	Weights: 42%, 16%, 42%

Numbers in bold in middle of table are used to identify rows.

Note that there are other permutations of these correlations which aren't shown here that would just be a re-ordering of a set of values included in the table. So for example suppose your portfolio has three assets: US bonds (D), S&P 500 (E) and NASDAQ (F); with correlations of -0.3 (DE), -0.2 (DF) and 0.8 (EF); which you would round to 0.0 (DE), 0.0 (DF), 0.9 (EF).

---

63. Alternatively some interpolation of weights could be done, but this makes this simple method rather complicated.
64. An asset with a negative correlation would get an unreasonably extreme allocation.

After reordering and mapping to ABC in the table the relevant row number 6 is 0.0 (DE mapping to AB), 0.9 (EF mapping to AC), 0.0 (DF mapping to BC) giving weights of 27% (A), 46% (B), 27% (C). Expressing that back in the original problem (E=A, D=B, F=C) the weights are US Bonds 46% (D), S&P 500 27% (E) and NASDAQ 27% (F).[65]

Let's think about the intuition of where these weights come from. Equities aren't very diversifying since they have a correlation of 0.90 with each other. But bonds are uncorrelated with the two equity indices, so add more diversification to the portfolio. So it makes sense that they get a higher weight, and the weight of the equities sinks lower.

Once every group has been processed you then allocate weights to groups, based on your guess or estimate of the correlation *between* groups.[66] Finally the weight of each asset in the overall portfolio is just the total weight of its group multiplied by the weight it has within the group.

Depending on the size and structure of the portfolio this process could be done with two levels as explained here, at just one level if all the assets fall readily into table 8 without needing subgroups, or with three or more levels.

To see how grouping works consider again the three asset portfolio of US bonds, S&P 500 and NASDAQ. Common sense and the correlations estimated above imply I should create one group for the single bond asset, and a second group for the two equity indices. Here is how I calculated the weights. The row numbers shown refer to the relevant rows of table 8.

First level grouping **Within asset classes**	Group one (bonds): One asset, gets 100%. Row 1.
	Group two (equities): Two assets, I place 50% in each. Row 2.
Second level grouping **Across asset classes**	I have two groups to allocate to, each gets 50%. Row 2.

Each equity index gets 50% (within group weight) multiplied by 50% (weight of group) which is 25%. The one bond asset gets the other 50%. The weights are shown in figure 9. They are fairly close to the ungrouped handcrafted weights, and to what the full **bootstrap** method gave us in its final iteration – despite both handcrafting methods taking only a few seconds and needing no computing power. Because I didn't use Sharpe ratios there isn't the slight overweight on bonds and S&P 500 that we have in the bootstrapped results. I'll address that shortcoming below.

---

65. If you didn't enjoy the mapping and un-mapping process you can find a larger table of weights on my website that doesn't require untangling in this way.

66. If you are going to use estimation then you would need to construct mini-portfolios for each group and **back-test** them to get their returns. Alternatively you can use the average (simple or weighted by intra group weights) of the correlation between the group members.

TABLE 9: HANDCRAFTED WEIGHTS ARE SIMILAR TO BOOTSTRAPPED WEIGHTS, BUT WITH LESS WORK

	Equal weight	Single period	Bootstrapped	Handcrafted ungrouped	Handcrafted grouped
US 20 year bond	33%	68%	53%	46%	50%
S&P 500 equities	33%	32%	27%	27%	25%
NASDAQ equities	33%	0%	20%	27%	25%

The table shows the final portfolio weights using equal weights, after optimising using both single period and bootstrapped methods with expanding windows, and using handcrafting without and with grouping.

A more complex example

Now for a harder challenge. Suppose I have a portfolio of three UK banks (Barclays, HSBC and RBS), two UK retailers (Tesco and Sainsburys), three US banks (JP Morgan, Citigroup and Bank of America), three US retailers (Safeway, Walmart and Costco), two UK government bonds (5 year and 10 year) and three US bonds (2 year, 20 year and 30 year). I grouped these, from the lowest grouping upwards as follows: equity sector, country and **asset class**, giving the grouping in table 10.

TABLE 10: GROUPING FOR LARGER EXAMPLE PORTFOLIO

	1st level	2nd level	3rd level	4th level
Barclays HSBC RBS	UK banks	UK equities	Equities	Whole portfolio
Tesco Sainsbury	UK retailers			
JP Morgan Citigroup Bank of America	US banks	US equities		
Safeway Walmart Costco	US retailers			
10 year UK bond 20 year UK bond	UK bonds		Bonds	
2 year US bond 20 year US bond 30 year US bond	US bonds			

Here is how I calculated the weights. Relevant rows of table 8 are shown.

First level grouping **By equity industry within country, by bond country**	Within equities I'm going to assume stocks have similar **correlations** if they're within the same industry and country. • UK banks: Assuming similar correlations allocate 33.3% to each. Row 3. • UK retail: Two assets so allocate 50% to each. Row 2. • US banks: Similar correlations so allocate 33.3%. Row 3. • US retail: Similar correlations so allocate 33.3%. Row 3. • UK bonds: Two assets so allocate 50% to each. Row 2. • US bonds: For the three US bonds things are a little more complex. From table 55 (page 294) the 2 year and 20 year bonds typically have 0.5 correlation, 2 year/30 year 0.5 and 20 year/30 year 0.9. This matches row 10 of table 8, giving weights of 42% in the 2 year bond and 29% in each of the 20 and 30 year bonds.

Second level grouping By country within asset class	• UK equities: Two groups (UK banks and UK retailers) so allocate 50% to each. Row 2.
	• US equities: Two groups (US banks and US retailers) so allocate 50% to each. Row 2.
	• UK bonds: 100% as only one group. Row 1.
	• US bonds: 100%, one group. Row 1.
Third level grouping By asset class	Equities: Two groups (US equities and UK equities) so allocate 50% to each. Row 2.
	Bonds: Two groups (US and UK bonds) so allocate 50% to each. Row 2.
Fourth level grouping Across asset classes	Two grouped assets (bonds and equities) allocate 50% to each. Row 2.

Final weights

The final weights for each asset, from multiplying the weights they are given at each grouping stage, are shown in table 11.

Notice I mostly didn't use correlations except in the US bonds group. If you can keep your groups down to one or two members, or your group members are similarly correlated, then you don't need to use correlations once you've determined your groups.

With 16 assets equal weights would have come out at 6.25% each. This was an unbalanced portfolio with more equities than bonds, and where it was unrealistic to assume identical correlations. In this situation we should be able to beat equal weights by giving more allocation to more diversifying assets.

TABLE 11: CONSTRUCTION OF WEIGHTS IN LARGER EXAMPLE PORTFOLIO

	1st	2nd	3rd	4th	Final
Barclays	33%	50%	50%	50%	4.2%
HSBC	33%	50%	50%	50%	4.2%
RBS	33%	50%	50%	50%	4.2%
Tesco	50%	50%	50%	50%	6.3%
Sainsbury	50%	50%	50%	50%	6.3%
JP Morgan	33%	50%	50%	50%	4.2%
Citigroup	33%	50%	50%	50%	4.2%
Bank of America	33%	50%	50%	50%	4.2%
Safeway	33%	50%	50%	50%	4.2%
Walmart	33%	50%	50%	50%	4.2%
Costco	33%	50%	50%	50%	4.2%
10 year UK bond	50%	100%	50%	50%	12.5%
20 year UK bond	50%	100%	50%	50%	12.5%
2 year US bond	42%	100%	50%	50%	10.5%
20 year US bond	29%	100%	50%	50%	7.3%
30 year US bond	29%	100%	50%	50%	7.3%

Calculation of weights is shown for each grouping stage, and in the last column we have the final portfolio weight, which is the product of the weights for each stage. Borders show grouping. There is some rounding.

Are we cheating?

The handcrafting method cannot easily be repeated automatically in multiple years, so is unsuitable for an **expanding** or **rolling out of sample back-test**.[67] You fit one single **in sample** set of portfolio weights, with knowledge of all past data. Arguably there is a danger that the resulting portfolio will be **over-fitted**. This is more likely if you're using

---

67. Actually it is possible to back-test the handcrafting method, and I have done so to validate it, but it requires historical estimates of correlation using only past data and an algorithm to cluster groups into a hierarchy. If you must use a back-tested method then the **bootstrap** method is much easier to implement. After all, the main benefit of handcrafting is its simplicity.

estimated **correlations**, although it's also an issue with correlations that are educated guesses, since both imply you knew the future at the start of the back-test.

Relax; you will be using information from the future but in mitigation the weights you'll produce will be much less extreme than an in sample **single period optimisation** will produce. Also correlations usually don't move enough that handcrafted weights would be dramatically different over time. So the weights you will produce using all data are likely to be very similar if you do them earlier in the back-test using only past data. Also for now the method ignores differences in **Sharpe ratio (SR)**, which also ensures weights are not extreme and relatively stable.

To illustrate this I fitted the trading system I outline in chapter fifteen for **staunch systems traders**. Using in sample handcrafting rather than rolling out of sample **bootstrapping** gave an insignificant advantage (Sharpe ratio of 0.54 rather than 0.52). In comparison in sample single period optimisation produced an unrealistically high SR of 0.84; although when I used the single period method to perform a rolling out of sample fit it did much worse, with an SR of 0.3.

Nevertheless the results of back-testing handcrafted portfolios should be treated with slightly more scepticism than a true out of sample method like bootstrapping.

Incorporating Sharpe ratios

The basic **handcrafting** method assumes all assets have the same expected **Sharpe ratio (SR)**. Usually you don't have enough data to determine whether historic SR were significantly different. However there might be times when you have a valid opinion about relative asset Sharpes.

One example which I'll return to later is when some assets have higher costs than others. Costs are known with much more certainty than raw performance, so you can usually have a statistically well informed opinion about their effect on returns.

Another scenario is where you are following my recommended procedure for trading rule selection outlined in the previous chapter. With my preferred method you don't remove unprofitable trading rules before deciding what their **forecast weights** should be. However if a rule is terrible in **back-test** you'll want to reduce its weight, although it will probably have some allocation, since it's hard to find sufficient evidence that one rule is definitely better or worse than another (as covered in the last chapter).

By experimenting with random data I calculated how **bootstrapped** portfolio weights change in a group of assets whose true SR are not equal. These adjustments can then be applied to handcrafted weights. These results are below in table 12. To avoid showing infinite permutations the results are in relative terms, so it's the SR relative to the average for the group that matters.

TABLE 12: HOW MUCH SHOULD YOU ADJUST HANDCRAFTED WEIGHTS BY IF YOU HAVE SOME INFORMATION ABOUT ASSET SHARPE RATIOS?

	Adjustment factor		
SR difference to average	(A) With certainty e.g. costs	(B) Without certainty, more than ten years' data	(C) Without certainty, less than ten years' data
-0.50	0.32	0.65	1.0
-0.40	0.42	0.75	1.0
-0.30	0.55	0.83	1.0
-0.25	0.60	0.85	1.0
-0.20	0.66	0.88	1.0
-0.15	0.77	0.92	1.0
-0.10	0.85	0.95	1.0
-0.05	0.94	0.98	1.0
0	1.00	1.00	1.0
0.05	1.11	1.03	1.0
0.10	1.19	1.06	1.0
0.15	1.30	1.09	1.0
0.20	1.37	1.13	1.0
0.25	1.48	1.15	1.0
0.30	1.56	1.17	1.0
0.40	1.72	1.25	1.0
0.50	1.83	1.35	1.0

The table shows the adjustment factor to use for handcrafted weights given the Sharpe ratio (SR) of an asset versus portfolio average (rows), certainty of SR estimate and amount of data used to estimate (columns). Column A: SR difference is known precisely, e.g. different trading costs. Column B: SR estimated using more than ten years of data or forecasted. Column C: SR estimated using less than ten years of data.

Initially my experiments assumed I knew the true SR difference. For cost adjustments this is a fair assumption. Column A shows the adjustment factor to multiply the starting portfolio weights by when we know differences with complete certainty.

However if you are using historical estimates of SR, or forecasting them in some other way, then you can't be as confident. You should use the less aggressive adjustment factors in column B. Finally if you're estimating SR based on less than ten years of data I advise not adjusting at all. As you might have seen in the last chapter estimates of SR are extremely unlikely to be statistically different after only a few years. Though it's trivial I've put this in column C of the table.

Follow these steps to adjust handcrafted weights for Sharpe ratio

Starting weights	Work out the handcrafted weights for the group. These will add up to 100%.
Get Sharpe ratios	In each group using historical data, cost estimates, or some other method, find the expected SR for each asset.
Sharpe versus average	Calculate the average SR for the entire group and then work out the relative difference higher or lower than this for each asset.
Get multiplier	Find the weight multiplier for each asset from column A, B or C in table 12, depending on how certain you are about the SR estimate, and if relevant how much data was used.
Multiply	Multiply each of the weights in the group by the relevant multiplier.
Normalise	The resulting weights in the group may not add up to 100%. If necessary normalise the weights so they sum to exactly 100%.

If you have two or more levels of grouping you'll need to repeat this process. When you move up to the next level you should estimate the SR of each group as a whole. You can do this by **back-testing** each group's returns, taking a weighted average of the SR for each individual asset in the group, or just using a simple average SR across the group's assets. The process for adjusting group weights is then the same as for within groups.

A simple example

Let's return to the simple three asset portfolio of two US equity and one bond market, using handcrafting with groups. My historic estimates of Sharpe ratios are around 0 for NASDAQ, 0.5 for S&P 500 and 0.75 for bonds. Here is what I did with the equity group (the bond group is still just 100% in a single asset):

Starting weights	NASDAQ: 50%, S&P 500: 50%
Estimate Sharpes	NASDAQ: 0, S&P 500: 0.5 (from historical data)
Sharpe versus average	Average: 0.25. Difference to average: • NASDAQ 0 - 0.25 = -0.25 • S&P 500 0.5 - 0.25 = 0.25
Get multiplier	I have uncertain estimates with over ten years of data so I use column B of table 12: • NASDAQ: 0.85 • S&P 500: 1.15
Multiply	NASDAQ: 50% × 0.85 = 42% S&P 500: 50% × 1.15 = 58%
Normalise	Total is 100% so no normalisation required.

Now for the second level where I mix bonds and equities

Starting weights	Equities: 50%, Bonds: 50%
Guess Sharpes	Equities: using a simple average of NASDAQ with SR of 0 and S&P 500 with SR 0.5, I get an average of 0.25 Bonds: 0.75 from historical data.
Sharpe versus average	Average across bonds and equities: 0.50. Difference to average: • Equities 0.25 - 0.50 = -0.25 • Bonds 0.75 - 0.50 = 0.25
Get multiplier	From column B of table 12: • Equities: 0.85 • Bonds: 1.15
Multiply	Equities: 50% × 0.85 = 42% Bonds: 50% × 1.15 = 58%
Normalise	Total is 100% so no normalisation required.

The final weights then are 18% NASDAQ (42% × 42%), 24% to S&P 500 (58% × 42%) and 58% to bonds. Though more uneven than before they are much less extreme than what I'd get with a **single period optimiser** using the same SR figures, as table 9 shows. They're also not dissimilar to my final bootstrapped weights, which also use Sharpe ratios in their calculation.

TABLE 13: HOW MUCH OF AN EFFECT DOES INCLUDING SHARPE RATIOS (SR) HAVE ON OPTIMISED PORTFOLIO WEIGHTS?

	Single period (uses SR)	Bootstrapped (uses SR)	Handcrafted: no SR	Handcrafted: using SR
US 20 year bond	68%	53%	50%	58%
S&P 500 equities	32%	27%	25%	24%
NASDAQ equities	0%	20%	25%	18%

When I bring in Sharpe ratio estimates, handcrafting up-weights better performing assets and produces similar results to bootstrapping, but does not result in extreme portfolios like single period optimisation.

Once again, are we cheating?

Now you're using **Sharpe ratios (SR)** to produce your handcrafted weights it's worth reiterating that this is a mild form of **in-sample back-test** cheating, since you only use the final SR averaged over all data history, which you wouldn't have at the beginning of the back-test.[68]

Again this is a fair criticism, but the problem is not that serious. The weights are still not extreme, so the effect on back-tested SR you get is modest compared to in-sample **single period** optimisation. However you should still be cautious of assuming that you'd be able to achieve the back-test SR in live trading. Table 14 shows you roughly how much you should degrade back-tested returns to get realistic achievable Sharpe ratios given a particular fitting technique for a system like the one I describe in chapter fifteen.

---

68. As with the standard handcrafted weights it's possible to back-test this by doing the SR adjustment on an **expanding window**. For the first ten years of data you shouldn't adjust the weights at all. After that you should use only past data to estimate the SR at each point in the back-test. But again this is much more work than using the **bootstrapping** method.

TABLE 14: WITH HOW MANY PINCHES OF SALT SHOULD WE TREAT BACK-TESTED SHARPE RATIOS?

	Pessimism factor
Single period optimisation, uses SR, in sample	25%
Single period optimisation, uses SR, out of sample	75%
Bootstrapping, uses SR, in sample	60%
Bootstrapping, uses SR, out of sample	75%
Handcrafted, no SR used, in sample	70%
Handcrafted, uses SR, in sample	65%

The table shows what proportion of back-tested returns are likely to be available in the future. Numbers shown are for the trading system in chapter fifteen, which has four trading rule variations and six instruments. More complicated trading systems will require larger corrections for overstated in sample performance. I assume 25% of past performance was due to unrepeatable secular trends in asset prices, as I discussed in chapter two (page 46).

Now you should be able to use fitting and optimisation safely we can move on to part three: my **framework** for trading systems.

PART THREE.

Framework

Chapter Five. Framework Overview

Now you have some theory and perhaps a few quantitative tools at your disposal you are ready to begin creating **trading systems**. In part three of this book I am going to describe a **framework** which will provide you with a template for the creation of almost any kind of strategy.

Chapter overview

A bad example	A trading system with some fatal flaws.
Why use a modular framework	The reasons why a modular framework makes sense for systematic trading strategies.
The elements of the framework	A brief road map of the various components in the framework.

The following chapters in part three will describe each component in more detail. In the final part of the book I'll show three examples of how this framework can be used, for **semi-automatic traders**, **asset allocating investors** and **staunch systems traders**.

A bad example

Here's an example of the kind of trading system you find in many books and websites.[69]

Entry rule	Buy when the 20 day moving average rises over the 40 day, and vice versa.
Exit rule	Reverse when the entry rule is broken, so if you are long close when the 20 day moving average falls behind the 40 day and go short.
Position size	Never trade more than 10 Eurodollar futures, 1 FTSE contract or £10 per spread bet point.
Money management	Never bet more than 3% of your capital on each trade.
Stop loss	Set a trailing stop to close once you have lost 3% of your capital. If you find yourself triggering stops too frequently, then widen them.

I am not going to discuss the entry or exit rule.[70] However the position sizing, money management and stop loss are a mess.

Firstly why 3%? Will this generate the right amount of risk? What if I'm particularly conservative, should I still use 3%? If I don't like a particular trade that much, what should I bet? I typically have 40 positions in my portfolio, so should I be putting 40 lots of 3% of my portfolio at risk at any one time (meaning 120% of my total portfolio is at risk)? Does 3% make sense if I am using a slower trading rule?

The position sizes above might make sense for someone with an account size of perhaps £50,000 and a certain risk appetite, but what about everyone else? They might be correct when the book was written, but are they still right when we read it five years later? What about an **instrument** that isn't listed, can we trade it? How?

Finally, setting a stop loss based solely on your capital and personal pain threshold is incorrect.[71] Someone with a tiny account who hated losing money would be triggering their very tight stops after a few minutes, whilst a large hedge fund might close a losing position after decades. Stops that would make sense in oil futures would be completely

---

69. This is a hypothetical example and as far as I know isn't identical to any publicly available system.

70. The rules aren't too bad, as they are purely systematic and very simple. However they are binary (you're either fully in or out) which isn't ideal, and having only one trading rule **variation** is also less than perfect.

71. This is recognised by most good traders. Here is Jack Schwager, in *Hedge Fund Wizards*, interviewing hedge fund manager Colm O'Shea: Jack: "So you don't use stops?" Colm: "No I do. I just set them wide enough. In those early days I wasn't setting stops at levels that made sense on the underlying hypothesis of the trade. I was setting stops *based on my pain threshold*. When I get out of a trade now it is because I was wrong. ... Prices are *inconsistent with my hypothesis*. I'm wrong and I need to get out and rethink the situation." (My emphasis.)

wrong in the relatively quiet USD/CAD FX market. A stop that was correct in the peaceful calm of 2006 would be absurdly tight in the insanity we saw in 2008.

The solution is to separate out the components of your system: **trading rules** (including explicit or implicit stop losses), position sizing, and the calculation of your **volatility target** (the average amount of cash you are willing to risk). You can then design each component independently of the other moving parts.

Trading rules and stop losses should be based only on expected market price volatility, and should never take your account size into consideration. Calculating a volatility target, how much of your capital to put at risk, is a function of account size and your pain threshold.[72] Positions should then be sized based on how volatile markets are, how confident your price forecasts are, and the amount of capital you wish to gamble.

Each of these components is part of the modular **framework** which together form a complete trading system.

Why a modular framework?

Remember that I drew an analogy between cars and **trading systems** in the introduction of this book. **Trading rules** are the engine of the system. These give you a forecast for **instrument** prices; whether they are expected to go up or down and by how much. In a car the chassis, drive train and gearbox translate the power the engine is producing into forward movement. Similarly, you will have a position risk management **framework** wrapped around your trading rules. This translates forecasts into the actual positions you need to hold.

As I said in the introduction the components of a modern car are modular, so they can be individually substituted for alternatives. The trading rules and other components in my framework can also be swapped and changed.

The words module and component could imply that these are complex processes which need thousands of lines of computer code to implement. This is not the case. Every part involves just a few steps of basic arithmetic which require just a calculator or simple spreadsheet.

Let's look in more detail at the advantages of the modular approach.

Flexibility

The most obvious benefit of a modular design is flexibility. Cars really can be any colour you like, including black. Similarly my framework can be adapted for almost any trading rule, including the discretionary forecasts used by **semi-automatic traders** and the

---

72. There are other considerations, such as the amount of leverage required versus what is available, and the expected performance of the system. I'll discuss these in more detail in chapter nine, 'Volatility targeting'.

very simple rule used by **asset allocating investors**. If you don't like the position sizing component, or any other part of the framework, you can replace it with your own.

Transparent modules

It's possible to have frameworks that are nicely modular but which contain entirely opaque black boxes. Most PCs are built like this. You can replace the hard disc or graphics card, but you can't easily modify them or make your own, so you are stuck with substituting one mysterious part with another.

In contrast each component in my framework is transparent – I'll explain how and why it is constructed. This should give you the understanding and confidence to adapt each module, or create your own from scratch.

Individual components with well defined interface

If you replace the gearbox in your car you need to be sure that the car will still go forward or backwards as required. But if the drive shaft output is reversed on your new gearbox you will end up driving into your front door when you wanted to reverse out of your driveway. To avoid this we need to specify that the shaft on the gearbox must rotate clockwise to make the car go forward, and vice versa.

Similarly if you use a new trading rule then the rest of the modular trading system framework should still work correctly and give you appropriately sized positions. To do this the individual components need to have a well defined *interface* – a specification describing how they interact with other parts of the system.

For example in the framework it will be important that a trading rule **forecast** of say +1.5 has a consistent meaning, no matter what style of trading or instrument you are using.[73]

Getting the boring bit right

The part of the **trading system** wrapped around the **trading rules**, the **framework**, is something that's easily ignored. Creating it is a boring task compared with developing new and exciting trading rules, or making your own discretionary forecasts. But it's incredibly important. By creating a standard framework I've done this dull but vital work for you.

The framework will work correctly for any trading rule that produces forecasts in a consistent way with the right interface. So it won't need to be radically redesigned for any new rules. Also by using the framework **asset allocating investors** and **semi-automatic traders** can get much of the benefits of systematic trading without using trading rules to forecast prices.

---

73. It will become clear in later chapters what this consistent meaning is.

Examples give you a starting point

Creating a new **trading system** from scratch is quite a daunting prospect. In the final part of this book there are three detailed examples showing how the framework can be used to suit **asset allocating investors, semi-automatic traders** and **staunch systematic traders**. Together these provide a set of systems you can use as a starting point for developing your own ideas.

The elements of the framework

Table 15 shows the components you'd have in a small **trading system** with two **trading rules**, a total of four trading rule **variations**, and two **instruments**. You first create a **trading subsystem** for each instrument. Each subsystem tries to predict the price of an individual instrument, and calculate the appropriate position required. These subsystems are then combined into a portfolio, which forms the final trading system.

TABLE 15: EXAMPLE OF COMPONENTS IN A TRADING SYSTEM

						Instruments		
Trading rule A, variation 1	A1 forecast for instrument X							
Trading rule A, variation 2	A2 forecast for instrument X	Combined forecast X				Subsystem position in X		Portfolio weighted position in X
Trading rule B, variation 1	B1 forecast for instrument X		Forecast weights	Volatility targeting	Position sizing		Instrument weights	
Trading rule A, variation 1	A1 forecast, instrument Y							
Trading rule A, variation 2	A2 forecast for instrument Y	Combined forecast Y				Subsystem position in Y		Portfolio weighted position in Y
Trading rule B, variation 1	B1 forecast for instrument Y							

Customising for speed and size

This trading system has two trading rules A and B; three rule variations A1, A2 and B1; and two instruments X and Y. Dotted lines show trading subsystems for X and Y.

Instruments to trade

Instruments are the things you trade and hold positions in. They could be any financial asset including directly held instruments such as equities and bonds, or **derivatives** like options, futures, contracts for difference and spread bets. You can also trade **collective funds** such as **exchange traded funds (ETFs)**, mutual funds, and even hedge funds.

Forecasts

A **forecast** is an estimate of how much a particular **instrument's** price will change, given a particular **trading rule variation**. For example a simple equities strategy might have three forecasts: two variations on a trend following rule, each looking for different speeds of trend, and a separate **equity value** trading rule with a single variation. If you are trading two instruments as in table 15 then there will be a total of 3 × 2 = 6 forecasts to make.

The trading rules which produce forecasts are the engine at the heart of all **trading systems** used by **staunch systems traders**. The biggest difference between strategies will be in which rules and variations are used, and which instruments are traded. In comparison the rest of the framework will be fairly similar.

Semi-automatic traders make discretionary forecasts, rather than using systematic rules. **Asset allocating investors** don't try and predict asset prices and use a single fixed forecast for all instruments.

Combined forecasts

You need a single forecast of whether an instrument will go up or down in price, and by how much. If you have more than one forecast you will need to combine them into one **combined forecast** per instrument, using a weighted average. To do this you'll allocate **forecast weights** to each trading rule variation.

Volatility targeting

It's important to be precise about how much overall risk you want to take in your trading system. I define this as the typical average daily loss you are willing to expose yourself to. This **volatility target** is determined using your wealth, tolerance for risk, access to leverage and expected profitability. Initially we'll assume that you're putting all of your capital into a single **trading subsystem**, for just one instrument.

Scaled positions

You can now decide how much of the underlying asset to hold based on how risky your instruments are, how confident you are about your **forecasts**, and your **volatility target**. The positions you will calculate assume for now that you're just trading one isolated instrument, in a single **trading subsystem**.

At this point you've effectively got a complete trading system, but for a single instrument. Just as the cells in the human body are each individual living organisms, these trading subsystems are self-contained units, but in the next stage you'll be putting them together.

Portfolios

To get maximum diversification you'd usually want to trade multiple instruments and put together a portfolio of **trading subsystems**, each responsible for a single instrument. This requires determining how you are going to allocate capital to the different subsystems in your portfolio, which you will do using **instrument weights.** After applying this stage you'll end up with **portfolio weighted positions** in each instrument, which are then used to calculate the trades you need to do.

Speed and Size

This isn't a separate component in the framework, but a set of principles which apply to the entire system. When designing trading systems it's important to know how expensive they are to trade, and whether you have an unusually large or small amount of capital. Given that information, how should you then tailor your system? I'll address both of these issues in detail in the final chapter of part three.

Chapter Six. Instruments

Instruments

Trading rule / variation	Forecast	Forecast weights	Combined forecast	Volatility targeting	Position sizing	Subsystem position	Instrument weights	Portfolio weighted position
Trading rule A, variation 1	A1 forecast for instrument X							
Trading rule A, variation 2	A2 forecast for instrument X		Combined forecast X			Subsystem position in X		Portfolio weighted position in X
Trading rule B, variation 1	B1 forecast for instrument X							
Trading rule A, variation 1	A1 forecast, instrument Y							
Trading rule A, variation 2	A2 forecast for instrument Y		Combined forecast Y			Subsystem position in Y		Portfolio weighted position in Y
Trading rule B, variation 1	B1 forecast for instrument Y							

Customising for speed and size

BEFORE YOU THINK ABOUT *HOW* YOU TRADE YOU NEED TO consider *what* you're going to trade – the actual **instruments** to buy or sell. It's likely you will know which **asset classes** you want to deal with, based on your knowledge and familiarity with different markets.

However there are certain instruments that should be completely avoided for systematic trading. Others have characteristics which make them worse than other alternatives, or would force you to trade them in a particular way. Finally there is often a choice of how you can access a particular market; you could get Euro Stoxx 50 European equity index exposure by buying the individual shares, trading a future, a spread bet, a contract for difference, a **passive index fund** or an **active fund**. Which is best?

Chapter overview

Necessities	The minimum requirements that need to be met before you can trade an instrument.
Instrument choice and trading style	Characteristics that influence instrument choice between alternatives and how to trade particular instruments.
Access	Different ways to get exposure to instruments, and the benefits and downside of each.

Necessities

There are a few points to consider when deciding whether an instrument is suitable for systematic trading.

Data availability

I'd like to be able to trade UK Gilt futures, but I don't have the right data licence so I can't get quoted prices. You can't trade systematically without access to prices and other relevant data.

At a minimum you will need accurate daily price information. Fully automated strategies that trade quickly or incorporate execution algorithms will need live tick prices. **Fundamental** trading strategies require yet more kinds of data. The costs of acquiring data on certain instruments, like Gilts perhaps, may be uneconomic for amateur investors.

Minimum sizes

Another future I would like to trade – but can't – is the Japanese government bond (JGB) future. The contract currently sells for around 150 million yen, which is well over a million dollars. If I put this into my portfolio the maximum position I would want is 0.1 of a contract, which obviously isn't possible. Few amateur investors will be able to trade these behemoths.

In stocks the minimum size is one share, normally costing less than $1,000, although the A class of Berkshire Hathaway shares currently sell for over $100,000. Even for cheaper stocks, it may not be economic to trade in lots of less than 100 shares.

Minimum sizes reduce the granularity of what you can trade. Your positions become binary – all or nothing (in the case of JGBs, always nothing). This is an important subject and I will return to it in chapter twelve, 'Speed and Size'. As you'll see in that chapter this problem also affects the number of instruments you can hold in your portfolio.

Why do prices move?

Do you know why bonds, equities and other instruments go up, or down, in price? "More buyers than sellers" is not an acceptable answer! I personally think it's important to have an understanding of what makes a market function; whether it be interest rates, economic news or corporate profits. This is vital if you're going to design **ideas first** trading rules.

It's also important to understand market dynamics once your system is running, if you want to avoid unpleasant surprises in markets that have become dysfunctional. As I'm redrafting this chapter, the Swiss government has just removed the peg which had held since 2011 fixing their currency at 1.20 to the euro, resulting in a massive Swiss franc (CHF) appreciation against all currencies. Thousands of traders including large hedge funds and banks were on the losing side, including many who were trading systematically.

Fortunately I wasn't trading the EUR/CHF or USD/CHF FX pairs. For me there didn't seem any point in trying to make systematic forecasts, since I knew the market was controlled by central bank intervention rather than the normal historic factors driving prices in the **back-test**. Keeping abreast of markets will help you to avoid similarly dangerous instruments.

Standard deviation

There is another reason why I excluded Swiss FX positions from my systematic trading strategies, which was the extremely low **volatility** of prices whilst the peg was in place. In principle my framework can deal equally well both with assets whose returns naturally have low **standard deviations** and those that are very risky. It can also cope with changes in volatility over time.

However instruments which have extremely low risk like pegged currencies should be excluded. Firstly, when risk returns to normal it is liable to do so very sharply, potentially creating significant losses. Secondly, these positions need more leverage to achieve a given amount of risk, magnifying the danger when they do inevitably blow up. Even if you don't use leverage they will limit the risk your overall trading system can achieve.[74] Finally, they also tend to be more costly to trade, as you will discover in chapter twelve, 'Speed and Size'.

Instrument choice and trading style

With your pool of available instruments narrowed by excluding those which don't have the necessary attributes mentioned above, you need to decide which of those remaining you prefer to trade. These characteristics will also influence *how* you'll trade the instruments you've chosen.

---

74. I'll return to this topic in chapter nine, 'Volatility targeting'.

How many instruments?

I like my portfolio of instruments to be as large and diversified as possible, as long as I don't run into issues with minimum sizes, for example as I would do with Japanese government bonds. The maximum number of instruments you can have will depend on minimum sizes, the value of your account and how much risk you're targeting (which you'll learn about in chapter nine, 'Volatility targeting').

In chapter twelve, 'Speed and Size', you'll see how to calculate the point at which you could run into problems with minimum instrument size. You will then be able to work out what size of portfolio makes sense.

Then in part four I will give some recommended portfolios in each example chapter, which have been constructed to be as diversified as possible given the level of the **volatility target** and the available instruments.

Correlation

If you already owned shares in RBS and Barclays then the last thing you would want to add to your portfolio is another UK bank like Lloyd's. Generally you should want to own or trade the most diversified portfolio possible, where the average **correlation** between the assets is lower than the alternatives. If there are a limited number of instruments that you can fit in your portfolio then it makes sense to pick those with lower correlations.

Costs

Given the choice between two otherwise identical instruments you should choose the cheapest to trade. So, if you can, use a cheap FTSE 100 future rather than an expensive spread bet to get exposure to the UK equity index.[75] Instruments that are expensive to trade are clearly less suitable for **dynamic** strategies, particularly those that involve faster trading.

Sometimes you have to trade an expensive instrument, if it's the only way of accessing a particular asset. In this case you should trade it more slowly. There is however a maximum acceptable cost depending on the type of trading that you're doing, so some instruments will be completely unsuitable. Because the cost of trading is so important it will be covered in great detail in chapter twelve, 'Speed and Size'.

Liquidity

Closely related to costs is **liquidity**. Less liquid instruments are likely to be more expensive to trade quickly or in larger amounts. This is more of a problem for large institutional investors and those trading fast. Liquidity is not constant and can reduce quickly in

---

75. I'll explain why the spread bet is more expensive in chapter twelve, 'Speed and Size'.

times of severe market stress, particularly for non exchange traded 'over the counter' instruments, as in the Credit Default Swap derivatives markets in 2008.

Again chapter twelve, 'Speed and Size', will explain how those with larger account sizes will need to understand costs and liquidity better than small investors.

Skew

Should you avoid negative **skew** in your portfolio from instruments like holding short VIX (US **equity volatility index**) futures? Remember I covered the skew of assets and trading rules in chapter two, 'Systematic Trading Rules'. **Static** strategies will inherit the skew of their underlying instruments, but the skew of a **dynamic** strategy also depends on the style of your trading rule. So using a positive skew rule like **trend following** on a negative skew asset will alleviate some of the danger.

As you will see in chapter nine, 'Volatility targeting', you need to be extremely careful if the overall returns of your **trading system** are expected to have negative skew. Instruments with extreme negative skew will often have very low **standard deviation** for most of the time, and should be excluded on those grounds.

Access

Finally you need to choose the route by which you access the underlying assets you're going to trade.

Exchange or OTC

Does your instrument trade on an exchange like shares in General Electric and Corn futures, or over the counter (OTC) like foreign exchange (FX)? There are often different ways of trading the same underlying asset, some via exchange, others OTC. So a spread bet on the CHF/USD FX rate is OTC, whilst the Chicago future on the same rate is exchange traded.

If you have a choice then, all other things being equal, should you trade on exchange or OTC? In the January 2015 Swiss franc meltdown traders using OTC brokers suffered a variety of difficulties, including dealers not accepting orders or displaying quotes, trades not being honoured and fills re-marked after the fact, and in extreme cases potential account losses as brokers went into liquidation.

Those who traded the CHF/USD future had difficulty finding deep liquidity, but otherwise the market operated as normal. In conclusion it's normally better to trade on exchange if you can.

Cash or derivative

'Cash' is simply where you own the underlying asset directly – perhaps a share in British Gas or a bond issued by General Electric. Alternatively you can own a **derivative** on an asset, like a future, Contract for Difference or spread bet.[76] The main advantage of derivatives is that they offer straightforward leverage. Without leverage it might be difficult to reach your **volatility target**, which will reduce the returns you can earn. There may also be different tax treatments; in the UK for example spread bets are treated as gambling, which means winnings are tax free but losses aren't deductible.

Various types of derivatives may have different trading costs, and also have different minimum sizes, liquidity and market access. For example a FTSE 100 future is cheaper to trade and more liquid than the corresponding spread bet. It also has the advantage of being accessed via an exchange, whereas the spread bet is OTC. But the future has a larger minimum size which precludes its use by smaller investors.

Funds

Other options for trading the FTSE 100 are to buy an **index tracker** like an **exchange traded fund (ETF)**. These are **collective funds** – instruments which buy you a share in a portfolio of assets. As well as ETFs, collective funds include US mutual funds, UK unit trusts and investment trusts. Normally for systematic trading you will be interested in **passive funds** like **index trackers**. These contain baskets of assets weighted to match an index like the FTSE 100 or S&P 500.

Passive funds normally have relatively low annual fees and minimum sizes, but frequently cost more than the relevant **derivative** to trade. But they can be useful instruments when leverage can't be used, or when a market can't be accessed another way.

In some cases you might want to use **active funds**, where the weights to different assets are determined by the fund manager. This might make sense if there is no relevant passive fund or derivative, but fees are higher on active funds, and the presence of any compensating manager skill or **alpha** is very hard to prove.

Collective funds can have quirks such as daily remarking, tax treatment, internal leverage and discounts to net asset value which you should fully understand before using them.

---

76. I've deliberately excluded options and other non-linear derivatives from this list, since these can't be used casually as substitutes for the underlying assets.

Summary of instrument choice

Data availability	At a minimum you need daily price data to trade an instrument systematically. For **fundamental** strategies you also need other relevant data, e.g. price:earnings if you're using an **equity value rule**.
Minimum sizes	For small investors large minimum trading sizes can be a problem.
Understand what moves returns	Don't trade from an ivory tower; have some idea of the factors driving returns. If unusual forces are at play then avoid that instrument.
Standard deviation of returns	Volatility must not be extremely low.
How many instruments?	Given the size of your account and the minimum size of each instrument you can determine whether you will run into problems given a particular sized portfolio. You should then hold the largest portfolio you can given those constraints.
Correlation of returns	You should always try and have a portfolio where assets are as diversified as possible.
Costs	Cheaper is better. Expensive instruments will need to be traded more slowly, and may be too pricey to trade at all.
Liquidity	For larger and less patient investors liquidity is vital.
Skew of returns	Assets with strong negative **skew** need careful handling and shouldn't dominate your portfolio. Using the right trading rules can improve skew to some degree.
Trading venue	Is the market accessed via exchange, or over the counter (OTC)? On exchange is preferable.
Cash or derivative	Should you trade the asset outright, or a derivative based on its value, and if so which one?
Collective funds	Investment through collective funds can make sense when derivatives can't be used.

Now you know *what* you are going to trade, the next step is to think about *how*. So the next chapter will cover the business of forecasting prices.

Chapter Seven. Forecasts

Instruments							
Trading rule A, variation 1	A1 forecast for instrument X						
Trading rule A, variation 2	A2 forecast for instrument X	Forecast weights	Combined forecast X	Volatility targeting	Position sizing	Subsystem position in X	Instrument weights	Portfolio weighted position in X
Trading rule B, variation 1	B1 forecast for instrument X						
Trading rule A, variation 1	A1 forecast, instrument Y						
Trading rule A, variation 2	A2 forecast for instrument Y		Combined forecast Y			Subsystem position in Y		Portfolio weighted position in Y
Trading rule B, variation 1	B1 forecast for instrument Y						
Customising for speed and size							

WHAT DO THESE TERMS ALL HAVE IN COMMON: BREAKOUTS, Elliott waves, Fibonacci waves, **exponentially weighted moving average crossover** and Bollinger bands? Answer: They can all form the basis of **trading rules**. These rules give you **forecasts** of what they think will happen to the prices of **instruments** you are trading or investing in.

Staunch systems traders use multiple systematic rules like these. But rules can also be extremely simple, like the single rule used by **asset allocating investors**. It's also possible to use my **framework** without any systematic rules at all, as a **semi-automatic trader** making your own discretionary forecasts.

Chapter overview

What makes a good forecast	Understand the important properties of the forecasts which trading rules produce.
Discretionary trading with stop losses	How semi-automatic traders can make forecasts that have the right characteristics.
The asset allocating investor's 'no-rule' rule	The simplest possible trading rule used by asset allocating investors – a constant and identical forecast for all assets.
Two systematic rules	A pair of suggested trading rules for staunch system traders.
Using other people's rules	How to adapt publicly available trading rules or invent your own.
Selecting trading rules and variation	A brief reminder of how I recommend selecting rules and variations.

What makes a good forecast

Parts of this section are quite technical; **semi-automatic traders** and **asset allocating investors** should read it but need only skim the content. However, **staunch systems traders** who will design their own trading rules need to understand it in detail.

A forecast is a scaled quantity

When I started trading options at a large investment bank I was encouraged to put on small proprietary positions outside of the normal customer flow trading. The idea was to give novices some practical experience in managing risk without exposing the book to large losses. Initially I was limited to trading single futures contracts.

Once I graduated beyond one contract I was faced with a dilemma. How big should my position be for a purchase of German 10 year bond futures (Bunds)? Should I stick to one contract, or increase my size? I asked for advice from a more experienced trader, Sergei.[77] He sighed, exasperated at the ignorance of youth, and turned towards me.

---

77. Not his real name.

"You need to know three things. First, *how much do you like this trade?* That comes from here," Sergei replied, pointing to his heart.

"Second thing, *how much can you afford to lose?* That is down here, in your gut," and he patted his extensive stomach.

"Last thing, *how risky is it?* You calculate that here." said Sergei, tapping his forehead.

His answer was unhelpful, completely lacking in any detail, but totally correct.

It's not enough to predict that prices are rising or falling; you also need to decide whether they will go up a lot, or a little. You need to decide *how much you like the trade*. You need a **forecast** – a prediction of how much prices are expected to go up or down. This chapter is about making forecasts. I'll return to the rest of Sergei's wisdom in subsequent chapters.

A forecast is a number: a positive value means you want to buy the asset because the price is expected to go up and a negative indicates you want to short the asset. Investors who don't use derivatives and can't **short sell** will only make positive forecasts. A forecast shouldn't be binary – buy or sell – but should be scaled. Forecasts close to zero indicate a small movement in prices and larger absolute values mean you expect bigger returns.

There are three reasons why scaled forecasts make sense. Firstly, if you were to examine the returns made by a trading rule given the size of its forecasts, you'd normally find that forecasts closer to zero aren't as profitable as those further away. Secondly, binary systems cost more to trade, since to go from long to short you'd need to sell twice a full size position immediately. Finally, the rest of the framework assumes that the forecasts you get are not binary or lumpy in other ways.[78] It's better to see forecasts changing continuously rather than jumping around.

It's relatively easy to design or adapt a trading rule to produce scaled forecasts, if you're a **staunch systems trader**. If you're a **semi-automatic trader** generating forecasts in a more discretionary way then you need to be able to quantify the strength of your convictions and I'll return to that problem later in this chapter. **Asset allocating investors** have it easy since they use a fixed forecast value.

Forecasts proportional to risk adjusted return

How do you set forecasts so that they embody how much you like a position, or to be precise how strong you think its subsequent rise or fall will be?

---

78. Technical notes: There are two main reasons for this. Firstly, forecasts should have well defined and relatively stable **standard deviations**, otherwise the risk properties of the trading system will not be well defined or stable. Secondly, as we'll see subsequently I recommend limiting absolute forecast values to twice their average. Forecast distributions which are more extreme than **Gaussian normal distributions** will see an undesirable level of forecast capping. Note that there is a special case where lumpy or even binary forecasts will work just fine. If we have a large number of relatively uncorrelated binary forecasts then once combined these will approach a desirable Gaussian normal.

Simple, you might think. As I was trading Bunds when I spoke to Sergei then I should set up my **trading rule** so a weak forecast of 50 would mean a purchase of 50 Bund futures. A strong forecast of 100 implies 100 contracts, and so on.

Unfortunately there are several flaws in this idea. What if you wanted to use my forecasting rule? You might not want to take a gamble on even five Bunds, or you could work in a large fund for whom an average position would be 50,000 contracts. This kind of forecast doesn't account for *different account sizes* or *varying appetite for risk*.

Secondly, what if the **standard deviation** of Bund prices were to double? A position of 50 contracts would now be twice as risky as you'd originally expected. The simple forecast doesn't account for *risk changing over time*.

Finally, you'd normally want to use the same trading rule across different **instruments**, because it's simpler and it allows you to pool data if you're **fitting**. However 50 Bunds expose you to much less risk than 50 Japanese government ten year bond futures, but to much more than 50 German Schatz (two year) bond futures. The rule can't cope with *instruments which don't have the same risk*.

The solution is to use my favourite technique, **volatility standardisation**. So in my framework forecasts are *proportional to expected risk adjusted returns*. For example suppose that the Bund has expected returns of 2% a year and an expected annualised standard deviation of 8%. Schatz futures have an expected return of 1% a year, but you only expect **volatility** of 2% a year. After adjusting for risk the expected return on Schatz (1% ÷ 2% = 0.5) is twice as much as on Bunds (2% ÷ 8% = 0.25).

That implies the forecast for Schatz should be twice the forecast for Bunds. This deals with instruments that have different risks. It also means any trading rule can be used without modification on all instruments and that if you fit trading rules you can do so with pooled data from multiple assets. If you continuously adjust your estimate of expected volatility then you also cope with risk changing over time.

Finally with forecasts like these different investors can use the same trading rules, but then scale positions depending on the size of their accounts and their appetite for risk. I show how this is done in chapter nine, 'Volatility targeting', and chapter ten, 'Position sizing'.

You've seen before that the ratio of average return to standard deviation of returns is the **Sharpe ratio**. So expected Sharpe ratios make good forecasts, which makes creating trading rules very intuitive.

Forecasts should have a consistent scale

I said above that a forecast needs to be *proportional* to the risk adjusted return. In the example above forecasts of 2.5 for Bunds and 5 on Schatz; 0.0000005 and 0.000001 respectively, or 5,000 and 10,000, are all valid. Which of these, or the infinity of other options, is best?

In truth it doesn't really matter, as long as you are consistent, but whichever scaling you choose here will affect the rest of your trading system. In particular the expected average absolute value of your forecasts is a key part of specifying the system. Life will be easier if you choose a scaling that is easy to work with. Very small or large numbers are difficult for humans to cope with and even computers struggle with floating point representation of tiny fractions.

My recommendation is to create forecasts which have an expected absolute value of 10. So +10 is an average buy and -10 an average sell. A forecast of +5 would be a weak buy, and -20 is a very strong sell. These forecast numbers may seem very abstract right now. Don't be too concerned as in chapter ten 'Position Sizing' I will show you how to translate them into actual positions.

If you're a **semi-automatic trader** using discretionary forecasts, it's straightforward to have the right scaling, as I will show you below. The rule used by **asset allocating investors** also has the appropriate scale. The example rules I provide for **staunch systems traders** later in the chapter are also correctly scaled. But if you're making your own rules, or adapting others, you will need to standardise their natural scaling, as I'll explain later in the chapter.

Should we allow forecasts to be as large as possible?

With an expected absolute value of 10, a forecast of +10 is bullish, and one of +20 is really bullish. What if you're confident that this is the chance of a lifetime, like the 2009 Barclays trade which I told you about in the introduction. Should you allow your rule to have a forecast of +100? I think not. Forecasts should be capped at a maximum absolute value and I recommend a limit of 20. Here's why:

Risk control	Diversification is the investor's best friend. But it's pointless diversifying if you then allow one part of your system to dominate your returns. You need to limit the risk that any **trading rule variation** can contribute to the overall system.
Limited data	When I **back-test** a profitable trading rule I normally find that positive forecasts are associated with price rises, and larger values mean larger rises. However for a properly scaled rule very large forecast values will appear rarely in a back-test. So there is a lot of uncertainty around whether extremely large forecasts translate into proportionally larger price movements, as I don't usually have enough data to support this finding. If a forecast had a **Gaussian normal distribution** you'd only see absolute forecast values over 20 around 5% of the time, so there is only limited evidence that forecasts of this magnitude are actually correct.

Extremes are often different	Normally markets trend with falls followed by further falls, but after very sharp drops subsequent one day rises are more likely; the so called 'dead cat bounce'. Similarly high yielding stocks do well, but those with dividend yields above 50% are probably going bankrupt, or at the very least about to cut their dividend. Many other patterns also reverse at extremes. These effects are not often strong or common enough to exploit directly, but they should give you concern about betting too much when you have very strong forecasts.
Higher realised return volatility	A high forecast could mean that you expect large returns, but equally might be due to very low **standard deviation** of returns. Unfortunately periods of subdued **volatility** are usually followed by jumps to much higher levels, often combined with reversals in price.
	I had very strong positive forecasts in the Japanese Bond markets in January 2013, mainly due to relatively low volatility. When Prime Minister Abe unveiled his latest set of economic reforms volatility spiked rapidly as prices dropped fast. Fortunately because my forecasts were capped the damage was contained.
Limited downside	If forecasts have a **Gaussian normal distribution** then it's rare, again around 5% of the time, that you'll see values bigger than 20. So the reduction in your returns from capping is quite small compared to the potential risk control benefits.

Staunch systems traders shouldn't ignore forecasts that are outside of the range -20 to +20, but cap them. A forecast of +25 from your trading rule should be reduced to +20. Increase any forecast lower than -20 to that level. All your forecasts will then be in the range -20 to +20.

For **semi-automatic traders** all your discretionary forecasts should be in the range of -20 to +20, with no exceptions, even for the trade of a lifetime. **Asset allocating investors** don't need to worry as you will have a fixed forecast of +10.

If we can't short an instrument, because of limited access to derivatives or difficulties **selling short**, then you'll also need to change all negative forecasts to zero.

Discretionary trading with stop losses

Semi-automatic Trader

If you're a **semi-automatic trader** then you won't use systematic trading rules but instead make **discretionary** forecasts either on gut feeling, or using complex analysis which can't be systematised, like my 2009 Barclays trade in the introduction.

As well as the sign of the forecast, positive for long and negative for short, you must indicate how strongly you feel about it. Your forecasts must be correctly scaled: the expected absolute value should be around 10, and they must be between the recommended limits of -20 and +20.

Forecasts don't have to be finely quantified, such as "I love the Nikkei today, about 8.7663." However, you should be able to give a rough indication of the strength of your passion for the Nikkei. You can then translate your opinion into a forecast number, as table 16 shows.

TABLE 16: TRANSLATING OPINIONS INTO A QUANTIFIED FORECAST

Very strong sell	Strong Sell	Sell	Weak sell	Neutral	Weak buy	Buy	Strong buy	Very strong buy
-20	-15	-10	-5	0	5	10	15	20

If you can't go short assets, because you're not using derivatives like spread bets or can't **short sell** in your account, then you'll need to limit yourself to positive forecast values.

You shouldn't change your forecast once a bet is open. Otherwise there is the risk of meddling, taking profits too early by reducing the conviction of your forecast or doubling up on a loss. Instead you will be using a systematic trailing stop loss rule to close all your positions. I'll explain this further in chapter thirteen, where I describe a semi-automatic trading system in more detail.

There are substantial advantages to using discretionary forecasts in my systematic **framework** with stop losses; you can make predictions about the behaviour of your live trading and measure expected risk more precisely. Your positions will always be the correct size for a given forecast, tolerance for risk, and account size. This will give you more time and energy to get the forecast right. Finally, by using stop losses you'll be trading somewhat like an 'early loss taking' **trend follower**, so it's more likely your strategy will have benign positive **skew**.

The asset allocating investor's 'no-rule' rule

Asset Allocating Investor

Think about a **static** portfolio of two **collective funds**: an S&P 500 equity and a US benchmark bond fund. Suppose you bought them in equal weights, with half your cash in each. As bond funds tend to have a quarter of the **volatility** of equities this portfolio will have 80% of its risk coming from stocks. As I explained in chapter two the solution is to hold the two assets in **risk parity**, each contributing the same amount of expected risk. This implies a cash weight to equities of roughly 20% and 80% to bonds.

By using the **framework**, instruments will automatically have identical expected **standard deviation** of returns for a given forecast level. This means if you have an equally weighted portfolio of two **trading subsystems**, one for equities and one for bonds, each with *identical forecasts* for their individual instrument, then you'd always have the same expected volatility for both equities and bonds. You'd effectively have a risk parity strategy where risk was being constantly adjusted, or what I described in chapter two as a 'fourth degree' static portfolio (page 38).

Hence the correct rule for an **asset allocating investor** is to have a constant forecast equal to the expected average forecast, +10 for all instruments at all times. I call this the 'no-rule' rule. You don't think you can predict how different assets will perform, so you buy them all. Remember all forecasts are proportional to return adjusted for standard deviation. So using an equal forecast for all instruments is equivalent to assuming all assets have the same expected **Sharpe ratio**.

There are certain advantages to using this constant forecast approach within the systematic framework, rather than just buying a normal risk parity portfolio. For starters you can probably do better than equal weights, as you will remember from chapter four, 'Portfolio allocation'. Secondly, many risk parity funds don't adjust for the standard deviation of returns changing over time, whereas you will.[79] As I'll discuss in chapter twelve, 'Speed and Size', that adjustment will be done after carefully considering the trading costs of our instruments. A DIY risk parity portfolio avoids paying the management fees you'd have with an external fund manager.

Finally, if you do decide to introduce expectations of asset returns there is a neat and relatively robust way to do this, by adjusting **handcrafted** portfolio weights in line with where you think prices will go. I'll give you more detail in the **asset allocating investor** example in part four of the book.

---

79. As you might recall from chapter two, page 38, many risk parity portfolios are 'third degree' with allocations set with initial expected risk, rather than the 'fourth degree' you will have (allocations adjusted as risk changes).

Two example systematic rules

Staunch Systems Trader

Semi-automatic traders and **asset allocating investors** can skip the remainder of this chapter, which is for **staunch systems traders** only.

The two examples of **trading rules** above aren't very interesting. I include them to show how my framework can still be used by people who don't believe that market returns can be forecasted, or others who think they can do it better than a simple rule can. However **staunch systematic traders** disagree with both of these groups and wish to forecast prices with fully systematic trading rules.

There isn't enough space in this book to include every trading rule in existence. Fortunately, there's a plethora of other books and websites available which contain explicit trading rules, or ideas from which they can be developed. Just one book, Perry Kaufman's *Trading Systems and Methods* has over 1000 pages and includes dozens of rules.[80] The next section in this chapter will show how you can create your own trading rules, or modify other people's.

In this section I will briefly outline two rules that I use in my own trading system.[81] If you want to use them you can find more detail in appendix B. In part four of this book I'll show how these rules can be incorporated into the framework to create a complete system for the staunch systems trader.

Trend following with the EWMAC rule

Many asset prices seem to show **momentum**: what goes up, usually carries on going up; and vice versa. This effect can be captured by using **trend following** rules. I am a big fan of these types of rules for several reasons.

Firstly, they work. As we saw in chapter one, the trend following 'early loss taker' rule made mincemeat of its opposition, the 'early profit taker'. There's a lot of academic research and real performance statistics supporting the use of trend following rules. Secondly, I like rules which I can explain; as I said in chapter two prospect theory justifies why these rules work, and should continue to do so. Also, trend following is an easy to implement **technical** strategy using only price data. Finally, it has benign positive **skew**.

---

80. There is a brief selection including this and other books in appendix A.
81. Although these two rules represent only part of my trading system these two rules alone would account for around 85% of **back-tested** performance. Unfortunately I'm unable to give a full description of every rule I use, partly because of space and also due to legal constraints.

Of course you could use the now familiar early loss taker rule for trend following, but there are better alternatives.[82] One of the most popular trading rules for capturing trends goes by the unwieldy name of **Exponentially Weighted Moving Average Crossover**, or **EWMAC** for short.[83] Fortunately the idea is simpler to implement than it is to say. You take two **exponentially weighted moving averages (EWMA)** of an asset's price. One average, the slower, looks back over a longer period than the faster average. When the faster is above the slower it means that prices are in an uptrend and you should buy; and vice versa.

FIGURE 18: RIDING THE DOWNTREND IN CRUDE OIL FUTURES WITH THE EWMAC TREND FOLLOWING RULE. WE SELL WHEN THE FAST EWMA CROSSES THE SLOW; AND BUY WHEN THIS REVERSES

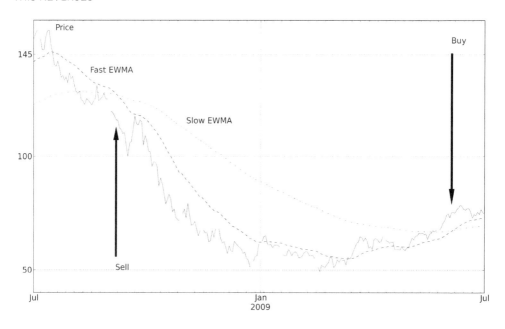

Figure 18 shows an example. Here we've got the price of crude oil futures from summer 2008 onwards. After a long uptrend in prices there is a reversal in July 2008. Within a few weeks the fast EWMA has gone below the slower and goes short. The gap gets bigger and the position is increased until January. A gentle bullish trend begins and the short

---

82. Early loss taker has some unpleasant attributes. First of all it gives a binary forecast; you are either long or short. Secondly, your current forecast depends on prices but also what positions you have recently had. This isn't a very nice property; amongst other things it means your precise **back-tested** behaviour will depend on where your price history began.

83. This is probably one of the oldest purely systematic trading rules in current use; ignoring the older, more subjective, technical analysis pattern matching tradition. There are academic studies of EWMAC dating back to the 1960s and it would have been used by traders prior to that.

is reduced, and then reversed once the fast EWMA climbs back above the slow in June 2009. There is a detailed specification of the EWMAC rule in appendix B.

The carry rule

EWMAC is a positive **skew** rule which needs prices to trend in one direction or another. To balance it out here is the **carry** rule which benefits when nothing happens. **Foreign exchange carry** is a well known strategy for exploiting stable markets; if you borrow in Japanese yen at 0.5% and invest the money in Australian dollars at 3.5% then you'll earn 3%, assuming that the JPY/AUD exchange rate doesn't budge. But what does carry mean for other assets?[84]

Carry, which is sometimes called roll down or contango, is the return that you will get if asset prices are perfectly stable. If the world doesn't change this will be equal to the yield on the asset, less the cost of borrowing (or the interest you would have got from holding cash). So if you buy shares in French supermarket Carrefour which currently has a dividend yield of 3%, and you pay 1% to borrow the purchase cost, then you earn 2% carry on the position if the share price is unchanged.

Similarly today I can buy June 2018 Eurodollar futures at 97.94, or March 2018 at 98.01. If there is no change in the shape of the yield curve then in three months' time June futures will rise to 98.01, earning 0.07 per contract.

Academic theory predicts that prices should move against us to offset these returns, but it often doesn't. Carry is usually earned steadily on these kinds of trades although occasionally they go horribly wrong and the relationship temporarily breaks down, giving this trading rule some evil negative **skew**. I think the rule is profitable as a reward for taking on this nasty skew and various other kinds of **risk premium** which tend to be correlated to carry trades.

Full details on how I calculate carry are given in appendix B, from page 285 onwards. There is an example of the carry trading rule in action in figure 19, again showing crude oil futures during the great crash of 2008. The price of the nearer futures contract dips below the contract we are trading in mid-August. This is a bearish carry signal and the rule sells to enjoy some of the continuing fall in price.

---

84. The first multi asset (rather than FX specific) academic research into carry appears to be the imaginatively titled working paper 'Carry' by Ralph Koijen, Tobias Moskowitz, Lasse Pedersen and Evert Vrugt from 2012. The specification of the carry rule here is identical to that paper. But rules like this have been used in the industry for much longer.

FIGURE 19: TRADING CRUDE OIL WITH CARRY IN 2008-10. WE ARE SLOW TO SELL AND STAY SHORT TOO LONG

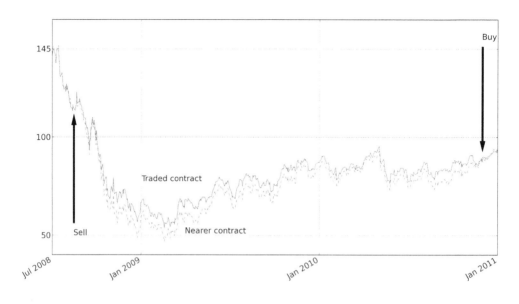

Unfortunately it remains bearish long after the market has turned, but you can't win them all. It makes sense to combine diversifying trading rules like the positive skew, trend following EWMAC rule, with a negative skew carry rule.

Adapting and creating trading rules

Staunch Systems Trader

The above trading rules, one positive and one negative **skew**, are sufficient to create a pretty good trading strategy. The benefits of adding further rules within the same styles are relatively limited. Just using these two simple rules would generate roughly 85% of the **back-tested** performance of my own more complicated system.

However you might still want to create your own rules, or adapt those you find elsewhere. Here are some pointers, with an example of how I modified a trading rule I read about whilst researching this chapter, which I've nicknamed 'Close to Open'.

Simplicity and objectivity	Trading rules in books tend to be quite complicated, with lots of conditionals and a degree of subjectivity. Try and pare the rule down to its essential elements, to create a simple and objective trading rule.
	The example rule I found could be reduced to 'Buy if the open is higher than yesterday's close'. (I haven't tested this rule and I have no idea if it will work or not.)
Continuous, not binary	Many trading rules are unfortunately of a buy or sell, binary, nature. If possible you should make them continuous. I converted the simple rule above to calculate the raw forecast as [Open price - Close price].
Not market specific; volatility standardised	The value of a forecast should be comparable across markets and across time. If a forecast is in price units, as in the simple example here, then you should **volatility standardise** it to get a forecast proportional to **Sharpe ratio**. So your forecast would be:
	[Open price - Close price] ÷ (Recent **standard deviation** of daily returns)
	This is the same standardisation that I use in the **EWMAC** and **Carry** rules.
Changing forecast	Separate entry and exit rules are not suitable for the framework.[*] Ideally a forecast should change continuously, independently of what our position is, throughout the life of a trade.
	This suggests that you should create rules which recalculate forecasts every time you have new data, and then adjust your positions accordingly. Normally this is simply a matter of modifying the entry rule. Rather than use the 'Close to Open' rule only for entries, you would calculate the forecast value every day.
Correct scaling	If you're going to create trading rules you need to rescale them from their natural scaling, so that the expected absolute value of the forecast is around 10. You do this by multiplying your raw forecast by a **forecast scalar**. You need to **back-test** the behaviour of the rule with real data to find the average forecast, but in line with my recommendations in chapter three, 'Fitting', you shouldn't look at performance data whilst doing this. See appendix D, page 297, for more details.
	The natural average absolute value of this rule is 0.33, implying the forecast scalar in this case is 10 ÷ 0.33 = 30.

---

[*] If you absolutely have to use an entry rule which doesn't adjust throughout the life of the trade, with a separate exit rule, then I strongly suggest you use the stop loss rule I advocate for **semi-automatic traders**. I don't recommend using any other kind of explicit exit rule as they are usually over-fitted and make life very complicated.

Selecting trading rules and variations

Staunch Systems Trader

Even if you don't adapt or create new rules and just use mine, there are still a theoretically infinite number of **EWMAC trading rule variations** on the menu. If you do get creative and make your own rules the number of options will explode. Which rules and variations should you use in practice?

As I said in chapter three, 'Fitting', I don't recommend using **back-tested** profitability to select trading rules or variations. Instead you should focus on behaviour such as the **correlation** between variations, and the speed they trade at, whilst ignoring **Sharpe ratio** and other performance metrics.

You should then use two selection criteria. The first is to avoid including any two variations with more than a 95% correlation to each other, as one of them will not be adding any value to the system. I discuss how to prune possible variations of the EWMAC rule in appendix B (in the section on EWMAC, from page 282).

Secondly, you must exclude anything which trades too slowly, or too quickly. As I mentioned in chapter two, very slow rules are unlikely to generate significant Sharpe ratio.[85] I suggest you remove any rule which holds positions for longer than a few months. At the other end of the spectrum for many instruments fast rules will be too expensive to trade. This could mean you end up choosing a different set of variations for each instrument. I'll return to this in chapter twelve, 'Speed and Size', where I'll show how to determine which variations should be excluded for a given level of trading costs.

The **staunch systems trader** example chapter in part four will give an overview of the rule selection process.

Summary of trading rules and forecasts

Where do forecasts come from	If you're **staunch systems traders** then each of your trading rules produces a forecast, including any variations that we're using; for example to capture different trend lengths.
	Asset allocating investors use a constant identical forecast for all instruments.
	Semi-automatic traders make discretionary forecasts on an ad-hoc basis for a changing set of instruments.

---

85. This also means we can't prove that they work statistically.

Forecast for every instrument and from each trading rule	For **staunch systems traders** each instrument will have a separate forecast for a given trading rule variation. So if you had ten instruments and three different kinds of trading rule, each with two variations, then you'd calculate 10 × 3 × 2 = 60 individual forecasts.
	Semi-automatic traders and **asset allocating investors** have one forecast per instrument.
Forecast sign is vital	Positive means you buy and go long the asset. A negative forecast means you go short. A zero forecast means you shouldn't have a position.
Forecast size is also important	Absolutely larger forecasts mean you are more confident of your opinion and expect a bigger rise (or fall) in prices.
	Forecasts should have an expected absolute value of 10.
Forecasts shouldn't be too big	Forecasts must lie in the range -20 to +20, unless you can't short an instrument in which case it would be between 0 and +20. If a trading rule produces a larger forecast then cap it at either end of the range.
Semi-automatic traders:	Make your own predictions and convert them into forecasts between -20 (strongly bearish) and +20 (strongly bullish). Positions are closed using systematic stop loss rule, as described in chapter thirteen.
Asset allocating investors:	Use a constant forecast of +10 for all assets.
Staunch systematic traders:	Use a combination of systematic trading rules like **EWMAC** and **Carry**, design your own rule or adapt others. Follow the advice earlier in this chapter, and in chapter three, when selecting trading rule variations.

You should now have one, or more, trading rules ready to go. **Asset allocating investors** will be using the single 'no rule' rule, and **semi-automatic traders** will be making discretionary forecasts. If you're in either of these groups you can skip to chapter nine.

Semi-automatic traders should either have developed their own rules, adapted a publically available rule, or be happy for now to use one or both of the rules I provided earlier in the chapter. If you have only one trading rule variation you can also skip the next chapter. But if you're using multiple rules or variations then you'll need to read chapter eight to discover how to combine forecasts from different rules.

Chapter Eight. Combined Forecasts

Staunch Systems Trader

This chapter is about combining forecasts from different trading rules, including variations of the same rule, so it's required reading for most **staunch systems traders**. If you're an **asset allocating investor** using the single 'no rule' rule or a **semi-automatic trader** you can skip ahead to chapter nine.

L IFE IS SIMPLE WHEN YOU HAVE ONLY ONE **TRADING RULE**. STRONG positive forecast? Then buy. Negative? Sell. But what if you have multiple rules and they disagree?

As you saw in the previous chapter, in late 2009 and 2010 one of my trading rules (the **EWMAC trend following** rule) had turned bullish on crude oil, but another (**Carry**) was still bearish (see figures 18 and 19). What should I have done – buy, sell, or do nothing? Multiple forecasts which disagree aren't conclusive – you need to create a single **combined forecast** for every instrument.

Chapter overview

Combining with forecast weights	How to use forecast weights to produce a single combined forecast for each instrument.
Choosing the forecast weights	Using the handcrafting method to find weights for each trading rule.
Getting the correct variation	Making sure the combined forecast has the right expected absolute value by correcting for diversification across the individual forecasts.
Capping combined forecasts	Just like the forecast from each trading rule you should limit the size of your combined forecasts.

Combining with forecast weights

How do you go from two or more **forecasts**, to a single **combined forecast** for each instrument? In the framework you need to use a *weighted average* of your forecasts, where the weights are **forecast weights**. These are a type of portfolio weight, where your portfolio consists of **trading rule variations**, and they should all be positive and add up to 100%.

So if you were trading crude oil in mid-2009, as shown in figures 18 and 19, then you might have had forecasts of +15 in the **EWMAC** trend following variation and -10 in **Carry**. With forecast weights of 50% in each rule your combined forecast would be 2.5.[86]

Choosing the forecast weights

How do you find the best weights to use when combining **forecasts**? This is an example of the problem of allocating a portfolio of assets, which we discussed in chapter four. But now the asset weights you have to choose are **forecast weights** for **trading rules** and their **variations**, rather than long positions in equities or bonds.

---

86. $(0.5 \times 15) + (0.5 \times -10) = 2.5$.

Forecast weights might be the same for all instruments, or different. I'll now show you how to use the **handcrafting** method I described in chapter four to find those weights, although you can also use **bootstrapping** if you're comfortable with that.[87] To find handcrafted weights you need both **correlations** and a way of grouping your assets.

You can **back-test** the performance of different trading rules to get historical estimates for correlations. Alternatively tables 56 and 57 in appendix C (from page 294) give some typical values for trading rules within the same instrument.

Once you have correlations the next step in the handcrafted method is to group your assets. The simplest way is to group the **variations** *within* a particular trading rule, then allocate *across* trading rules. Let's take a simple example. Suppose we're using the two rules from the last chapter, **trend following (EWMAC)** and **Carry**. For now assume that EWMAC has three variants, with fast look-backs of 16, 32 and 64 for the moving averages.[88] The carry rule has a single variation. Here is how I calculated the weights.

First level grouping Within trading rules	• Group one (EWMAC): From table 57 in appendix C (page 295) I get the correlations between EWMAC variations: 0.90 between adjacent variations, and 0.7 between the variations with fast look-backs 16 and 64. Using table 8 (page 79) row 11 I get weights of 16% in look-back 32, and 42% in look-backs 16 and 64.
	• Group two (Carry): One asset. Using table 8 row 1: 100% in Carry.
Second level grouping Across trading rules	Using table 8 row 2: 50% in the EWMAC and 50% in Carry.

This gives us the weights in table 17. By the way it's also possible to have a three level grouping, if you are mixing rules of different styles.

---

87. Naturally this should be done on an **out of sample** basis, so your weights change during the back-test. After cost performance must be used when generating portfolio weights. I discuss costs more in chapter twelve, 'Speed and Size'.

88. The slow look-back is 4 times the fast, as discussed in appendix B, page 284.

TABLE 17: EXAMPLE HANDCRAFTED FORECAST WEIGHTS

	1st level	2nd level	Final weights
EWMAC 16, 64	42%	50%	21%
EWMAC 32, 128	16%	50%	8%
EWMAC 64, 256	42%	50%	21%
Carry	100%	50%	50%

Notice that I haven't shown you how to incorporate different performance between rules, the effect of costs, or how to decide if different instruments should have different weights. If you've followed my advice from chapter three, and not fitted or selected trading rules based on **Sharpe ratio**, then you risk having some poor rules in your portfolio, on which you could want to reduce the allocation. It's also quite likely faster rules will have worse after-cost performance than slower ones.

I'll discuss these issues in detail in chapter twelve, 'Speed and Size'. There will also be a more realistic example using performance and cost estimates in the **staunch systems trader** example chapter in part four.

Getting to 10

I recommended in chapter six that all your individual forecasts should have the same expected variability – equivalent to an expected absolute value of 10. But unless your trading rules are perfectly correlated it's likely that the **combined forecast** will end up on a smaller scale. It's the same general effect you get from putting less than perfectly correlated assets into any portfolio, where the overall portfolio will always end up with lower risk than its constituents. The magnitude of the fall in **standard deviation** will depend on the degree of diversification.

However the trading system **framework** will not work consistently if combined forecasts have a low and unpredictable scaling. You need your combined forecasts to maintain the same expected absolute value of 10 as you required for individual forecasts. To fix this the combined forecast is multiplied by a **forecast diversification multiplier**.

CONCEPT: DIVERSIFICATION MULTIPLIER

If you have two stocks, each with identical return **volatility** of 10%, with half your money in each, what will be the volatility of the whole portfolio? Naturally it will depend on how **correlated** the two assets are.

If they are perfectly correlated then the portfolio will have a return **standard deviation** of 10%; the same as the individual assets. But if the correlation between the two assets was 0.5, the portfolio volatility would come out at 8.66%.[89] Similarly a correlation of zero gives a volatility of 7.07%. More diversified portfolios have lower **volatility**.

In the framework we are concerned with putting together **volatility standardised** assets that have the same expected average **standard deviation** of returns; and to do this we need forecasts to have the same average absolute value. To ensure this is always the case you need to multiply the forecasts or positions you have to account for portfolio diversification, so that your total portfolio also achieves the standard volatility target.

This multiplication factor is the **diversification multiplier**.[90] If the correlation between the two assets in the simple two stocks example is 1.0, then because the portfolio has the same volatility as its members (10%) no adjustment is required, and the multiplier will be 1. A correlation of 0.5 implies a multiplier equal to the target volatility of 10%, divided by the natural portfolio volatility of 8.66%. This will be 10 ÷ 8.66 = 1.15. Finally if the two assets were completely uncorrelated with portfolio volatility of 7.07%, then the multiplier would be 10 ÷ 7.07 = 1.44.

You will get even higher values with negative correlations. However this will result in dangerously large multipliers, so I strongly recommend you floor any estimated correlations at zero.

You can use two possible sources for correlations to do this calculation. Correlations can be estimated with data from **back-tests**, or using rule of thumb values from the tables in appendix C.[91]

You can do the actual calculation with the precise equation, or alternatively table 18 gives a rule of thumb which will give a good approximation.[92]

---

89. You can replicate this result with one of the many online portfolio calculators, such as www.zenwealth. com/businessfinanceonline/RR/PortfolioCalculator.html

90. The diversification multiplier is also a measure of the number of independent bets in the portfolio, as used in the **law of active management**.

91. A couple of technical points. Firstly strictly speaking diversification multipliers should be calculated on a **rolling out of sample** basis if based on **back-tested** data. However as you're not optimising a parameter based on profitability, estimating these single multipliers won't cause serious problems with **over-fitting**. Secondly when estimating forecast diversification multipliers you can either use the forecasts from each individual instrument, or pool back-tests of different instruments (which is my preferred approach), before calculating correlation matrices.

92. The precise formula and spreadsheet method is in appendix D (page 297).

FIGURE 20: COMBINING DIFFERENT FORECASTS REDUCES VARIABILITY. RESCALING FIXES THIS

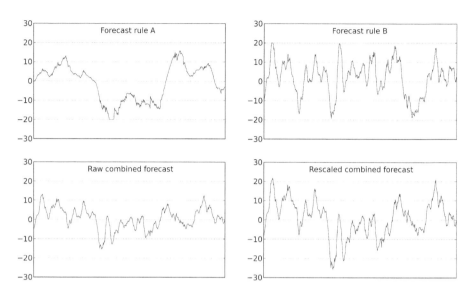

Figure 20 shows this effect for two uncorrelated forecasts A and B, which I've combined with a 50% weight to each. They cover the range from -20 to +20. But the **combined forecast** is much less variable than I want, with a smaller range of -15 to +12. Scaling the combined forecast up with a **forecast diversification multiplier** fixes the problem.

TABLE 18: MORE ASSETS AND LOWER CORRELATIONS MEAN MORE DIVERSIFICATION AND A HIGHER MULTIPLIER[93]

| | Diversification multiplier | | | | |
| | Average correlation between assets | | | | |
Number of assets	0.0	0.25	0.5	0.75	1.0
2	1.41	1.27	1.15	1.10	1.0
3	1.73	1.41	1.22	1.12	1.0
4	2.0	1.51	1.27	1.10	1.0
5	2.2	1.58	1.29	1.15	1.0
10	3.2	1.75	1.35	1.17	1.0
15	3.9	1.83	1.37	1.17	1.0
20	4.5	1.86	1.38	1.18	1.0
50 or more	7.1	1.94	1.40	1.19	1.0

The table shows the approximate diversification multiplier given the number of assets in a portfolio (rows) and the average correlation between them (columns). Beware of using very high multipliers.

I'll now explain how to calculate the **forecast diversification multiplier**. If you don't have **back-tested** forecast values then you can estimate likely correlations from tables 56 and 57 in appendix C (from page 294). Correlation between selected variations of the same rule tends to be high; up to 0.9 but averaging around 0.7. Across different trading rules within the same style it is around 0.5. Using different styles of rules, correlations for trading rules within an instrument are around 0.25.

For the simple example with four rule variations from earlier in the chapter I populated a correlation matrix using the information in appendix C, which is shown in table 19.

---

93. These values assume that you have equal weights in your portfolio and all **correlations** are identical. So they are an approximation, but very close to the real answer except for extreme portfolios.

TABLE 19: CORRELATION OF TRADING RULE FORECASTS IN SIMPLE EXAMPLE

	EW16	EW32	EW64	Carry
EWMAC 16,64	1			
EWMAC 32,128	0.9	1		
EWMAC 64,256	0.6	0.9	1	
Carry	0.25	0.25	0.25	1

Values shown are correlations, populated using values in appendix C tables.

You could now use tables 18 and 19 to find an approximate forecast diversification multiplier for the four rule variations. The matrix in table 19 has a rounded average correlation of 0.50,[94] which with four assets in table 18 gives a multiplier of 1.27. As a comparison the precise value is 1.31 using the actual forecast weights calculated above and the formula on page 297.

Finally, a word of warning. It's possible, as table 18 shows us, to get very high multipliers if your trading rules are sufficiently diversified, even if you cap negative correlations at zero. As you'll see in a moment I recommend that combined forecasts are limited to a maximum value of 20, so having a high multiplier would mean having capped forecasts most of the time, and effectively behaving as if you had a binary trading rule which is either fully long or fully short.

To avoid this I advocate using a maximum diversification multiplier of 2.5, regardless of what your actual estimate is.

Capped at 20

In the previous chapter I recommended that you limit the forecast from individual rules to the range -20 to +20. However it's possible in theory for a combined forecast to go above 20 if the **forecast diversification multiplier** is greater than 1, as is usually the case. To take a simple example, if the **Carry** rule and a single **EWMAC** variation both had forecasts of +16, with forecast weights of 50% on each rule, and a diversification multiplier of 1.5, then the combined forecast would be 24.[95]

---

94. You shouldn't include the self **correlation** '1' values when working out the average.
95. The weighted average of the two forecasts is $(16.0 \times 50\%) + (16.0 \times 50\%) = 16.0$. After applying the multiplier the combined forecast is $16.0 \times 1.5 = 24$.

All the reasons cited in the previous chapter for limiting individual forecasts apply equally to combined forecasts, so I strongly encourage you to limit combined forecasts to absolute values of 20 or less. Any value outside this range should be capped.

Summary for combining forecasts

Instrument forecasts for each trading rule and variation	You start with the forecasts for each trading rule variation for an instrument. So if you have two rules, each with three variations, then you'd have six possible forecast values per instrument.
	I recommended in the previous chapter that each individual forecast has an expected average absolute value of around 10 and should be limited to between -20 and +20.
Forecast weights	Each rule variation should have a positive **forecast weight**. The weights must add up to 100%. These weights can be the same across instruments, or different.
Raw combined forecast	Using the **forecast weights**, take a weighted average of the **forecasts** from each rule variation.
Forecast diversification multiplier	This is needed to get the expected absolute value of the combined forecast up to the recommended value of 10.
	Estimated **correlations** are needed; from **back-test** results, or the rule of thumb tables in appendix C. You can then calculate the multiplier approximately from table 18 or precisely using the equation on page 297.
	The multiplier is at least 1.0 and I recommend a maximum of 2.5.
Rescaled combined forecast	This is the raw combined forecast multiplied by the **forecast diversification multiplier**.
	Because of the diversification multiplier it will have an expected average absolute value equal to the expected variability of the individual forecasts, which I recommend to be 10.
Final combined forecast	I recommend you cap the rescaled combined forecasts within the range -20 to +20, as for individual forecasts.

Now you can forecast price movements for a particular instrument you are ready to translate that into actual trades. The first step in doing this is to decide how much money you are willing to put at risk, as you'll see in the next chapter.

Chapter Nine. Volatility targeting

Instruments

Trading rule A, variation 1	A1 forecast for instrument X					
Trading rule A, variation 2	A2 forecast for instrument X	Combined forecast X			Subsystem position in X	Portfolio weighted position in X
Trading rule B, variation 1	B1 forecast for instrument X					
Trading rule A, variation 1	A1 forecast, instrument Y					
Trading rule A, variation 2	A2 forecast for instrument Y	Combined forecast Y			Subsystem position in Y	Portfolio weighted position in Y
Trading rule B, variation 1	B1 forecast for instrument Y					

Forecast weights · Volatility targeting · Position sizing · Instrument weights

Customising for speed and size

D O YOU REMEMBER SERGEI, DISPENSER OF OPAQUE TRADING advice in chapter seven? He told me that there were three issues to consider when deciding how big a position we should have. The first thing to consider was how much we liked the trade. You've dealt with that by creating a single forecast for each instrument you're trading – either a discretionary forecast for **semi-automated traders**, a constant forecast for **asset allocating investors**, or a **combined forecast** for **staunch systems traders**. Now we're ready to return to Sergei's second question, "How much can you afford to lose?"[96]

---

96. Many trading books use the term 'money management' to cover both volatility targeting and position sizing (which is discussed in the next chapter), but I prefer to separate them out for the reasons I explained in chapter five, 'Framework Overview'.

Chapter overview

The importance of risk targeting	Why getting your appetite for risk right is so important and the key issues involved.
Setting your volatility target	The measure of how much risk you're prepared to take and how to calculate it.
Rolling up profits and losses	How your volatility target should be adjusted when you lose or make money.
What percentage of capital per trade	Relating the volatility targeting concept to traditional money management where you limit bets to a specific percentage of capital.

The importance of risk targeting

Deciding your overall trading risk is the most important decision you will have to make when designing your trading system. Nearly all amateur traders lose money and most do so because their positions are too large compared to their account size.[97] Suffering painful losses is the main reason why both amateurs and professionals meddle with trading systems rather than letting them run unimpeded.

Making this decision correctly involves understanding two things. Firstly you must *understand your system*, in particular its likely performance and whether it's likely to have positive or negative **skew**. You must avoid **overconfidence**, as I discussed in chapter one. You should not extrapolate over-fitted **back-test** results to create high expectations of return. Are you sure your strategy can generate a **Sharpe ratio** of 2.0 after costs? Are you really, really sure?

Next you must *understand yourself*, in a complete and honest way. Can you face the possibility of regularly losing 5%, 10% or 20% of your own capital in a day?

These points also apply to those paid to manage other people's money. Additionally professionals need to understand their clients' tolerance for losing money. If investors aren't truly comfortable with the risks being taken then you will see them redeeming in droves when large losses occur.

---

97. The other reason is that they trade too much, which is covered in chapter twelve, 'Speed and Size'.

Setting a volatility target

Imaginary conversation between a financial advisor and myself:

Financial 'expert': "How much risk do you want to take?"

Me: "What do you mean by risk?"

Financial 'expert': "Er... well how would you define your tolerance for losing money?"

Me: "Well it could be how much I'm prepared to lose next year. Or tomorrow. Or next week. Are you talking about the absolute maximum loss I can cope with, or the average, or the worst loss I'd expect 95 days out of 100 (the so called 'Value at Risk')? Which question would you like me to answer?"

Financial 'expert': "Hold on. I need to speak to my supervisor..."

Joking aside, how do we answer this deceptively simple question? To keep things simple I use a single figure to measure appetite for risk – an expected **standard deviation**, which I call the **volatility target**. You can measure this as a percentage, or in cash terms, and over different time periods. So for example the **daily cash volatility target** is the average expected standard deviation of the daily portfolio returns. As it's a cash value you need to specify the currency that your account or fund is denominated in.

When I first discussed risk on page 39 I talked about **predictable** and **unpredictable risks**. Your volatility target is the long-term average of expected, predictable, risk. The exact predictable risk you have on any given day will depend on the strength of your **forecasts**, and on the current expected **correlation** of asset prices. You'll also face unpredictable risks if your forecast of volatility or correlations is wrong. In any case the actual amount you lose or gain on any given day will be random, since even a perfect estimation of risk only tells you what your *average* gains and losses will be.

I find it's easier to look at an **annualised cash volatility target**, which will be the annualised expected daily standard deviation of returns. As before you annualise by multiplying by the square root of time; given there are around 256 trading days in a year this will be 16. Beware: the annualised volatility target isn't the maximum, or even the average, you might expect to lose in a year.[98] Indeed it's quite probable you will sometimes lose more than that in a year.

---

98. There are several reasons why your expected average annual loss wouldn't be equal to the annualised expected daily standard deviation. Firstly, if your **Sharpe ratio** is greater than zero then your expected average annual loss will be smaller than one **sigma**. Secondly, in the event of losses you'd probably reduce your positions if you're using **trend following rules** or stop losses. Thirdly, as you'll see in the next chapter 'Position Sizing', you should reduce your positions when price volatility rises, which reduces losses in periods of rising risk. Also, as you'll see later in this chapter, you'd reduce your risk target throughout the year if you made losses, and vice versa. More technically if consecutive returns aren't independent, and have time series autocorrelation, then annualising by multiplying by 16 is a poor approximation.

It's also easier to separate out your cash account value and the appropriate level of risk to run on that money. The amount of cash you are trading with is your **trading capital**. You then decide what your volatility target will be as a percentage of that capital. If you multiply this **percentage volatility target** by your trading capital, then you'll get your volatility target in cash terms. So with a million dollars of trading capital and an annualised 10% percentage volatility target, you would have an annualised cash volatility target of $100,000.

In the rest of the chapter I'll be dealing with the implications of where you set your trading capital and percentage volatility target, rather than setting your cash volatility target directly. This means that amateur traders with £1,000 in their account can use the same guidelines to set percentage volatility target as multi-billion Euro hedge funds.

Here are the points to consider when setting your trading capital and percentage volatility targets:

1. **How much can you lose?**: How much money do you have to trade or invest?

2. **How much risk can you cope with?**: Can you afford to lose it all? Can you afford to lose half? What probability of losing half would you be comfortable with? What probability of losing 90% of it over ten years would make you lose sleep?

3. **Can you realise that risk?**: Given the instruments you are investing in and the safe amount of leverage (if any) you can use, can you actually hit the risk target?

4. **Is this level of risk right for your system?**: Given the characteristics of your trading system, expected **Sharpe ratio** and **skew**, does the amount of risk make sense?

How much can you lose?

The initial **trading capital** is the amount of cash you start with, bearing in mind that there is a chance that you might lose all or nearly all of it, although hopefully that's quite unlikely. I'll show you below how to set your **percentage volatility target** based on exactly how relaxed you are about losses.

For an institutional investor things are usually straightforward; you are given £100 million and you would use 100% of it. Sometimes you might not go 'all in' if you have guaranteed some of the capital, or need to retain cash for potential redemptions.

If you're investing your own money then your trading capital will depend on your savings and how much you are willing to commit to such a risky endeavour. In any case – and I can't emphasise this enough – never put in more than you can afford to lose. Never trade with borrowed money, or money earmarked to pay off debts.[99] Even if you follow the advice in this book to the letter there is still a remote chance that you will be unlucky enough to burn through virtually your entire account.

---

99. This isn't a ban on **leverage**, but if your trading capital is £100,000 you should actually have that available to lose, and none of it should be borrowed. I'll discuss leverage in more detail below.

Can you cope with the risk?

Let's say you decide to put $100,000 of **trading capital** into your account and run with a 200% **volatility target**; equating to an **annualised cash volatility target** of $200,000. Could you cope with losing $20,000 in one day? What about having a cumulative loss, or draw-down, of over $60,000? If it isn't your money, could your client cope with it?

I hope so because you're likely to see those kinds of losses within the first few weeks of trading! As table 20 shows, a $20,000 loss would typically be seen every month, and a $62,000 cumulative loss around 10% of the time.[100]

TABLE 20: WHAT KIND OF LOSSES DO WE SEE FOR A PARTICULAR VOLATILITY TARGET?

	Percentage volatility target			
Expected	25%	50%	100%	200%
Worst daily loss each month	$2,500	$5,000	$10,000	$20,000
Worst weekly loss each year	$6,900	$14,000	$28,000	$55,000
Worst monthly loss every ten years	$16,000	$32,000	$63,000	$80,000
Worst daily loss every 30 years	$5,400	$11,000	$22,000	$43,000
10% of the time, the cumulative loss will be at least	$9,300	$15,000	$30,500	$62,000
1% of the time, the cumulative loss will be at least	$11,000	$18,500	$37,000	$75,000

The table shows various expected losses (rows), and different percentage volatility targets (columns), given trading capital of $100,000, assuming Sharpe ratio 0.5 and zero skew with Gaussian normal returns.

Now, table 20 assumes you have zero **skew** in your returns. Are you running a positive skew **trend following** system, or a negative skew **relative value** or **carry** rule? Systems with different **skew** have varying risk properties. As table 21 shows, the worst days, weeks and months for a negative skew strategy are much nastier than with zero skew. For positive

---

100. I've assumed a **Sharpe ratio (SR)** of 0.5 here, and the returns are drawn from a **Gaussian normal distribution**. Using a different SR won't affect these numbers much, although the annual loss figures will be slightly better (worse) if the true Sharpe is higher (lower).

skew strategies large losses are much less likely, as you can see in table 22. However the typical cumulative loss is higher.

With negative skew it's vital to have sufficient capital to cope with the very bad days, weeks and months you will occasionally see. This is especially true with high leverage and the risk your broker will make a margin call at the worst possible time. With positive skew the difficulty is psychological; committing to a system when you spend most of your time suffering cumulative losses.

TABLE 21: HOW DO TYPICAL LOSSES LOOK WITH NEGATIVE SKEW? INDIVIDUAL LOSSES ARE HIGHER THAN IN TABLE 20, BUT CUMULATIVE LOSSES ARE SMALLER

Expected	Percentage volatility target	
	25%	50%
Worst daily loss each month	$3,100	$6,100
Worst weekly loss each year	$8,500	$17,000
Worst monthly loss every ten years	$18,100	$36,000
Worst daily loss every 30 years	$11,500	$23,000
10% of the time, the cumulative loss will be at least	$3,700	$7,400
1% of the time, the cumulative loss will be at least	$7,100	$14,000

The table shows various expected losses (rows) and different percentage volatility targets (columns), for a negative skew option selling strategy given trading capital of $100,000.[101] The strategy has a Sharpe ratio of 0.5 and skew of around -2.

---

101. Results are from a **back-test** of a strategy which involves persistently selling futures option straddles.

TABLE 22: HOW DO LOSS PATTERNS CHANGE FOR POSITIVE SKEW? WITH POSITIVE SKEW INDIVIDUAL LOSSES ARE MUCH BETTER THAN IN TABLES 20 AND 21, BUT AVERAGE CUMULATIVE LOSSES A LITTLE WORSE

Expected	Percentage volatility target	
	25%	50%
Worst daily loss each month	$2,000	$4,000
Worst weekly loss each year	$6,100	$12,000
Worst monthly loss every ten years	$15,000	$30,000
Worst daily loss every 30 years	$2,800	$5,700
10% of the time, the cumulative loss will be at least	$11,000	$22,000
1% of the time, the cumulative loss will be at least	$12,000	$24,000

This table shows various expected losses (rows) given different percentage volatility targets (columns), for a positive skew trend following strategy, with trading capital of $100,000.[102] The strategy has a Sharpe ratio of 0.5 and skew of around 1.0.

Earlier I said you could frame risk by how much you are prepared to lose in a lifetime. That's difficult to quantify without knowing your life expectancy, so let's assume you will trade for ten years. In table 23 I show the chances of ending a decade-long trading career with less than half, and less than 10%, of your **trading capital** left, given a certain percentage target volatility.

Only you know how much risk you can cope with. However you, or your clients, must be able to stomach the likely losses involved. If you can't then you should set a lower percentage volatility target, or if possible consider using less initial trading capital.

---

102. Figures from **back-testing** a futures system using a mixture of relatively fast **trend following rule variations**.

TABLE 23: WHAT ARE THE CHANCES OF LOSING ALL, OR MOST, OF MY MONEY?

	Percentage volatility target			
	25%	50%	100%	200%
Chance of losing half	<1%	10%	40%	93%
Chance of losing 90%	<1%	1.1%	22%	88%

The table shows chances of ending a ten-year trading career losing a given proportion (rows), of initial trading capital given different percentage volatility targets, assuming Sharpe ratio is 0.50 and zero skew.[103]

Can you realise that risk?

If you're investing in leveraged derivatives like futures and spread bets then very high levels of risk are attainable, even if they aren't desirable. Such systems can easily run at over 100% annualised **target volatility** with margin to spare.

But if you can't get enough, or any, leverage then you might have a problem achieving your target volatility. If you are buying short-term government bonds with an expected volatility of perhaps 5% a year, then without leverage it's impossible to create a portfolio with a 50% volatility target. With no leverage you are restricted to the amount of *natural* risk that your **instruments** have. With only 100% leverage you are limited to twice that natural risk, and so on.

Because it's mostly a problem for non-leveraged **asset allocating investors** I'll go into more detail about this in the relevant part of part four, chapter fourteen.

Is there too much leverage?

Even if you are able to leverage up as required to hit a particular **percentage volatility target**, it would be very unwise if excessive gearing is needed. This is particularly problematic for negative **skew** instruments and trading strategies, which tend to have low natural risk – until they blow up.

I've mentioned before the huge appreciation of the Swiss franc that happened in just minutes in January 2015. At the start of the day in question the natural risk of holding a position in EUR/CHF was tiny, at around 1% a year. If this was the only instrument you were trading then to achieve a 50% annualised volatility target would have needed

---

103. The results would be slightly worse for negative **skew**, and slightly better for positive skew. For example with a 200% **volatility target** the chances of losing half your capital over ten years are 90% with positive skew of 1.0 and 97% with negative skew of -2.0.

50 times leverage. Retail FX brokers had no compunction in allowing this, with leverage up to 500 times available from some providers.

If you had been on the wrong side of this move, with your entire trading capital leveraged 50 times, then a 2% appreciation would have wiped you out. But the actual move was over 16%! Only those with leverage of 7 times or less would have survived the day, which implies a maximum achievable 7% volatility target.

You should ensure that with a given percentage volatility target any individual position would not wipe you out after the largest conceivable move. Diversifying amongst many different **instruments** will also help, and we'll return to that in chapter eleven, 'Portfolios'. A 16% move with 50 times leverage would have been just about survivable if EUR/CHF was only 10% of your portfolio, assuming no other losses had occured elsewhere.

Ideally such low **volatility** instruments, requiring insanely high leverage, should be excluded from any trading system.

Is this the right level of risk?

Suppose you've decided on a 200% **volatility target**. You've got the leverage you need; but you haven't got carried away. Furthermore you're confident that you will cope with the spectacularly bumpy ride tables 20 to 23 imply you'll be getting. Assuming you are a profitable trader, should you then set your target at 200% and expect to end up incredibly wealthy through the magic of compound interest?

The short answer is no. There is a Goldilocks level of risk – not too little and not too much. Even if you are willing and able to go above this level you shouldn't, as you will end up with more than your tongue getting burnt.

Naively if you expect to be profitable then you should bet as much as you're allowed to. However this ignores the *compounding* of returns over time. Suppose you have a fantastic expected average return of 100% on each trade for a given bet size. You then lose 90% of your capital on your first trade and make 190% on your next trade. Unfortunately there is only 29% of your cash left, even though you've achieved the expected average return of 100% per trade.[104] To maximise your final profits, the optimal bet to make is actually a quarter of the original size.

Nearly all professional gamblers, many professional money managers and some amateurs in both fields know that this optimal point should be calculated using something called the **Kelly criterion**.[105] Kelly has some useful but potentially dangerous implications for how you should set your **percentage volatility target**.

---

104. After the first loss you have 10% of your capital left. A 190% return on this generates another 19%, for a total of 29%.
105. The Kelly criterion maximises the geometric mean of returns, which is what we get from compounding. It was invented by physicist John Kelly in 1956. There is an excellent and highly readable book on this subject – *Fortune's Formula* by William Poundstone.

A simple formula can be used to determine how you should set your volatility target, given the underlying **Sharpe ratio (SR)** of your trading system. You should set your volatility target at the same level as your expected SR. So if you think your annualised SR will be 0.25 then you should have a 25% annualised volatility target.

You can see this in figure 21, where for an SR 0.5 system the best performance is achieved with the optimal 50% volatility target. This is true for all three systems shown, regardless of **skew**.

FIGURE 21: KELLY CRITERION IMPLIES THE OPTIMAL RISK PERCENTAGE FOR A SHARPE RATIO 0.5 SYSTEM IS 50%. WITH HIGHER RISK THINGS GO BADLY, ESPECIALLY FOR NEGATIVE SKEW STRATEGIES.

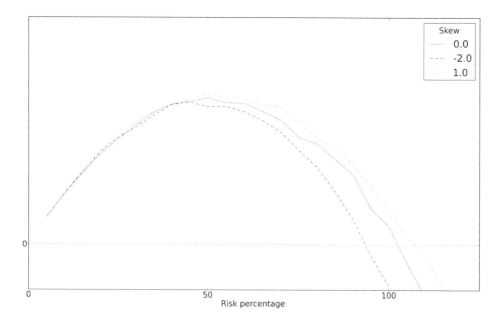

The X-axis shows the percentage volatility target and the Y-axis the geometric mean of returns which Kelly optimises.

TABLE 24: BIG SHARPE MEANS BIGGER RISK AND EXPONENTIALLY BIGGER PROFITS

Expected Sharpe ratio	Optimum percentage volatility target	Expected return
0.2	20%	4%
0.5	50%	25%
0.75	75%	56%
1.0	100%	100%
2.0	200%	400%

The table shows the expected annual return (as a percentage of trading capital), given different Sharpe ratio (SR) (rows) and using the optimal Kelly percentage volatility target. Expected return is SR multiplied by percentage volatility target.

This finding is potentially dangerous when used by an over confident investor. It's very easy with **back-testing** software to get **over-fitted** performance with a Sharpe ratio (SR) of 2, 3 or even higher. If you believe those are attainable then a risk percentage of 100% or 200% seems justified. As table 24 shows, running at a 200% risk with SR of 2.0 implies huge returns of 400% a year!

Unfortunately many people with capital of $20,000 will conclude it's possible to earn 400% a year, or $80,000, as full-time traders. There are also plenty of brokers who will happily provide them with the necessary leverage. Most of these people will quickly lose their $20,000, as they won't achieve their expected SR. It's very difficult to know exactly what your true Sharpe ratio really would have been in the past, with back-tests giving you only a rough upwardly estimate, and it's utterly impossible to know what SR to expect in the future.

Even if you had a crystal ball, and knew your expected Sharpe precisely, you could be unlucky and have a decade or more of sub-par performance. Figure 21 shows that if you realise an SR of only 0.5 then a 200% volatility target will see you ending up deep underwater. In general if you get your estimate of SR wrong and bet more than the optimal then you have a high chance of losing your shirt.

Recommended percentage volatility targets

I run a highly diversified futures trading system with around 45 **instruments**, eight **trading rules** drawn from four different styles, and 30 **trading rule variations**. In a 35 year **back-test**, conservatively fitted with **out of sample bootstrapping**, it has a **Sharpe ratio (SR)** of around 1.0 after costs, but the highest **volatility target** I'd advocate using for it is 37%, rather than the 100% suggested by the **Kelly criterion** and the back-tested SR.[106] Why such a conservative number – am I a wimp?

There are several reasons for my caution. Firstly, it's unlikely a back-tested SR will be achieved in the future. On average realised performance is never as good as in back-tests. This is because it's very easy to over-fit if you ignore the advice in chapters three and four. Additionally it's difficult with **ideas first** testing to avoid using only trading rules that you already know would have worked.

Even if you could avoid over-fitting actual profits are unlikely to be as high as they could have been in the past. This is because future asset returns are likely to be lower than in the historical data set we usually use for back-testing, as I discussed in chapter two, 'Systematic Trading Rules', in the section on achievable Sharpe ratios (from page 46).

To find realistic achievable SR from back-test results a good rule of thumb is to use the ratios in table 14 (page 90). These suggest that for an out of sample bootstrap, as I've used in my own system, a ratio of 0.75 should be applied to find a more realistic Sharpe ratio. Much lower ratios should be used if you haven't been as careful with your fitting. I also said in chapter two that I think the absolute maximum SR that **staunch systems traders** should expect to achieve is 1.0, regardless of how good their back-test is.

Secondly, using the full Kelly criteria is far too aggressive, because of the risk of getting a poor run of luck and the large drawdowns that can result, even if SR expectations are correct.[107] In table 23 someone using the correct Kelly target of 50% would have a 10% chance of losing half their money after ten years; which most people would find worrying. It's far better to use **Half-Kelly** and set your risk at half the optimal. Column A of table 25 shows the recommended percentage volatility target for a given realistic back-tested SR.

For my own system I started with the back-tested Sharpe ratio of 1.0. Multiplying by 0.75 (as I'm using out of sample bootstrapping) from table 14, this gives me a realistic SR of 0.75. With full Kelly criterion betting that would be a 75% volatility target, which I then halved to get 37% (rounding down).

This assumes your trading system, like mine, has zero or positive **skew**. You should be very careful if you have expected negative skew. As figure 21 shows, the penalty for too much risk is greater with negative skew than when skew is positive, or zero. As I discussed in chapter two, many negative skew strategies have fantastic SR in back-test, but I advise you to run them at half the risk you'd use for a more benign trading system. Column B of table 25 shows the recommended percentage volatility target for negative skew systems.

---

106. At the time of writing I'm using a 25% **volatility target**, reflecting my relatively low appetite for risk.
107. Here is famous Kelly fan, hedge fund manager and Blackjack card counter Ed Thorpe: "My experience has been that most cautious ... investors who use Kelly find the frequency of substantial bankroll reductions to be uncomfortably large." (Quoted in *Fortune's Formula*.)

TABLE 25: WHAT VOLATILITY TARGET SHOULD STAUNCH SYSTEMS TRADERS USE?

Realistic back-tested SR	Recommended percentage volatility target	
	(A) Skew>0	(B) Negative skew
0.25	12%	6%
0.40	20%	10%
0.50	25%	12%
0.75	37%	19%
1.0 or more	50%	25%

The table shows the recommended percentage volatility target for those who can back-test their dynamic trading systems, depending on the skew of returns (columns) and achievable back-tested Sharpe ratios (SR) (rows) after making adjustments to simulated results from table 14 on page 90. Optimal volatility target is calculated using Half-Kelly. For negative skew strategies this is cut in half again. We assume a maximum SR of 1.0 is achievable.

The returns of **asset allocating investors** are limited by their use of a **static** trading strategy. With a small, relatively undiversified portfolio you shouldn't expect high Sharpe ratios. As I said in chapter two, if you're holding a dozen equities in different industries but from the same country then you probably will achieve an SR of around 0.20. Those with larger portfolios diversified across multiple **asset classes** could get a maximum realistic SR of 0.4.

Column C of table 26 shows the correct targets given asset allocators' SR expectations. However, as you'll see in chapter fourteen, it's unlikely even this level of volatility can be achieved as these investors don't use leverage.

Semi-automatic traders have systems which cannot be back-tested and usually have a small, relatively un-diversified, set of ad-hoc instruments. I would initially assume an achievable SR of 0.20 unless you are very experienced, are trading across multiple asset classes, and have a good track record with real money. As you saw in chapter two, in my opinion an SR of 0.5 is the maximum safe achievable level, so you should set the volatility target at no more than 25%.

Again the target should be halved if you are trading a strategy that is likely to have negative skew, such as selling option volatility, or exhibits a similar return pattern with steady profits on most bets with occasional large losses. Columns D and E of table 26 show the appropriate volatility targets for this type of trader.

TABLE 26: WHAT VOLATILITY TARGET SHOULD ASSET ALLOCATING INVESTORS AND SEMI-AUTOMATIC TRADERS USE?

Expected SR	Recommended percentage volatility target		
	(C) Asset allocating investor	(D) Semi-automatic trader, zero or positive skew	(E) Semi-automatic trader, negative skew
0.20	10%	10%	5%
0.30	15%	15%	7%
0.40	20%	20%	10%
0.5 or more	20%	25%	12%

This table shows the recommended percentage volatility target depending on the type of trader and expected skew (columns), and Sharpe ratio (SR) expectations (rows). The optimal volatility target is calculated using Half-Kelly. We assume asset allocators shouldn't expect more than 0.40 SR and semi-automatic traders won't get more than 0.50 SR. Asset allocators are assumed to have zero skew. We halve volatility targets for negative skew semi-automatic trading.

This implies that nobody will use more than a maximum 50% volatility target and most people should use less. Tables 20 to 23 illustrate that a 50% annualised volatility will mean some pretty substantial losses from time to time. Just because the volatility targets in tables 25 and 26 are optimal it doesn't mean they will suit you, or that your broker will permit them. It just means you should *never* run a higher risk target than this.

When the percentage volatility target should be changed

I don't advocate changing your **percentage volatility target** since there is a potential risk of *meddling*; reducing it when you don't trust your system and increasing it when it agrees with you. The exception is if you have grossly miscalculated your tolerance for risk. You begin trading on day one with a 50% target, but the first big loss then sends you or your investors into a panic. In this case you should significantly reduce your percentage target. However it should ideally be a one off change and only ever downwards.

To avoid this scenario it's better to start with significantly lower **trading capital** and gradually increase it until you have the full amount invested. Keep the percentage volatility target fixed and allow your cash volatility to increase up to the point just before you get uncomfortable. This also helps with gaining confidence in your trading strategy and testing any automated systems.

Rolling up profits and losses

Once set your **percentage volatility target** shouldn't need changing. However your **trading capital** will definitely change from its initial value. This implies that your **cash volatility target** will also be adjusted over time.

Let's imagine you have trading capital of $100,000 and after reading this chapter you've decided on a 30% volatility target. You begin trading with the appropriate $30,000 **annualised cash volatility target**. Then on day one you lose $2,000. Should you continue to use a $30,000 volatility target?

You should not. The implication of the **Kelly criterion** is that you should adjust your risk according to your current capital. You did have $100,000 of capital, but now you only have $98,000. Instead of having a 30% volatility target ($30,000 of $100,000) you effectively have a target of $30,000 divided by $98,000 = 30.6%. This might not seem a big deal, but you are now betting more than you intended and you've slightly increased your chances of going bankrupt. If you make further losses the situation could deteriorate fast.

The correct thing to do is to reduce your volatility target to 30% of your current capital of $98,000, or $29,400.

Now suppose things start to improve and you make $2,000 back. Your accumulated losses have reduced to zero and your volatility target will be back to 30% of $100,000, or $30,000. After another profitable day making $3,000 you're now in positive territory with an account value of $103,000 – higher than your starting capital. Should you now increase your risk appetite above its initial level?

If you want to maximise your wealth then Kelly says you should roll up your profits and increase your capital.[108] The new volatility target will be 30% of $103,000, or $30,900. This means you will be compounding your returns, which over the long run will increase them faster.

You should also reduce your trading capital, and hence your cash volatility target, if you withdraw money from your trading account or investors redeem. Similarly if you put more funds in then you would normally increase your maximum capital. There are exceptions such as if you are putting cash into a leveraged account to meet margin or reduce borrowing, but you don't want to increase the amount of capital at risk.

In my own trading an automated process checks my account value, and adjusts risk accordingly, on an hourly basis. If your system is not automated and if you are running with more than a 15% volatility target I would recommend checking at least daily. With a lower target you can check more infrequently, but if you're using leverage I'd advise always calculating your volatility target at least once a week.

---

108. Someone who is trading as a hobby and starting with a small stake would probably do this. Those investing other people's money should also add all profits after fees to their trading capital, so that returns are compounded, unless they are committed to paying coupons or guaranteeing a certain proportion of the initial investment made. If you are more risk averse then rolling up profits might not make sense, if for example you live partly or wholly off your trading income. This is the approach that I take.

What percentage of capital per trade?

Traditional money management systems allocate a certain percentage of **trading capital** to be risked on each trade or bet. If you're familiar with these systems you might be wondering how this relates to the volatility targeting done here. It is possible to infer the **percentage volatility target** that is implied for a particular trading system if you know the approximate holding period, the average number of positions held and the maximum amount of capital put at risk on each trade. You just need to assume that the average bet is half the maximum, which is the same ratio between my recommended average forecast of 10 and maximum of 20.

Table 27 gives the results, assuming an average of two positions are held at once. If a greater or fewer number are traded on average, then you just need to multiply or divide the figures appropriately. So with an average of four positions you'd double them, and for a single position halve them.

TABLE 27: WHAT IS THE VOLATILITY IMPLIED BY A TRADING SYSTEM'S HOLDING PERIOD AND BET SIZE?

	Implied percentage volatility target				
	Maximum percentage of capital at risk per trade				
Average holding period	1%	2.5%	5%	10%	20%
1 day	40%	100%	200%	!	!
1 week	16%	40%	80%	160%	!
2 weeks	8%	19%	38%	76%	152%
6 weeks	4%	10%	21%	41%	82%
3 months	3%	7%	13%	27%	53%

The table shows the implied annualised percentage volatility target for a given average holding period (rows) and maximum percentage of capital allocated to each bet (columns), assuming an average of two bets are held in the portfolio. "!" indicates volatility greater than 200% per year.

As an example take the system which I briefly discussed in the introductory chapter. This held positions for around a week, with no more than 10% of capital at risk. Let's assume on average that two bets are made at once, although the author wasn't clear on this point (a common shortcoming in trading books).

This all sounds fairly sedate but from the table this works out to a suicidal 160% volatility target. If this target is **Kelly optimal** then the achievable **Sharpe ratio** must be at least 1.6, implying an expected return of 1.6 × 160% or 256% a year! There is some serious overconfidence at work here. Worse still, this is nowhere **near** the most aggressive system I've ever seen.

Summary of volatility targeting

Percentage volatility target	Desired long run expectation of annualised **standard deviation** of percentage portfolio returns. A maximum of:
	• The level of risk that you are comfortable with given tables 20 to 23.
	• What is practically attainable given your access to **leverage** and the natural risk of your **instruments** (see the **asset allocating investor** example in part four for more details).
	• The highest level that is safe given the natural volatility of your instruments, and how much leverage they need. Avoid very low **volatility** instruments requiring insanely high leverage.
	• The recommended percentage volatility in tables 25 and 26, depending on the **back-tested** or expected **Sharpe ratio** and **skew** of your trading system, and the type of trader or investor you are.
	Percentage volatility target should remain unchanged.
Trading capital	The amount of capital you currently have at risk in your account.
	Every day you should add profits and any injections of funds. Deduct any losses and withdrawals made from the account.
	Measured in currency.
Annualised cash volatility target	Long run expectation of annualised **standard deviation** of daily portfolio returns. Equal to the **trading capital** multiplied by the **percentage volatility target**.
	Measured in currency.
Daily cash volatility target	Long run expectation of daily standard deviation of daily portfolio returns. **Annualised cash volatility target** divided by 'the square root of time', which for a 256 business day year is 16.
	Measured in currency.

In the next chapter I will come back to the final piece of advice I got from Sergei and think about how the risk of an instrument determines what size position we should take.

Chapter Ten. Position Sizing

Trading rule A, variation 1	A1 forecast for instrument X					
Trading rule A, variation 2	A2 forecast for instrument X		Combined forecast X		**Subsystem position in X**	Portfolio weighted position in X
Trading rule B, variation 1	B1 forecast for instrument X					
Trading rule A, variation 1	A1 forecast, instrument Y					
Trading rule A, variation 2	A2 forecast for instrument Y		Combined forecast Y		**Subsystem position in Y**	Portfolio weighted position in Y
Trading rule B, variation 1	B1 forecast for instrument Y					

Instruments

Forecast weights · Volatility targeting · Position sizing · Instrument weights

Customising for speed and size

LET'S COME BACK TO SERGEI'S THREE QUESTIONS FROM CHAPTER seven. First, how much do you like this trade? This is the **forecast** for each instrument. Secondly, how much can you afford to lose? You should know how many chips of **trading capital** you're willing to put down on the hypothetical casino baize depending on your desired **target volatility**.

So far, so good. But how many shares, bonds, spread bet points or futures contracts should you actually buy or sell? What does a **combined forecast** of -6 and a £1,000,000 **annualised cash target volatility** mean in practice if you're trading crude oil futures in New York? To answer this we need to come back to Sergei's third question: how risky is your trade?

153

Once you know this you can move from the abstract world of forecasts and trading rules to deciding the size of actual positions in real financial **instruments**.

Chapter overview

How risky is it?	If you own one unit of an instrument how much risk does that expose you to?
Volatility target and position risk	What is the relationship between your cash volatility target and the risk of each instrument?
From forecast to position	Given how confident you are in your forecasts, the cash volatility target you have and the position risk, what size position should you be holding?

How risky is it?

What is the expected risk of holding an **instrument**?[109] If you own one Apple share or one crude oil futures contract, how much danger are you exposed to?

Position block and block value

Let's start by asking a philosophical question. What exactly is 'one' of an instrument? I define this as the **instrument block**. If 'one' of an instrument goes up in price by 1% how much do you gain or lose? This is the **block value**.

These definitions will seem trivial to equity investors. 'One' Apple share is exactly that – one Apple share. If a share has a price of $400 it will cost exactly $400 to buy one block. If the price goes up by 1% from $400 to $404 then you will gain $4. Apple shares, and most other equities, have a natural **instrument block** of one share and a block value of 1% of the price. Sometimes though to reduce costs you'll trade in larger blocks, usually of 100 shares. In this case the block value will be 100 × 1% × share price, which is equal to the cost of one share.

But life isn't always that simple. For example you can use a UK financial spread betting firm to bet on the FTSE falling at £10 a point. If the FTSE rises 1% from 6500 to 6565 you would lose £650. Here the block value is ten times 1% of the price.

Futures contracts also have non-trivial block values. WTI crude oil futures on NYMEX are quoted in dollars per barrel. But each futures contract is for 1000 barrels. This means

---

109. Notice we're dealing here with expected, **predictable risk**, as discussed on page 39.

a 1% move up in price from $75 to $75.75 will net you $750 on a long position of one contract, giving a block value of $750.

A Eurodollar future represents the cost of nominally borrowing $1 million for three months and is priced at 100 minus the annual interest rate. If the price rises by 1% from 98.00 to 98.98 then the rate of interest payable has fallen from 2% to 1.02%. Because three months is a quarter of a year you will have saved $1 million × 0.98% × 0.25 = $2,450 in interest on your loan. The block value is $2,450.[110]

Price volatility

We've established that a 1% fall in quoted price will cause a certain degree of pain, equal to the **block value**, for each **instrument block** of an instrument that you're long. But how likely is a 1% fall in price? Equity prices can easily change by 1% or more in minutes, but a two-year bond might not see a 1% move over several months. How should you take these different levels of risk into account?

This is another job for **volatility standardisation**. You need to calculate an expected **standard deviation** of daily instrument percentage returns, which I'm going to define as the **price volatility** of an instrument. So for example the price volatility of an average equity is around 1%, whereas as I write this the German two-year Schatz bond future has a daily standard deviation of just 0.02%.

CONCEPT: MEASURING RECENT STANDARD DEVIATION

Remember that my standard definition of **predictable risk** (from page 39) is the expected daily **standard deviation** of prices. One of the simplest ways to estimate future **volatility** is to use a measure of recent standard deviation. This works surprisingly well because volatility tends to persist; if the market has been crazy over the last few weeks it will probably continue to be crazy for a few more weeks.

I recommend using one of three methods to calculate recent standard deviation.

The first method is to eyeball the chart. If you look at figure 22 you can see that the average daily change in crude oil futures over the last month of the chart is around $1.0 a day, or 1.33% of the final price of $75. This method is fine for **semi-automatic traders** who will probably be staring at charts anyway, but I don't recommend it for others.

The second method is to calculate the precise standard deviation of price changes over a moving window of time – the **volatility look-back period**. You can use a

---

110. There are even more complicated cases such as options, interest rate swaps and credit derivatives but I do not cover these here.

short window like ten business days (around two weeks), or a longer one such as 100 days.

As the upper panel of figure 23 shows, shorter windows mean your volatility estimate is noisy, which as you'll see in chapter twelve will mean higher trading costs, but reacts very quickly to changes. The slower estimate is smoother, however it takes longer to adjust to new volatility environments. It's not obvious which look-back would be best.

In my research I found almost no difference in performance before costs for look-back periods from a few days up to six months in length.[111] Rather than risk **over-fitting** I decided on a default look-back of 25 business days, or five weeks. This corresponds to the most popular value used across the industry, for example by the RiskMetrics (TM) system.[112] I'll discuss in chapter twelve, 'Speed and Size', when and why you'd use a longer look-back for **instruments** that are expensive to trade.

The lower panel of figure 23 shows the volatility estimation using a 25 day look-back. It also shows the estimate coming from my third method, which is to use an **exponential weighted moving average (EWMA)** of standard deviation.

This gives a smoother measure than a simple moving average that still reacts quickly to significant changes in the state of the market. I've chosen the default look-back for this as 36 days, which is equivalent to a 25 day window for a simple moving average.[113] Details of how to calculate volatility with both kinds of moving average are shown in appendix D on page 298.

Using recent price volatility is generally a good way to get the right risk adjusted position size. However it would be a disaster if you were using this method to trade **Credit Default Swaps** in early 2007, the front of the Eurodollar futures curve at any time in the US zero interest rate period, or for that matter Swiss franc FX in early January 2015.

During all of these periods there was really low price volatility. If volatility is low then you would buy large numbers of instrument blocks, since each block has very little expected risk. But after periods of calm markets have a nasty habit of becoming crazy overnight, leaving you with dangerously large positions.

As I've already mentioned in earlier chapters, holding very low volatility assets is generally a bad idea, and this is yet another reason to avoid them.

---

111. Much slower than six months and performance gets steadily worse.
112. As of 2015 RiskMetrics (TM) is owned by MSCI but it was originally developed by JP Morgan. It uses an **exponentially weighted moving average** whose half-life is equivalent to that of a 25 day simple moving average.
113. The two measures have the same half-life when using a 25 day look-back for the simple moving average, and 36 days for exponentially weighted.

FIGURE 22: PRICE AND DAILY CHANGES IN CRUDE OIL FUTURES

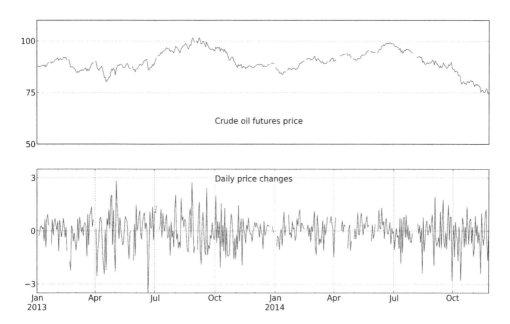

FIGURE 23: MEASURING CRUDE OIL PRICE VOLATILITY USING SIMPLE MOVING AVERAGE (MA) AND EXPONENTIALLY WEIGHTED (EWMA) STANDARD DEVIATIONS WITH VARIOUS LOOK-BACKS, IN DAYS

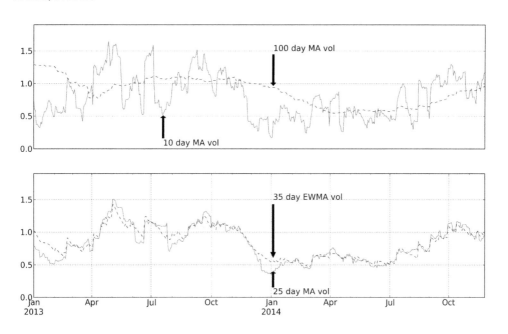

Returning to the example I opened the chapter with, if you use the bottom panel of figure 23 the price volatility of crude oil futures here is around $1 per day, which is 1.33% of the final price shown ($75).

Instrument currency volatility

If one oil futures contract has a **block value** of $750, and a **price volatility** of 1.333%, then what is the risk of owning one contract? This is the **instrument currency volatility**; it's the expected **standard deviation** of daily returns from owning one instrument block in the currency of the instrument. For oil futures you'd expect on any given day to see a price move of around 1.33% and since each 1% price move will cost you $750, your daily profit or loss will average around 1.33 × $750 = $997.50. So the instrument currency volatility for WTI crude oil futures is $997.50. This value shouldn't be rounded.

In general instrument currency volatility is equal to the block value multiplied by the price volatility. It will be in the same currency in which the block value is measured.

What's that in real money?

This is all fine if you are a US investor trading crude oil futures, a Brit trading UK equities, or a Euro area investor buying German bonds. However many investors and traders will want to buy and sell in currencies that are different from their trading capital. The **instrument currency volatility** isn't good enough. Instead you need to know the volatility of the instrument value in the currency of your account, which will be the same currency as your **cash volatility target**. I call this the **instrument value volatility**.

The instrument currency volatility needs to be converted to an instrument value volatility using an appropriate exchange rate. The exchange rate will have the currency of the instrument as the numerator, and the account value currency as the denominator.

As an example for a UK investor with a GBP account, the instrument currency volatility of a crude oil future ($997.50) will need to be multiplied by the current USD/GBP exchange rate, to work out what those dollars are worth in British pounds. As I write this paragraph the USD/GBP rate is 0.67, giving an instrument value volatility of $997.50 × 0.67 = £668.325. Again you shouldn't round any numbers yet. Note I'm using USD/GBP, rather than GBP/USD which is normally quoted. Be sure you are using the correct rate.

Volatility target and position risk

Now let's relate this back to your **cash volatility target** – the risk you require and are comfortable with from your trading account. From the previous chapter on volatility targeting (page 137) your **daily cash volatility target** is your long-term expected daily standard deviation of returns, measured in the currency of your **trading capital**.

Let's refer back to the example I opened the chapter with. We had an investor with a £1,000,000 **annualised cash target volatility**, implying a daily target of one-sixteenth of that, £62,500.[114] I worked out above that the crude oil future had an **instrument value volatility** of £668.325 for a UK investor. This is the daily risk of owning one instrument block – a single futures contract. How many of these blocks of crude oil should this investor hold?

For now let's assume we are putting together a **trading subsystem** for the investor; a trading system which only has a single instrument. We'll be achieving the entire cash volatility target by having positions in just one instrument; in this case crude oil. This assumption will be relaxed in the next chapter, when we look at creating a portfolio of subsystems.

We also assume that we get the required target risk by having a constant amount of expected volatility from owning a fixed long position in the asset. So we won't worry yet about the value of any **forecast** for the instrument. I'll consider forecasts in the next section of this chapter.

For the investor in the example to get the entire required daily standard deviation of £62,500 from being long crude oil futures they need to buy £62,500, divided by the risk of one contract, £668.325, or 93.52 contracts. The value of 93.52 is a scaling factor which accounts for the difference between an instrument's natural volatility and the required volatility of the portfolio. I call it the **volatility scalar**.

In general the volatility scalar is equal to your daily cash volatility target, divided by the instrument value volatility. You'll notice that both of these variables are in the same currency as your trading capital. Also please note that you should not round the volatility scalar to a whole number.

From forecast to position

I've shown that the investor in the simple example for this chapter would need to own a long position in 93.52 crude oil futures (the **volatility scalar**) to realise their desired **volatility target**. This however ignores any **forecast** that the investor has made; either a **combined forecast** from multiple **trading rules,** or the single forecasts made by **asset allocating investors** and **semi-automatic traders**. At the start of the chapter I'd assumed that the forecast is -6 in the example. Clearly the investor is going to want to be short, rather than long, but by how much?

To work this out you need to think about *average* forecasts. Over a long period of time you'll still want to be hitting your **volatility target** for returns, no matter what your daily forecasts are. In chapter seven (page 112) I recommended that forecasts should have a

---

114. Remember to go from annual to daily volatility you divide by the 'square root of time'. As there are roughly 256 business days in a year, the appropriate divisor is 16.

long run average absolute value of 10. This implies that to hit your target over the long run you'd want your positions to have the same average expected variation as if you had a constant forecast of +10.

Effectively then the volatility scalar gives you a position which is consistent with having a constant forecast of +10. If you're currently more optimistic with a larger positive forecast you should buy more blocks; and if you're pessimistic you should have fewer blocks, or go short if the forecast is negative.

In the example above I calculated a volatility scalar of 93.52 crude oil futures contracts. This will be consistent with the long run forecast, so a forecast of +10 equates to buying 93.52 contracts (ignoring for the moment that you can't hold fractional contracts). If the forecast falls to +5 you'd only be half as confident, and want half the original position, 46.76 contracts. A forecast of -20 would mean you'd want to go short twice the original position, a sell of 187.04 blocks.

The resulting quantity of blocks is the **subsystem position.** It's a subsystem position because, as I said earlier, we're assuming in this chapter your entire capital is invested in a subsystem trading one instrument, rather than in a complete **trading system** running across a number of instruments.

A subsystem position is equal to the volatility scalar multiplied by the forecast, then divided by the long average of 10. So for the crude oil example with a forecast of -6, and where I've worked out the volatility scalar to be 93.52, the subsystem position will be $(93.52 \times -6) \div 10 = -56.11$, implying a short of 56.11 contracts. Again you shouldn't do any rounding of non integer positions for now.

If you're an **asset allocating investor** you've probably spotted that with a constant forecast which is always equal to +10 (from the single 'no-rule' rule), your position will always be equal to the **volatility scalar**.

For other traders and investors your position will depend on your forecast and on the components of the volatility scalar (your **cash volatility target** for your portfolio and the **account value volatility** of the instrument). Higher absolute forecasts, bigger account sizes, a greater appetite for risk and lower instrument price volatility will mean larger positions; and vice versa.

Summary for position sizing

Instrument forecast	**Staunch systems traders:** This is the **combined forecast** calculated in chapter eight by weighting your **trading rule forecasts** for an instrument and accounting for the **forecast diversification multiplier.**
	Asset allocating investors: Equal to a constant value of +10.
	Semi-automatic traders: Single discretionary forecast.
	All groups will end up with one forecast per instrument. It will have an expected average absolute value of 10 and it is limited to a range of -20 to +20.
Annualised cash volatility target	This is the **percentage volatility target** multiplied by the **trading capital**, from chapter nine. It's an annualised measure of expected risk from your portfolio.
	It will be in units of the currency your trading capital is in.
Daily cash volatility target	**Annualised cash volatility target** divided by 'the square root of time'; with approximately 256 business days in a year you should divide by 16.
Price volatility	Expected daily **standard deviation** of instrument price changes. Watch out for very low standard deviations.
	It will be in units of percentage of price.
Instrument block	This is the size you trade instruments in. For equities this would usually be one share, though 100 shares might make sense if trading fewer is uneconomic. For futures this will be a single contract and for spread bets it is the minimum bet per point.
Block value	This is how much each 1% change in the price of a **block** translates into monetary value.
	It will be in units of instrument currency, i.e. $ for US equities.
Instrument currency volatility	This is the daily standard deviation of instrument value. Equal to **block value** multiplied by the **price volatility**. It will be in units of instrument currency.
Exchange rate	This is the exchange rate between instrument currency (numerator) and the currency your **trading capital** is in (denominator).
Instrument value volatility	Daily standard deviation of instrument value, measured in your trading capital currency. Equal to **instrument currency volatility** multiplied by the **exchange rate**.
	It will be in units of your account currency.

Volatility scalar	Number of position units to hold if you are investing your entire **trading capital** in one instrument, ignoring forecasts. Equal to **daily cash volatility target** divided by the **instrument value volatility,** both in your currency.
	It's in units of position blocks.
Subsystem position	How many blocks do you need to hold given your forecast? Equal to the **instrument forecast**, multiplied by **volatility scalar,** divided by 10.
	This is in units of position blocks.

Worked example for position sizing

From the start of the chapter the investor in this example has an annualised £1,000,000 **volatility target** and is investing in WTI Crude oil futures contracts, with a forecast of -6.

Instrument forecast	-6
Annualised cash volatility target	£1,000,000
Daily cash volatility target	**Annualised cash volatility target** divided by 16: £62,500
Price volatility	For crude oil the bottom panel of figure 23 shows average returns of $1 a day, which with a price of $75 equates to 1.33%.
Instrument block	One futures contract
Block value	For a WTI Crude contract of 1000 barrels with price $75 a 1% price move will equate to $0.75 × 1000 = $750.
Instrument currency volatility	This is the **block value** multiplied by the **price volatility**.
	For crude this is $750 × 1.33 = $997.50
Exchange rate	Numerator is instrument currency, USD. Denominator is account value currency, GBP. The USD/GBP exchange rate is currently around 0.67.
Instrument value volatility	This is the instrument currency volatility multiplied by the exchange rate.
	$997.50 × 0.67 = £668.325

Volatility scalar	Daily **cash volatility target** divided by the instrument value volatility, both in the investor's currency.
	£62,500 divided by £668.325 equals 93.52 contracts.
Subsystem position	Final combined instrument forecast, multiplied by volatility scalar, then divided by 10.
	(-6 × 93.52) ÷ 10 = short 56.11 contracts (no rounding).

You can now answer all of Sergei's questions and you've finally got positions for a trading system that has a single instrument, the **subsystem position**. But any good trading system will have multiple assets and even **semi-automatic traders** normally have more than one bet on the table at a time. The next chapter examines how you can put several subsystems together into a portfolio.

Chapter Eleven. Portfolios

	Instruments					
Trading rule A, variation 1	A1 forecast for instrument X					**Portfolio weighted position in X**
Trading rule A, variation 2	A2 forecast for instrument X	Combined forecast X		Subsystem position in X		
Trading rule B, variation 1	B1 forecast for instrument X					
Trading rule A, variation 1	A1 forecast, instrument Y					
Trading rule A, variation 2	A2 forecast for instrument Y	Combined forecast Y		Subsystem position in Y		**Portfolio weighted position in Y**
Trading rule B, variation 1	B1 forecast for instrument Y					

Forecast weights · Volatility targeting · Position sizing · Instrument weights

Customising for speed and size

QUESTION: WHAT DO MANY TRADERS AND AMATEUR INVESTORS who buy individual equities rather than invest in **collective funds** have in common? Answer: They both tend to have too few assets in their portfolios.

Research into individual investors finds many hold less than five shares, whilst traders often only prefer to deal with one or two markets where they feel most expert. So far I haven't helped solve this problem, since in the last chapter I showed you how to put together a **trading subsystem** which holds positions in just a single instrument.

But diversification really is the only free lunch in investment. Allocating across different **asset classes** can easily double your expected **Sharpe ratio**, as we saw in chapter two (page 46). It's best to simultaneously run a *portfolio* of as many trading subsystems and instruments as possible and allocate your **trading capital** between them. To allocate within this portfolio you will use **instrument weights**. Even though **semi-automatic traders** don't have a fixed set of assets they should also try and hold a number of positions in several instruments at once.

Chapter overview

Portfolios and instrument weights	What is a portfolio of trading subsystems and what are instrument weights?
Instrument weights – Asset allocators and Staunch systems traders	How to allocate weights when you are trading a fixed set of trading subsystems.
Instrument weights – Semi-automatic traders	The special case of semi-automatic traders who have multiple bets on, but not necessarily in the same instruments.
Instrument diversification multiplier	Accounting for diversification between subsystems for different instruments.
A portfolio of positions and trades	Calculating what position you should hold, given your instrument weights, and what trades you should generate.

Portfolios and instrument weights

This section is suitable for all readers

In an earlier chapter I used an example of a three asset portfolio to illustrate the black art of **portfolio optimisation**. The three assets were the S&P 500, NASDAQ and a 20 year US Bond. Suppose now that you're **asset allocator investors** who are trying to allocate capital between these **instruments**, or **staunch systems traders** who have forecasting rules that predict their returns. Alternatively, imagine that you're a **semi-automatic trader** who happens to have placed bets on each of these three assets.

Using the methods in the previous chapter you would calculate three **subsystem positions**, one for each instrument. Each position will depend on your **forecast** and how risky each instrument is. You would also have pretended to put all of your **trading capital** into trading each one of these systems. Effectively you will create three **trading subsystems**, each of which nominally uses your entire capital to trade one instrument.

In practice though you're going to share your capital across a *portfolio* of subsystems; similar to the way I created a portfolio with the same three underlying assets in chapter four. Each instrument's trading subsystem will get a positive **instrument weight**, with weights summing to 100%. Your **portfolio weighted position** will be the instrument's subsystem position, multiplied by the relevant instrument weight to reflect its portfolio share. Once you have this you can work out what trades are needed for each instrument.

As I'll show you later in the chapter you also need to account for the effect of portfolio diversification. But first we need to consider how to calculate the instrument weights.

Instrument weights – asset allocators and systems traders

Asset Allocating Investor

Staunch Systems Trader

Asset allocating investors run a fixed portfolio of **trading subsystems**, one per **instrument**, each consisting of a single **trading rule** – the 'no-rule' rule producing a constant identical forecast. **Staunch systems traders** have a group of **trading rules** whose forecasts are combined and then scaled into a position. In both cases you are allocating your **trading capital** between subsystems relating to a fixed set of instruments. This is different to traditional portfolio allocation, where you allocate capital directly to positions in each instrument.

Because of your hard work in the last couple of chapters all the subsystems will be **volatility standardised** and have the same expected **standard deviation** of returns. As you saw in chapter four, this makes the job of **portfolio optimisation** simpler. You can easily use the **handcrafting** method introduced in chapter four to determine the instrument weight each subsystem gets. It's also possible to use **bootstrapping** as an alternative.[115]

To handcraft your weights you need to group the assets and for this you need **correlations**. There are two alternatives that can be used to find these. Firstly you can estimate them using **back-tested** data. Alternatively if you don't have back-tested correlations then tables 50 to 55 (from page 291 in appendix C) give indicative correlations between instrument returns.

But you need the correlations between trading subsystem returns, *not* the returns of the underlying instruments. For **dynamic** trading systems the correlations between subsystem returns tend to be lower than those of the underlying instruments. A good approximation is that the correlation between subsystem returns will be 0.70 of the correlation of

---

115. To use bootstrapping you need to be able to **back-test** the performance of each of the **trading subsystems** separately. Ideally this should be done on a **rolling out of sample** basis. As I'll discuss in chapter twelve, 'Speed and Size', any returns that are calculated should be after costs.

instrument returns. So if two assets have a correlation of 0.5 between their instrument returns in appendix C, then their subsystems will have a correlation of $0.7 \times 0.5 = 0.35$.

Because asset allocating investors use a **static** strategy, the correlation of your subsystems is likely to be much closer to what you'd have with fixed long positions in the underlying instruments. So rather than multiplying the correlations in appendix C by 0.7, I recommend that you use them without adjustment.

In chapter four I showed you how to change portfolio weights if you had evidence that assets had different Sharpe ratios. But I wouldn't recommend adjusting instrument weights for Sharpe ratios, since there's rarely enough evidence of different performance between subsystems for different instruments, even once we account for different levels of costs. I come back to this in the chapter on 'Speed and Size'.

Let's look at an example. Here's how I would handcraft the instrument weights for the simple example of three instruments (S&P 500, NASDAQ, 20 year bond). Row numbers refer to the relevant rows of table 8 (page 79).

First level grouping	Group one (bonds): One asset, so 100% in 20 year bond. Row 1.
Within asset classes	Group two (equities): Two assets, 50% in each. Row 2.
Second level grouping	I have two groups to allocate to, each gets 50%. Row 2.
Across asset classes	

This gives me the same weights I had in chapter four for the actual assets, as shown in table 28. Of course this wouldn't normally be the case; it's only because this is a trivial example with no more than two assets in each group, and the same groupings as before.

TABLE 28: IN THIS SIMPLE EXAMPLE HANDCRAFTED WEIGHTS FOR TRADING SUBSYSTEMS ARE THE SAME AS FOR THE ASSETS THEMSELVES

	Handcrafted weight
US 20 year bond	50%
S&P 500 equities	25%
NASDAQ equities	25%

I give more complex examples of handcrafting instrument weights in each of the example chapters in part four.

Instrument weights – semi-automatic trading

Semi-automatic Trader

Semi-automatic traders don't have fixed portfolios of **instruments**, always creating **forecasts** and holding positions in each and every instrument. Instead you're likely to have a relatively small number of opportunistic positions (bets) on your books at any one time, drawn from a larger pool of potential trading ideas. Each time you enter a new bet for a different instrument you need to make a forecast, and then size your positions according to the size of your account and the risk of the instrument.

This presents a problem because the make-up of your portfolio, and hence the **correlation** of returns, will change over time as different instruments come in and out. The simplest thing to do is to allocate trading capital *equally* between potential opportunities. To ensure your risk is properly controlled you must also limit the *maximum* number of bets that can be placed at any time.

So you should allocate your risk equally between a notional maximum number of concurrent bets, each of which represents a potential **trading subsystem**. For example if the notional maximum number is ten bets this implies each **instrument weight** will be 100% divided by 10, which equals 10% for each **instrument**.

For reasons that will become clear later in this chapter, I recommend that this maximum shouldn't be more than 2.5 times the *average* number of bets you expect to be holding over time.

Instrument diversification multiplier

Once you've parcelled out your **trading capital** to each **trading subsystem** you're faced with a problem you might have seen before in chapter seven, which is the issue of diversification reducing your risk. If you skipped that chapter please go back and read the concept box on page 129. Diversified portfolios of **volatility standardised** assets like **trading subsystems** nearly always have a lower expected **standard deviation** of returns than the individual assets they are trading. The lower the average **correlation**, the worse the undershooting of risk will be.

You already know that the correlation between the two equity indices and the bond in the simple example is very low (the rule of thumb value from table 50 in appendix C is 0.1, and the estimated value I calculated in chapter four was negative). The correlation between the subsystem returns is likely to be even lower. So it's very unlikely that you'll get the same desired level of average risk from a portfolio of these three instrument subsystems as you would if you ran each one individually.

As in chapter seven you're going to need to apply a factor to account for the diversification in your portfolio: an **instrument diversification multiplier**. You multiply the portfolio weighted positions you've calculated by this multiplier to ensure that the overall portfolio has the right level of expected risk.

Staunch Systems Trader

Asset Allocating Investor

Asset allocating investors and **staunch systems traders** should use the **correlations** between the returns of each instrument **trading subsystem** to calculate the expected degree of diversification in the portfolio.

You have the option of either using estimated correlations from a **back-test**, or using rule of thumb correlations.[116] Once again be warned that tables 50 to 55 (from page 291 in appendix C) give indicative correlations between instrument returns. **Staunch systems traders** can multiply these by 0.7 to give the correlation between trading subsystem returns. **Asset allocating investors** should use instrument return correlations without adjustment.

Once you have the correlations, from whichever source, you have two options for the calculation: either use the formula in appendix D on page 297, or the approximations in table 18 (page 131). The number of assets in table 18 will be the number of subsystems you are running.

Let's return to the simple three asset example. From table 50 the correlation between bonds and equities is 0.1, and from table 54 the correlation between the S&P 500 and NASDAQ is around 0.75.[117] I'll assume for the sake of the example that I have a **dynamic** trading system, so I'm not a **static** asset allocator. This implies I should multiply correlations by 0.7, giving the correlation matrix in table 29. The average correlation is around 0.25, and from table 18 with three assets I get a diversification multiplier of 1.41.[118]

It's possible to get very high values for the diversification multiplier, if you have enough assets, and they are relatively uncorrelated. However in a crisis such as the 2008 crash, correlations tend to jump higher exposing us to serious losses – an example of **unpredictable risk**. To avoid the serious dangers this poses I strongly recommend limiting the value of the multiplier to an absolute maximum of 2.5.

---

116. Any negative correlations you estimate should be floored at zero to avoid an excessively large multiplier.
117. Actually table 54 in appendix C tells us the correlation between equities of different industries. Given the technology heavy nature of the NASDAQ compared to the S&P 500 this seems a good enough approximation, and is very close to the real number which we estimated in chapter four.
118. You should remove the self correlation values of 1.0 before calculating the average.

TABLE 29: CORRELATION MATRIX OF TRADING SUBSYSTEMS FOR THREE EXAMPLE ASSETS

	Bond	S&P	NASDAQ
US 20 year bond	1		
S&P 500	0.07	1	
NASDAQ	0.07	0.53	1

Correlations are 0.7 of the indicative correlations of instrument returns from tables 50 and 54 in appendix C.

Semi-automatic Trader

For **semi-automatic traders** I recommend using the following simple calculation. The instrument diversification multiplier should be your *maximum* numbers of bets divided by the *average* number of bets.[119] So if you had an average of four bets on at any given time, with a maximum of five, then your multiplier would be 5 ÷ 4 = 1.25.

I advocate that the multiplier is limited to a maximum of 2.5, since if you end up frequently trading more than your average then your expected risk will be too high. As I said earlier this means it's advisable that the maximum number of bets isn't more than 2.5 times the expected average.

A portfolio of positions and trades

This section is relevant to all readers

You're now in a position to see how a complete **trading system** for the simple three asset example could work.

I'm assuming that I use futures to trade these assets and that I have an **annualised cash volatility target** of €100,000. The price volatility and exchange rates are correct as I

---

119. This essentially assumes that all of a semi-automatic trader's bets are always perfectly correlated, which is very conservative. Here is the proof of this result. Suppose you're aiming for a daily **volatility target** of $1,000 and have an average of five bets, with a maximum of 10. All portfolio weights are 100% ÷ 10 = 10%. Each **trading subsystem** will also have a volatility target of $1,000. Once multiplied by the portfolio weight each subsystem position will have an average volatility of $100. On average with five bets, all of which are perfectly correlated, your daily portfolio returns will be 5 × $100 = $500 (note had they all been uncorrelated the risk would only be $223). So to hit the overall target of $1,000 you need a diversification multiplier of 2.

write, but I've used some arbitrary forecasts to make this example interesting but not too specific. You'll see some more specific examples in part four.

First of all tables 30 and 31 are there to remind you of the calculations in earlier chapters for each of the three **trading subsystems**.

TABLE 30: CALCULATING THE INSTRUMENT VALUE VOLATILITY FOR THE THREE ASSETS IN THE EXAMPLE PORTFOLIO

	(A) Price volatility % per day	(B) Block value	(C) Instrument currency volatility A × B	(D) Exchange rate USD/EUR	(E) Instrument value volatility C × D
US 20 year bond	0.52	$1500	$780	0.88	€686
S&P 500 equities	0.84	$1145	$956	0.88	€841
NASDAQ equities	0.87	$880	$766	0.88	€674

Values in table assume we're using futures and assuming a Euro investor. Figures correct as of January 2015.

TABLE 31: CALCULATING THE SUBSYSTEM POSITION FOR THE THREE TRADING SUBSYSTEMS IN THE EXAMPLE PORTFOLIO

	(F) Instrument value volatility	(G) Daily cash volatility target	(H) Volatility scalar G ÷ F	(J) Combined forecast	(K) Subsystem position (H × J) ÷ 10
US 20 year bond	€686	€6,250	9.11	10	9.11
S&P 500 equities	€841	€6,250	7.43	-10	-7.43
NASDAQ equities	€674	€6,250	9.28	-15	-13.9

The investor has a €100,000 cash volatility target, which implies a €6,250 daily target.[120] Forecasts are arbitrary.

---

120. To go from annualised to daily we divide by the 'square root of time', assuming a 256 day business day year that means you should divide by 16.

The **subsystem positions** in column K assume one instrument is traded with the entire trading capital. In table 32 I bring in the **instrument weights** and **instrument diversification multiplier** that I calculated earlier in this chapter. So to get the final **portfolio instrument position** I just need to multiply each **subsystem position** by the relevant instrument weight and the multiplier which compensates for the diversification in the portfolio.

TABLE 32: CALCULATING THE PORTFOLIO INSTRUMENT POSITION FOR THE EXAMPLE PORTFOLIO

	(K) Subsystem position	(L) Instrument weight	(M) Instrument diversification multiplier	(N) Portfolio instrument position K × L × M
US 20 year bond	9.11	50%	1.41	6.42
S&P 500 equities	-7.43	25%	1.41	-2.62
NASDAQ equities	-13.9	25%	1.41	-4.91

The table is using the instrument weights and diversification multiplier derived earlier in the chapter.

The final table 33 shows how I generate actual trades. To begin with I round the instrument position to get a **rounded target position**. This is the first time that I've rounded in my calculations. I then compare this to the current position which I already have. If I'd only just started trading this will be zero, but column P shows some arbitrary current positions to demonstrate the logic.

Finally I can calculate the size of any trade needed. I recommend that if the current position is within 10% of the rounded target position, then you shouldn't trade. I call this **position inertia**.

So for example if I had a target position of 50 crude oil contracts and my current position was between 45 and 55 contracts then I wouldn't bother trading. Conversely if the current position was 42 contracts versus a target of 50, I'd buy 8 contracts to hit my target. In the table the positions are relatively small so position inertia isn't used.

TABLE 33: CALCULATING THE REQUIRED TRADE GIVEN THE ROUNDED TARGET POSITIONS AND SOME ARBITRARY CURRENT POSITIONS

	(N) Portfolio instrument position	(P) Rounded target position Round (N)	(Q) Current position	(R) Trade P - Q
US 20 year bond	6.42	6	4	Buy 2
S&P 500 equities	-2.62	-3	-2	Sell 1
NASDAQ equities	-4.91	-5	-5	None

CONCEPT: POSITION INERTIA

Position inertia is a way of avoiding small frequent trades that increase costs without earning additional returns.

For example suppose your desired unrounded position is 133.48 Italian government bond futures, which is 133 contracts rounded. If your desired position goes to 133.52, 134 rounded, you'd buy one contract. If it drops back to 133.48 you would sell again. But the changes in desired position were only 0.04. Is it worth buying and selling, paying two lots of commission and market spreads, for such a small adjustment? Probably not.

The solution is to avoid trading until the target position is more than 10% away from the current position. For Italian bond futures the first movement in the desired position to 133.52 wouldn't result in a trade, since your current position of 133 would only be 0.75% away from the desired rounded position of 134. In fact the target position would have to go to 147 blocks before you traded.

Position inertia significantly reduces trading costs, which as you'll see in the next chapter can seriously affect your returns. My research shows position inertia usually has a negligible effect on pre-cost performance, so there is no downside to using it.[121]

---

121. This seems to be true for trading rules with holding periods of greater than a few days. If you're trading faster you probably shouldn't use position inertia (or use a lower value than 10%), but as we'll see in chapter twelve it's very hard to trade that quickly and make money.

Trades can be done manually or by an algorithm if you have a completely automated system. There is information on how I automate my own trading with simple algorithms on my website (see appendix A).

Summary for creating a portfolio of trading subsystems

Subsystem position	This is the number of **instrument blocks** you hold in each **trading subsystem,** given your **forecasts,** the instrument riskiness and your **daily cash volatility target,** as calculated in chapter ten. It is in instrument blocks.
Instrument weights	Each **trading subsystem** should have an **instrument weight.** Weights should add up 100%. **Staunch systems traders** and **asset allocating investors** can use **handcrafting** or **bootstrapping** to find weights. **Correlations** can be estimated from a **back-test** of trading subsystems, or using rules of thumb. In the latter case you should multiply instrument return correlations from appendix C by 0.7 if you're trading a **dynamic** strategy, or by 1.0 if you're asset allocating investors using fixed constant forecasts. **Semi-automatic traders** should use equal instrument weights of 100% divided by the maximum number of possible bets.
Instrument diversification multiplier	For **asset allocating investors** and **staunch systems traders** this is calculated using the correlation of **trading subsystem** returns. The multiplier can be calculated precisely using the formula in appendix C on page 297 or approximately using table 18 on page 131. For **semi-automatic traders** this will be equal to the maximum number of bets divided by the average number of bets. I recommend that in all cases the multiplier is limited to a maximum value of 2.5.
Portfolio instrument position	Equal to **instrument subsystem position** multiplied by **instrument weight** and then by **instrument diversification multiplier.**
Rounded target position	This is the **portfolio instrument position** rounded to the nearest integer number of **instrument blocks.**
Desired trade	After calculating the rounded target position you compare this to your actual current position and generate the necessary trade. If the current position is within 10% of the target then you don't need to trade (**position inertia**).

This completes the main part of the framework. I've now shown you how to create a complete **trading system**, consisting of a portfolio of **trading subsystems**. In the next chapter we will consider how to design systems which cope with the varying costs you'd see trading at different speeds, and with larger or smaller amounts of capital.

Chapter Twelve. Speed and Size

Instruments		Forecast weights	Volatility targeting	Position sizing	Instrument weights	
Trading rule A, variation 1	A1 forecast for instrument X					
Trading rule A, variation 2	A2 forecast for instrument X	Combined forecast X			Subsystem position in X	Portfolio weighted position in X
Trading rule B, variation 1	B1 forecast for instrument X					
Trading rule A, variation 1	A1 forecast, instrument Y					
Trading rule A, variation 2	A2 forecast for instrument Y	Combined forecast Y			Subsystem position in Y	Portfolio weighted position in Y
Trading rule B, variation 1	B1 forecast for instrument Y					

Customising for speed and size

SO FAR EVERYTHING YOU'VE SEEN IN THE **FRAMEWORK** IS EQUALLY relevant to a nimble amateur trader, holding 100 share positions for a few hours, and the portfolio manager of a massive hedge fund, following trends lasting for months. However in practice these two people will need to trade quite differently to account for the frequency and size of their trades.

In this chapter I will look at how you should design your **trading systems** given these two interrelated issues of speed and account size.

Chapter overview

Speed of trading	The thorny question of how quickly you should trade given the costs of doing so.
Decomposing and calculating the cost of trading	How to work out what you expect to pay in costs, given which instruments you are trading and the characteristics of your trading system.
Using trading costs to make design decisions	Once you know your costs, how you should adjust your system to cope.
Trading with more or less capital	The issues of trading with relatively small or large amounts of capital.
Determining overall portfolio size	Having a smaller account of capital limits how many instruments you can trade. I'll explain how best to determine the size and shape of your portfolio.

Speed of trading

How fast should you trade? If you go long USD/EUR FX at 11:05am on Tuesday 23 September 2014, should you expect to be selling at 11:06? Or by Thursday? Perhaps you will be holding on until December, or even March the following year?

The answer to this question depends on two things: how you expect prices to behave and the cost of each trade. Suppose you have a crystal ball and know with certainty that prices will increase by 10 cents in the next week. If it costs you 1 cent to trade then you should buy as you'll definitely make 8 cents by next Tuesday.[122]

Unfortunately crystal balls are in short supply. Instead we have **forecasts** which don't provide certainty, but hopefully shift the odds in our favour. You might have a **trading rule** where after looking at the **back-test** you expect to get a **Sharpe ratio (SR)** of 1.5 before costs. But this strategy pays out two-thirds of its profits in trading costs, so the after-cost SR is just 0.5. If you were running at a 20% **volatility target** you'd be expecting pre-cost returns of 30% a year, annual costs of 20% and net returns of just 10%.[123] Is it wise to trade this rule?

---

122. 10 cents raw profit, less 1 cent to buy in and 1 cent to sell out.

123. Annual returns are the expected annualised standard deviation of percentage returns (**percentage volatility target**) multiplied by Sharpe ratio. For pre-cost returns 20% × 1.5 = 30%. For after cost returns 20% × 0.5 = 10%. Hence you must be paying 30% - 10% = 20% in costs.

Personally I think it is very unwise indeed. If the actual pre-cost SR turned out to be less than 1.0, giving raw returns below 20% a year, then the strategy will lose money after costs. You'd be trading far too quickly relative to the available pre-cost performance.

Overtrading is a result of overconfidence, one of the **cognitive biases** I discussed in chapter one. Only someone who was very bullish would assume the realised pre-cost SR would definitely be 1.0 or over in actual trading. You shouldn't trade systems like this and hope for the best. Instead it's much better to design trading systems that aren't vulnerable to such high levels of costs.

In the next part of the chapter I'm going to show you how to calculate the cost of trading a particular instrument at a given speed, and how to work out the likely costs you'll face. Then you'll see how to construct trading systems to ensure you won't be making more money for brokers and market makers, than for yourself.

Calculating the cost of trading

The cost of execution

The first kind of cost we'll analyse is **execution cost**. **Back-tests** nearly always assume that when executing a trade you will pay the mid-price. But in practice the difference between the mid and the price you achieve will depend on how large your trades are compared to the available volume. This difference is the execution cost. Look at figure 24, which shows a snapshot of the order book for the Euro Stoxx European equity index future. At this point the mid-price was halfway between the bid of 3,369 and the offer of 3,370; equal to 3,369.5.

Smaller traders can assume they will pay at most half the usual spread between bid and offer in execution cost, which is what you get from submitting a market order that crosses the spread and hits the best bid or offer. If you're selling 437 contracts or fewer then the price you'd receive is 3,369. Similarly if you're buying fewer than 8 contracts the most you would pay is 3,370. In this example the expected execution cost is 0.5 of a point (half of the one point spread between 3369 and 3370). If you placed limit orders you might do better, but it's better to be conservative and assume costs are higher than you'd hope.

This assumption is reasonable if your typical trade is less than the usual size available on the inside of the spread. Larger traders cannot assume this, and I discuss this further in the final part of this chapter. Also remember that this is not a book about high frequency trading. These assumptions are wrong if you are constantly submitting orders every few seconds or fractions of a second, as the order book will be affected by each of your successive trades.

FIGURE 24: ORDER BOOK FOR EURO STOXX INDEX MARCH 2015 FUTURES, AS OF 23 JANUARY 2015 11:13 GMT

Product		Product ID	
Euro Stoxx 50 Index Futures		FESX	
Avg. Pr.	Cum. Qty.	Quantity	Bid
3,369.00	437	437	3,369.00
3,368.43	1,013	576	3,368.00
3,367.89	1,633	620	3,367.00
3,367.32	2,330	697	3,366.00
3,366.81	2,988	658	3,365.00
3,366.30	3,659	671	3,364.00
3,365.91	4,144	485	3,363.00
3,365.37	4,814	670	3,362.00
3,364.63	5,797	983	3,361.00
3,364.07	6,587	790	3,360.00
	Contract	Last	Volume
	Mar 2015	3,368.00	652,226
Ask	Quantity	Cum. Qty.	Avg. Pr.
3,370.00	7	7	3,370.00
3,371.00	540	577	3,370.99
3,372.00	1,147	1,724	3,371.66
3,373.00	696	2,420	3,372.05
3,374.00	647	3,067	3,372.46
3,375.00	1,017	4,084	3,373.09
3,376.00	831	4,915	3,373.58
3,377.00	502	5,417	3,373.90
3,378.00	1,131	6,548	3,374.61
3,379.00	571	7,119	3,374.96

Source: EUREX

Types of cost

The **execution cost** I calculated above is a key element of costs, but it's not the only one. There are also fees: commissions and taxes to pay. Here is a list of the types of cost you might face.

Expected execution cost per block	This is the **execution cost** you saw above; the difference between the mid-price and what you get when you actually trade.
	Smaller traders can usually assume they will pay at most half the usual spread between bid and offer, as in the 0.5 points for Euro Stoxx in figure 24. As a percentage of 3,370 this will be 0.01484%.
	To get the cost in cash terms multiply the percentage spread in price points by the value of each 1%.* For Euro Stoxx futures at a price of 3,370 this happens to be €337, so the execution cost is equal to 0.01484 multiplied by 3,370, which is €5.**
Fee per ticket	Many UK retail brokers impose a per trade commission regardless of the trade size. £5 to £15 is typical.
Fee based on trade size	Other brokers charge per 100 shares or single futures contract traded. My broker charges €3 per contract to trade Euro Stoxx futures.
Percentage value fee	Certain jurisdictions charge a percentage tax on the value of the trade, such as UK stamp duty at 0.5%. Some brokers also charge percentage commissions on larger transactions; 0.1% is typical.

* Remember this was defined in chapter ten, 'Position sizing', page 154, as the **block value**, the amount we make in cash terms when a price moves by 1%.

** For Euro Stoxx each one point move in the futures price costs €10. So a 1% move of 33.7 points is worth €337.

There may also be a *holding* cost for certain instruments. Futures, spread bets and contracts for difference require rolling over monthly or quarterly. Nearly all **collective funds** impose an annual charge. These holding costs are usually relatively small compared to trading costs, and they don't affect decisions about speed, so we'll ignore them.[124]

Standardising cost measurement

Suppose it costs €8 in total to trade one Euro Stoxx futures contract (€5 in **execution costs** and €3 in brokerage fees). Is this a lot? How does it compare with €5 to trade a German 2 year bond Schatz futures contract? Naively, €5 sounds cheaper than €8, but the

124. There may also be interest payments, gains or losses on FX translation, data feeds, account management fees, various business costs for professionals, and if you do well capital gains or income taxes. All these costs should be taken into account when determining a trading system's likely net profitability.

answer is not as simple as you might expect. What if you have to buy 20 Schatz versus 10 Euro Stoxx to achieve the same amount of risk? (This is the volatility **scalar** from chapter ten, page 159.) Despite Schatz looking like a bargain it's going to cost you €100 versus €80 to put equivalent positions on, so Euro Stoxx is actually cheaper to trade.

This is another opportunity to use the technique of **volatility standardisation**. You should use a measure of costs that accounts for how risky different instruments are. The measure is defined as follows: if you buy one **instrument block** and then sell it, how much does that round trip cost when divided by the annualised risk of that instrument? This **standardised cost** is equivalent to how much of your annualised raw **Sharpe ratio (SR)** you'll lose in costs for each round trip.

To calculate it you take the cost to trade one block in instrument currency C, and double it because a round trip is two trades. You then divide by the annualised **standard deviation** of the value of one block of an instrument. This is the annualised version of the daily **instrument currency volatility** ICV (which was defined on page 158). Remember that to annualise daily volatilities you need to multiply by 16.[125] So the standardised cost will be $(2 \times C) \div (16 \times ICV)$.

An important implication of this formula is that the effective cost of trading is higher for instruments with lower price volatility. This is another reason to exclude very low risk instruments from your portfolio.

As I'm writing this, the price of the Euro Stoxx future has volatility of around 1.5% a day (the **instrument riskiness** defined on page 155), and as each 1% move is worth €337 (the **block value** I discussed on page 154) this equates to a daily standard deviation of the contract value of €506 (the ICV or **instrument currency volatility**). When I annualise this I get 506 × 16 = €8,096. Given the cost of trading at €8 per block, this is a standardised cost of 2 × €8 divided by €8,096, or 0.002 SR units.

Like most futures this is cheap to trade.[126] Average standardised costs in 2014 for the futures contracts I traded ranged from around 0.001 SR for the most liquid like the FTSE 100, up to around 0.03 SR for Australian interest rate futures.[127]

Now let's look at a spread bet[128] on the FTSE 100, where I am betting £1 per point. First I need to work out the **instrument currency volatility**.

---

125. This is the usual 'square root of time' factor of 16, assuming a 256 business day year.

126. **Staunch systems traders** will use futures in the example in part four.

127. These are the conservative costs assuming you pay half the spread each time. In practice I paid a fraction of this by using simple automated execution algorithms. Nevertheless, I still use the more conservative costs when **back-testing**.

128. This is what **semi-automatic traders** will use in the example in part four.

Price volatility	Currently 0.75% a day.
Instrument block	£1 per point.
Block value	With the FTSE at 6600 a 1% move will be 66 points, the value of which at £1 per point will be £66.
Instrument currency volatility (*ICV*)	This is the **price volatility** multiplied by the **block value**: 0.75 × £66 = £49.50.

Now I can work out the costs.

Expected execution costs per block	Half the typical spread is 4 points, i.e. £4.* There are no fees or taxes.
Total cost per block (*C*)	£4
Instrument currency volatility (*ICV*)	From above £49.50.
Cost in SR units	2 × C ÷ (16 × ICV) = 2 × £4 ÷ (16 × £49.50) = 0.01 SR

* This is for a quarterly forward bet – spreads on spot FTSE are tighter but with my typical holding period they would end up being more expensive.

This is about ten times larger than for the FTSE 100 future, which isn't surprising as the spread bet is a retail product with a smaller block size.[129] Generally bets on most major indices come in around the 0.01 SR level, although those on individual shares will usually cost more. I'll use 0.01 SR as the benchmark cost for spread bets.

The third type of instrument we'll consider is **exchange traded funds (ETFs)**. Like many equities, these are cheaper to trade in 100 share blocks. The precise cost will depend on volatility, and the volatility for ETFs depends on the underlying assets and whether any leverage is used. I will be conservative and check the cost of a relatively low volatility instrument, the iShares IGIL global inflation linked bond ETF, which is one of the ETFs I use in the **asset allocator** example in part four.

---

129. Spread bets generally have higher trading costs than futures, and are OTC traded rather than on exchange. On the upside as well as smaller block sizes they offer tax free returns under current UK legislation.

Price volatility	Around 0.43% a day in early 2015.
Instrument block	100 shares.
Block value	100 shares at $144 per share is $14,400. 1% of this is $144.
Instrument currency volatility	This is the **block value** multiplied by the **price volatility**: $144 × 0.43 = $62

Now for the costs.

Expected execution cost per block	The typical bid offer on this ETF is 70 cents wide or 0.486% of the current price of $144.
	The block value is $144. So if I pay half the spread I'd pay 0.486 × $144 × 0.5 = $35 for each block.
Fee per ticket	My broker charges me $5.00 per trade. I assume there are no other fees or taxes due.
Total cost per block (*C*)	$35 + $5 = $40
Instrument currency volatility (*ICV*)	$62 (from above).
Cost in SR units	2 × C ÷ (16 × ICV) = 2 × $40 ÷ (16 × $62) = 0.08 SR

ETFs with higher price volatility, such as equities, will cost less than this on a risk normalised basis, but to be safe I'll use the figure of 0.08 SR as my expected cost for ETFs. The costs in these examples are correct given current market conditions and the brokerage fees I'm paying, but you should calculate your own figures before making any decisions.

Introducing turnover

What is the point in knowing it will cost us 0.08 **Sharpe ratio (SR)** units, 0.01 SR or 0.002 SR, to buy and sell a risk adjusted amount of each instrument? It's pointless having just a standardised measure of costs; you also need a standardised measure of how quickly you're trading. Since you know the cost per round trip in annualised SR units you'll need to count the number of round trips done annually, where a round trip is a buy and then a sell.

I measured standardised costs by making them **volatility standardised.** Similarly each buy and sell should be of a volatility standardised quantity of **instrument blocks**. Because of the way the **framework** works, this is equivalent to your expected average absolute position, or the position you'd have with an average sized **forecast** (defined as the **volatility scalar** in chapter ten, page 159).

The number of round trips per year is the **turnover**. A turnover of 1 unit means you expect to do one buy and one sell of an average sized position per year; so your average holding period will be 12 months. Similarly a turnover of 52 units would imply you're hanging on to positions for an average of one week. Because turnover is volatility standardised it means you can consider the trading pattern of each instrument in isolation (the so called **trading subsystem** that was defined in chapter ten), without worrying about the rest of your portfolio.

For example suppose it costs a standardised 0.01 Sharpe ratio units for each round trip in spread bets, and your turnover is 10 units of average position each year. Then over a year of ten round trips (ten buys and ten sells), you'd lose 10 × 0.01 = 0.10 SR in costs. That means an SR of 0.5 would be reduced to 0.5 - 0.1 = 0.4.

Where does turnover come from?

Before continuing you also need to understand where turnover comes from. For what reasons would you want to trade? Here's a list, in order of descending importance.

Forecast	A change in forecast from one or more of the **trading rules** used by **staunch systems traders**, or because a **semi-automatic trader** is placing new bets or closing old ones. This is the main source of position changes, except for **asset allocating investors** for whom forecasts do not change.
Instrument currency volatility	Movements in the expected daily **standard deviation** of the value of each instrument block (**price volatility** multiplied by **block size**). This is the second most important reason for position changes.
Trading capital	Changes in the amount of capital you currently have at risk. This is determined by your profits and losses and by any additional funds you add or withdraw. Ignoring withdrawals and injections of money, with the highest recommended 50% **volatility target**, this will change by an average of 3% each day.
	You can't reduce the trades that result from this component, except by using a lower percentage volatility target. So with a target of 16% it would move by around 1% a day.
Exchange rate	This is the exchange rate between an instrument's currency and the currency your current trading capital is in. Rates usually move by less than 1% a day in major currencies.
	You can't reduce these trades, which in any case are relatively small.

System parameters	These are parameters in the trading system which should only change infrequently if at all: **Forecast weights, Instrument weights,** forecast and instrument **diversification multipliers,** and the **percentage volatility target.**
	You can eliminate the trades that result from this element by not meddling with your system!

In the rest of this chapter I will focus on how **forecasts** and changes in **price volatility** influence trading speed, since these can readily be adjusted and have the biggest effect.

Estimating the number of round trips

You can now calculate the expected costs of trading each instrument, given the units of **turnover** of the trading system and the **standardised costs**. But how do you find the turnover? There are three ways to estimate it.

Sophisticated back-test	If you have access to decent **back-testing** software, or can write your own, then you can include a function that estimates turnover directly.
Simple back-test	More rudimentary back-testing tools can give you an estimate of the average number of **instrument blocks** traded each year and the average absolute number of blocks you held. You can then calculate turnover as:
	Average number of blocks traded per year ÷ (2 × average absolute number of blocks held)
Rule of thumb	The third alternative is to use rules of thumb. This approach is fine for **semi-automatic traders** whose turnover will depend on the tightness of their stop loss, **asset allocating investors** who don't get turnover from forecast changes, and for those **staunch systems traders** who are using only the trading rules I provided in chapter seven (the **carry** and **EWMAC** rules).
	There will be relevant rules of thumb later in this chapter and in the example chapters of part four.

Using trading costs to make design decisions

Setting a speed limit

Let's return to the Euro Stoxx future, which had a **standardised cost** of 0.002 **Sharpe ratio (SR)**. Suppose you have a rule with a **back-tested** pre-cost return of 0.40 SR, and a **turnover** of 50 round trips per year. You'd expect to pay 50 × 0.002 = 0.10 SR annually in costs and receive 0.30 SR of net performance.

What if you had an alternative rule, with a turnover of 100, but with a pre-cost return of 0.60 SR? Though your costs have doubled to 0.20 SR, the net return has increased to 0.40 SR. Surely you should choose the more expensive option?

In chapter three when I discussed **fitting** I pointed out that there is always considerable uncertainty about expected pre-cost performance. An implication of that is you need a lot of historical data to prove that a **trading rule variation** is likely to be profitable (as shown in table 5 on page 62), let alone make enough money to cover its costs.

It also means you need a lot of data to make it probable that one trading rule had better performance in the past than another. So considerable evidence is required to justify trading a faster, and apparently superior, variation rather than a slower, cheaper and supposedly inferior alternative (see table 6 on page 64).

The relative pre-cost Sharpe ratio you will achieve in practice is extremely uncertain, whilst expected costs can be predicted with much more accuracy. There is one further danger in blindly accepting the back-test results of expensive systems. What I've shown you in this chapter is an estimate of *current* costs, which could be very different from what they were 20 years ago. In many markets trading costs were much higher in the distant past than they are now.

A fast trading rule might look great in the past, but if the market was very expensive nobody could have actually exploited it. Now costs have fallen there is a good chance the effect will vanish.

To ensure you don't chase performance, or trade faster than was viable in the past, I recommend that you set a **speed limit**; a maximum expected turnover you will allow your systems to have.

At the start of this chapter I said I wouldn't trade a strategy which paid two-thirds of its profits out as costs, amounting to 1.0 in SR annually. I personally think it's foolhardy to pay more than a third of your expected profits in trading costs and I use that to set my own speed limits. If you're being realistic then the Sharpe ratio from trading each instrument using its **trading subsystem** is unlikely to be higher than 0.4 on average.[130]

---

130. For more discussion on this refer back to chapter two, page 46.

This implies you should *never* pay more than a third of 0.4, or 0.13 SR, in costs, regardless of how good your back-test is. Remember that cost in SR terms is equal to the **standardised cost** multiplied by the turnover in round trips per year. So dividing 0.13 by the standardised cost of an instrument will give you the turnover speed limit for that instrument.

For a relatively cheap futures market like the Euro Stoxx this implies a maximum turnover of 0.13 ÷ 0.002 = 65 round trips per year, or an average holding period of just under a week. With the very cheapest instruments like NASDAQ futures you might be able to double that turnover to give a holding period of a couple of days.

However this precludes day trading, which with two or more round trips per day would be a turnover of at least 500 round trips each year. To trade that fast without spending more than a third of your returns on costs you'd need to get a significantly higher pre-cost Sharpe ratio, or reduce your standardised cost to around 0.13 ÷ 500 = 0.00025 SR units. That level of costs is around a quarter of what the cheapest futures can achieve.

As it happens about a quarter of the standardised costs of these super cheap futures are commissions of around $1 per contract, with the rest coming from **execution costs**. So to day trade you'd need to get your execution costs down to zero, which means consistently achieving the mid-price or better. To trade even faster, with three or more round trips a day, you'd have to be getting consistently *negative* execution costs.

In conclusion then, to day trade even the cheapest instruments you will need to achieve very high pre-cost Sharpe ratios, or have an execution strategy that consistently captures the spread. This isn't impossible, but clearly only those with a proven record of achieving these goals should contemplate trading this quickly. This capability is relatively rare in practice, which is why the vast majority of amateur day traders are unprofitable.

With a cost of 0.13 SR a year if you're using the maximum suggested 50% **volatility target** (as defined on page 137 in chapter nine), then you'll be paying 0.13 × 50% = 6.5% a year in costs. This is a reasonably large drag on performance and personally I wouldn't want to see anything bigger.

As discretionary **semi-automatic traders** can't use back-tests they need to avoid over-confidence about their performance expectations. Rather than a maximum **Sharpe ratio (SR)** of 0.40 on each instrument, you should conservatively expect to get at most 0.25 SR.[131] This implies paying no more than a third of 0.25, or 0.08 SR in costs annually. **Asset allocating investors**, whose **static** trading systems will have similar performance to the underlying assets, should also use this lower figure.

You're now ready to think about how you can customise your trading systems with an understanding of costs. There are several areas in the framework where performance expectations are used. These decisions should now be made using costs as well as expected pre-cost performance.

---

131. Again refer back to chapter two, page 46.

Which instruments to trade	It's going to be difficult to trade **instruments** with costs which are too high for the kind of system we want to use.
Deciding average holding period by setting stop losses (semi-automatic traders)	**Semi-automatic traders** should use stop losses which target a particular average holding period for positions. When setting the level of these stops you need to consider the costs of your preferred instruments.
Selecting, fitting and calibrating trading rules (staunch systems traders)	If you decide to **fit** your trading rules then you must consider both pre-cost **Sharpe ratio** and costs. Remember that you have more certainty of costs than of pre-cost performance.

With my preferred method of fitting you shouldn't look at pre-cost performance but should still exclude **trading rule variations** whose likely costs will be too high. |
Setting forecast weights (staunch systems traders)	You need to use likely costs to avoid overweighting trading rule variations which perform well but are also relatively expensive to trade.
Setting the risk percentage	When checking your Sharpe ratio to set the **risk percentage**, you should use after-cost performance.
Setting the look-back for estimating price volatility	After **forecast** changes this is the next key source of turnover in your **trading systems**. The costlier your trading is, the slower you should update your estimate of **price volatility**.
Allocating instrument weights (semi-automatic traders and asset allocating investors)	You should consider giving less weight to more expensive instruments, unless you think additional pre-cost performance compensates you.

Which instruments to trade?

There are two routes to take when designing your trading systems so that they don't exceed any **speed limits**. Firstly you could decide what sort of speed you wish to trade at and then choose **instruments** that are cheap enough to trade that quickly. Alternatively if you have a preference for particular instruments then that will limit how fast you could trade them. So for example if you can't trade futures and prefer **ETFs**, then that will heavily curtail your trading speed.

If you use my recommended maximum of 0.08 **Sharpe ratio (SR)** units paid annually in costs for **asset allocating investors** and **semi-automatic traders**, then table 34 gives the maximum possible standardised cost for a given holding period and **turnover**. It also shows instruments which typically have that level of cost. You can then infer which instruments to trade for a given speed of trading, or how quickly to trade given a preferred set of instruments.

The table also shows the lower limit on how slowly you can trade a particular kind of system, with a minimum achievable turnover in round trips per year. Given your limit on what you're willing to pay in costs, you can imply from this turnover which instruments will be too expensive to trade at all.

TABLE 34: WHAT SPEEDS AND HOLDING PERIODS CAN SEMI-AUTOMATIC TRADERS AND ASSET ALLOCATING INVESTORS TRADE WITH PARTICULAR INSTRUMENTS?

Holding period	Typical turnover	Maximum cost SR	Likely instruments	
1 day	256	0.00031	None	
3 days	85	0.001	Cheapest futures, e.g. NASDAQ	
1 month	12	0.0067	Nearly all futures except short maturity bonds, STIR*	
6.5 weeks	8	0.01	Index spread bets, e.g. FTSE	
3 months	4	0.02	Individual equity spread bets	
6 months	2.0	0.04	Cheapest ETFs, e.g. equity indices	Slowest semi-automatic trader
One year	1.0	0.08	Benchmark inflation linked bond ETF	
2.5 years	0.4	0.20	Most individual equities	Slowest asset allocating investor

The table shows for different holding periods the turnover in round trips per year, maximum instrument cost if we pay no more than the recommended 0.08 SR a year, and typical instruments at each cost level (estimates as of January 2015).

* Short term interest rate futures

Asset allocating investors can get down to an annual turnover of 0.40 round trips per year, implying that a cost of 0.08 ÷ 0.40 = 0.20 SR is affordable.[132] So ETFs, which we estimated will cost at most 0.08 SR, will be fine. As I explain in the next section, **semi-automatic traders** with very wide stop losses will realise a turnover of 2.0 round trips a year. A cost of 0.08 ÷ 2.0 = 0.04 SR is the maximum they could pay. This rules out ETFs but allows spread bets, which we costed at 0.01 SR.

I've done a similar analysis for **staunch systems traders**, for whom I recommend a maximum of 0.13 SR units of cost per year. Table 35 gives the figures and I've also shown how each level of turnover relates to the trading rules I presented in chapter seven, 'Forecasts'.

TABLE 35: WHAT SPEED SYSTEMS CAN STAUNCH SYSTEMS TRADERS USE?

Typical turnover	Maximum cost SR	Likely instruments	
128	0.001	Cheapest futures, e.g. NASDAQ	
54	0.0024	Average future, e.g. WTI Crude	Fastest single trend following rule I use (this the **EWMAC** 2, 8 rule)*
28	0.0046	Most futures except short end bonds, equity volatility indices, STIR	Second fastest single trend following rule (this is the **EWMAC** 4, 16 rule)
12.5	0.01	Nearly all futures, index spread bets	Set of rules used in chapter 15
7.5	0.017	Cheaper individual equity spread bets	Slowest trend following rule I use (this is the **EWMAC** 64, 256 rule)

The table shows for different levels of turnover in round trips per year the maximum standardised instrument cost if you pay no more than the recommended 0.13 SR a year for staunch systems traders, and typical instruments at each cost level (estimates as of January 2015).

* Defined in chapter seven, 'Forecasts', and appendix B (page 282).

---

132. As you'll see later in the chapter on page 195, this requires using a very slow look-back of 20 weeks for volatility estimation.

I've also shown the level of turnover that you'll get with the set of trading rules that I advocate using in chapter fifteen, where I explain in detail the design of the staunch systems trader example. Staunch systematic traders who use this recommended set of trading rules, which is fairly slow, will get a turnover of 12.5 round trips per year.[133] You'd get a maximum **standardised cost** of 0.13 ÷ 12.5 = 0.01 SR, which is fine for nearly all major futures markets and index spread bets.

Deciding average holding period by setting stop losses

Semi-automatic trader

How should **semi-automatic traders** determine how quickly to trade? You might think it depends on how trigger happy you are, with itchy fingered day traders clicking in and out every few minutes, and relaxed macro traders trading every few weeks or months.

But I advocate that traders exclusively use a systematic stop loss to exit positions, no matter how they decide to enter them. This means the average holding period will depend mainly on how tight, or loose, your stops are set. You should then ensure that your trading style, and the horizon you are trying to predict price movements for, is in line with your stop levels.

If stops are set very tight then you'll have short holding periods and high **turnover**. You won't be able to trade more expensive **instruments** with tight stops, since with a **speed limit** on what you're willing to pay in **Sharpe ratio (SR)** costs there will be a maximum viable **standardised cost**.

Table 34 shows that with the cheapest futures you can use a relatively tight stop, with a holding period of three days. However this would be far too expensive if you're using spread bets. I mentioned a particular spread betting system in the introductory chapter which held positions for around a week. This would have a turnover of 52 round trips per year. The standardised cost I'm using for spread bets is 0.01 SR, so this gives costs of 52 × 0.01 = 0.52 annually.

Earlier (page 150) I calculated the implied **volatility target** of that system at 160%. This implies you'd need to make 0.52 × 160% = 83% a year on your **trading capital** before costs – just to break even!

Table 34 shows that with spread bets you can't use stops with holding periods of less than about six weeks. Furthermore it's unlikely that any trader will be happy with a holding period of more than six months. So the slowest turnover you can get is 2 round trips a year, which is the figure I used earlier in the chapter when looking at instrument selection.

---

133. This figure is calculated when we cover the **staunch systems trader** example in chapter fifteen on page 251.

Selecting trading rules

Staunch systems trader

In chapter three I said I don't like to fit or calibrate **trading rules** using real performance. But that prohibition only applies to pre-cost performance. I positively encourage you to **back-test** and find the expected **turnover** of your trading rules and then reject **variations** which are too expensive.

Using my recommended guideline for setting **speed limits** from above you don't want costs greater than 0.13 **Sharpe ratio (SR)**. So you should be rejecting trading rules with turnovers greater than 130 round trips per year for the very cheapest futures (cost 0.001 SR for each unit of turnover), over 65 round trips for the Euro Stoxx future (cost 0.002), and with turnovers over 13 for a spread bet with a standardised cost of 0.01 SR.[134]

It is simplest to use the same trading rules and variations for all the **instruments** you trade. This means you will need to drop any rules which are too fast for the most expensive instrument you have; remaining rules will automatically be fine for the cheaper ones. You'll see how this is done in more detail in part four, chapter fifteen, which is the example chapter for the **staunch systems trader**.

However if the set of instruments you have features trading costs that vary significantly you might consider using faster variations only with the cheapest instruments, and using a slower set of variations for the expensive ones. Costs in my own portfolio vary by a factor of 40 across the futures that I trade, so this is the approach I use.

Trading slower rules – Weights to trading rules

Staunch systems trader

How should you determine the **forecast weights** to use when forming a **combined forecast**? Unless you think that faster rules will give you a pre-cost **Sharpe ratio (SR)** advantage which compensates for their costs you're going to have less weight on higher turnover rules, especially in **instruments** which are expensive to trade.

If you use **bootstrapping** to determine weights on a **rolling out of sample** basis then you can include a correction for costs in estimates of returns. Bootstrapping will automatically

---

134. As I showed you earlier, trading rules aren't the only source of turnover; we also have changes in price volatility, which we'll discuss later in the chapter. The costs you actually pay will also be inflated by the effect of the **forecast diversification multiplier**. But for faster rules these are more than compensated by the effect of **position inertia**: not trading position changes of less than 10%. All this makes it very hard in practice to estimate the expected costs of trading a particular rule. Looking solely at the turnover of the forecast is the simplest approach and is usually conservative enough.

determine the right weights, accounting for predictable costs and uncertain profits. By comparing the weights found when pooling results across the portfolio with those from individual instruments it will also tell you if different forecast weights make sense, or if you should use the same weights.

Personally I've never found consistent evidence in my own system that faster trading rules, whether in general or as variations of a single rule, have a higher pre-cost **Sharpe ratio (SR)**.[135] So if you're deciding weights using **handcrafting** then I recommend that you assume the same pre-cost SR for all trading rules, but account for their different trading costs. You can then adjust forecast weights for trading rules based on your estimate of the SR of costs, as we did in chapter four on page 86.

How do we do this?

Remember from chapter four that the adjustment is done by comparing the SR of an asset versus the average across the portfolio. For each instrument and **trading rule variation**, you should use the cost per round trip and the turnover to calculate the total cost in SR units per year. If you've decided to keep the same set of trading rules for all instruments you may want to use the same adjustments on every instrument, which means using the highest and most conservative instrument standardised cost to do your adjustment, rather than the specific cost for each instrument.

On a given instrument you should then take the average cost in SR points over all rules you are finding weights for. Because costs are fairly predictable you should use column A 'With Certainty' of the SR adjustment table 12 in chapter four (page 86). As an extreme example, if you think that a particular rule is going to cost 0.13 SR per year, versus an average for all rules of 0.03 SR, then the performance difference is 0.10 SR worse than average and you should multiply its weight by 0.95.

With my recommended **speed limit** applying to exclude any trading rules with costs of more than 0.13 SR, the adjustments made here will never be larger than 0.95 or 1.05. In most cases they will be much smaller and not worth bothering with. However if you're using a higher speed limit then adjusting for trading rule costs could significantly alter your weights.

---

135. The set of rules in my own system have turnovers of between 65 and six times a year, i.e. holding periods of between four business days and a couple of months. As rules get slower than a turnover of six their performance does start to worsen, and I exclude these rules entirely. For a turnover between six and 65, pre-cost performance is relatively similar across variations of the same trading rules (and is often worse for quicker **trend following rules** as most markets do not trend well at shorter horizons). However some kinds of rules show better performance at shorter holding periods and you should do your own **bootstrapping** with realistic costs to check this.

More conservative estimation of Sharpe ratio to set risk percentage

This section is relevant to all readers

Back in chapter nine, 'Volatility targeting', I said that you should have realistic expectations of likely **Sharpe ratio (SR)** to determine the optimal level of risk to take. If you're doing your own **back-test**, or estimating your likely performance in some other way, this needs to be done on an after-cost basis.

Alternatively if you're using the suggested figures for Sharpe ratio in the relevant chapters of part four, then there's nothing more to do as all these assumptions are post-cost.

Slower estimation of price volatility

This section is relevant to all readers

After forecasts the next source of **turnover** is the adjustment of positions to cope with changes in the risk of each instrument – the **instrument currency volatility**, which I defined on page 158. This in turn depends on how quickly you update your estimate of the **standard deviation** of daily percentage returns, the **price volatility**, which was also defined in chapter ten.

I mentioned three ways of estimating price volatility in that chapter. Two of these methods involved formally calculating the standard deviation of price changes over a **volatility look-back period**, either with a **moving average** or an **exponentially weighted moving average (EWMA)**. I suggested that these should be used by **asset allocators** and **staunch systems traders**, with a default look-back of 25 business days, or 36 days with an EWMA. The other method involved eyeballing the chart, which I recommended for **semi-automatic traders**.

Asset allocating investor

Staunch systems trader

If you're measuring **price volatility** using a simple **moving average**, or the equivalent exponentially weighted **EWMA**, should you use my recommended look-back of 25 days (five weeks of trading days), or a slower look-back of ten, or even 20 weeks? On page 157, figure 23 showed that slower look-backs are very sluggish to react to changes in risk. My research suggests that look-backs over 20 weeks lead to much poorer trading system performance. However faster look-backs change very frequently and will generate additional **turnover** and thus cost more to trade.

First let's quantify the effect of higher costs. You need to check the turnover for each **trading subsystem**. This is all the trading that you'll be doing for a particular instrument. It will be what you get from any changes in **forecasts**, plus additional turnover as your estimate of price volatility changes. You can ignore the other reasons for trading that I discussed earlier, as these are relatively unimportant.

If you have multiple trading rules then you need to work out the trading coming from your **combined forecast** across all trading rules. To get this first take the weighted average, using **forecast weights**, of the turnover in round trips per year for each individual trading rule. Then multiply this by the **forecast diversification multiplier** to get the turnover of the combined forecast.

If you're an **asset allocating investor** using the 'no-rule' rule of a constant forecast then there are no forecast changes and you'll have a zero turnover from trading rules.

You then need to apply a correction for the effect of changing your estimate of **price volatility**, which always increases turnover. At the same time, you must also account for the effect of **position inertia,** which I introduced on page 174 – not trading any position change greater than 10%. This slows trading down.

You can see the net result of these two corrections in table 36. The table shows that changing the look-back has almost no effect if the turnover of the original **combined forecast** is five or more round trips per year. So if you're trading fast trading rules, on cheap instruments, then you can safely use the default look-back.

For slower rules it will depend on the precise costs of your instruments. Take the 'no-rule' rule used by asset allocating investors. As before let's assume you're trading ETFs with a **standardised cost** of 0.08. With zero turnover in forecasts you should refer to the top row of the table. Using the default five week look-back to estimate price volatility gives a turnover of 1.6 round trips per year. You'd have costs of 1.6 × 0.08 = 0.13 **Sharpe ratio (SR)** units annually. This violates the recommended **speed limit** of paying 0.08 SR in costs for asset allocating investors, who are unlikely to see high performance from their **static** portfolios.

In contrast with a 20 week look-back, giving a turnover of 0.40, you'd only pay 0.40 × 0.08 = 0.032 SR. This is a quarter of the original cost, saves a substantial 0.10 SR units, and is well within the speed limit. Notice that a turnover of 0.4 round trips per year is the lowest an asset-allocating investor can achieve without slowing down their estimate of price volatility beyond the maximum recommended 20 weeks.

TABLE 36: WHAT EFFECT DOES SLOWING DOWN YOUR ESTIMATE OF PRICE VOLATILITY HAVE? A SLOWER ESTIMATE CAN REDUCE FINAL SYSTEM TURNOVER, IF UNDERLYING TRADING RULES ARE ALSO SLOW

Starting turnover of trading rules	Look-back of price volatility estimate*		
	20 weeks	10 weeks	5 weeks
0 (no-rule rule)	0.4	0.8	1.6
1	1.2	1.5	2.5
5	4.7	5.0	5.7
10	9.4	9.8	10.2
12.5	11.7	12.2	12.6
20	19.1	19.2	19.7
40	39.2	39.2	39.4
60	60	60	60

The table shows the final turnover, in round trips per year, we get from changing the look-back for price volatility (columns) given a starting level of turnover from trading rules (rows). Five weeks (25 business days) is the default look-back. Starting turnover is the average turnover of your trading rules, weighted by forecast weights, multiplied by forecast diversification multiplier. Position inertia is used to slow down trading.

* Using a simple **moving average**. For an **exponentially weighted moving average** the relevant look-backs are 144 days instead of 100 days, 72 days instead of 50 days, and 36 days instead of 25 days.

Semi-automatic Trader

The first method of estimating price volatility I discussed in chapter ten was eyeballing; looking at the chart and figuring out what a typical daily move was. It's obviously very difficult to **back-test** this method as everyone's perception is different. However you should usually use a one month window on a chart to find the **price volatility**, since this will give similar results to the 25 day **volatility look-back** I recommended for more formal **moving average** methods. This is fine if you're trading cheap **instruments** like futures.

With more expensive assets, like spread bets and **ETFs**, then I'd suggest you still use a one month window. However I would recommend that you also compare your estimate of the cash risk of an existing position (the **instrument currency volatility** defined on page 158) to the value you had yesterday. If the estimate hasn't changed by more than 25% from its last value then don't bother to adjust it.

Just like **position inertia** this will reduce any trading caused by updating the volatility estimate on existing positions and keep your costs down. However when opening new positions you should use the most up-to-date estimate of volatility to work out your initial trade size.

Choice of instrument weights

Asset allocating investor

Staunch systems trader

This isn't relevant to **semi-automatic traders** who don't trade a fixed set of **trading subsystems**.

Suppose you're running a portfolio including a cheap **instrument** like a Euro Stoxx future, and a more expensive one like two year German bond (Schatz) futures. Perhaps you've managed to find **trading rules** that make sense for each instrument and fitted some **forecast weights** to them; or you could be an **asset allocating investor** who is going to use the single 'no-rule' rule with a constant **forecast**. As in chapter eleven you must now allocate your **trading capital** and think about the appropriate **instrument weights** to give to each of these two **trading subsystems**.

Will you get lower after-cost performance from running trading systems for the more expensive Schatz? If so then you should obviously give it a lower instrument weight. But this is not a clear-cut decision. Academic research shows that the extra costs of owning less liquid instruments are often outweighed by higher profits, such as the additional returns you get from investing in the equities of smaller firms. As I briefly mentioned in chapter two, 'Systematic Trading Rules', we tend to get rewarded for being exposed to illiquid assets.

My own research shows that more expensive instruments usually perform somewhat better even once costs are taken into account; but only if they're traded relatively slowly, with a **turnover** of less than 15 round trips per year. The improvement isn't usually strong enough to warrant a higher allocation, but it does mean that under-weighting costly instruments doesn't make sense. For asset-allocating investors (whose turnover from table 36 will be at most 1.4), and slower **staunch systems traders**, there is no need to consider adjusting instrument weights in light of costs.

If you're a fast systems trader, with a turnover of more than 15 round trips per year, then my research shows that you will see worse relative performance after costs for expensive instruments. However if you've followed the advice I gave earlier then you wouldn't be trading them that quickly anyway, since you'd be breaking the speed limits implied by the recommended limit of 0.08 **Sharpe ratio (SR)** units or 0.13 SR units, per year spent on costs.

When you stick to the speed limit then only the very cheapest instruments would have access to quick trading rules. So in general you'd either be trading cheaper instruments more quickly than expensive ones, or trading all your instruments at the same relatively slow pace. In my own research into systems with these features I don't find any difference in after-cost returns between instruments, regardless of their standardised costs.

In conclusion, unless **bootstrapping** tells you differently, I would recommend assuming the same post-cost SR for all trading subsystems. If you're using **handcrafted** instrument weights this means no Sharpe ratio adjustment is needed to account for different cost levels.

Trading with more or less capital

This section is relevant to all readers

Trading with a lot of capital

Let's have another look at the order book in figure 24. An investor who wants to sell 437 contracts or fewer can assume they will pay at worst half the spread, 0.5 price units, as they're selling at 3,369 compared to the mid-price of 3,369.5. But a large hedge fund which needs to sell more than this, like 5,000 lots, has a problem.

They have three options when they submit the order. Firstly they can cross the spread and submit a single market order. They will get 3,369 for the first 437 lots, but the next 576 lots will go for 3,368, then 620 at 3,367 and so on. The average price received per lot will be 3365.2, which compared to the original mid of 3,369.5 gives an **execution cost** of 4.3 points. The exact cost for any given trade will depend on the depth of the order book when it is submitted.

Secondly they can offer 5,000 lots at 3,370, adding to the 7 lots already on the order book. They might get lucky and meet a large buyer who takes their offer. This would beat the mid-price by half a point, and get an effectively negative execution cost. But it's much more likely that on seeing this huge order other traders will push the price down, leaving the order unfilled and the market at a worse level.

Finally the funds human traders or execution algorithims can break the order up into chunks and execute it gradually. The order will take longer to execute and there will be a lot of uncertainty about the fill level, and even if each chunk is small other market participants will see the individual orders coming through and react accordingly, which will probably result in the price drifting down.

In none of these three cases is the execution cost guaranteed to be exactly 0.5 points. If you are trading in large size, in relatively illiquid markets and relatively quickly, you can't casually assume you will pay half the spread. If your typical order size is going to be greater than the usual depth available at the inside spread, you need to do serious research to calculate your expected trading costs, and to work hard at optimising your execution.

Trading with relatively little capital

Those with much lower fund values have a different problem. Think back to the example in table 32 on page 173. The imaginary investor there had a €100,000 **annualised cash volatility target**, and after working out the target positions they needed to short 2.62 S&P 500 futures contracts, based on the **combined forecast** of -10. But what if you are an amateur investor with only €40,000? Running at the maximum recommended 50% percentage volatility target would give you a mere €20,000 cash volatility target. With one-fifth of the risk you'd get one-fifth of the target position. However you can't short the 0.524 contracts this equates to. You'd have to short a rounded position of just one contract.

With a €20,000 volatility target if your S&P 500 combined forecast doubles from -10 to -20, you'd still be short just one contract.[136] With a forecast of -20 if the **price volatility** then doubled, you'd still have just the single short.[137] Your risk is much 'lumpier' than if you could trade fractional contracts. The problem occurs because the minimum size of the S&P future is quite big.[138]

As I explained in chapter six, 'Instruments', the minimum block size is relatively large for many other instruments. Equities with very high prices – like Berkshire Hathaway A shares, currently trading at $220,000 each – are obviously going to be an issue, whilst UK spread betting firms may not allow you to trade in bets of only £1 per point on some indices.

Apart from the S&P, many other futures contracts tend to have large nominal values including long maturity bonds, CME currency futures, and some energy and agricultural commodities. An extreme example is the Japanese 10 year bond future which currently has a price of around 150 million yen, or $1.3 million. In some cases there are mini versions of these large contracts, but these might not be liquid enough.

Even without a large minimum it may be impractical or uneconomic to trade small sizes. With a per ticket cost of €4 to buy ETFs it doesn't make sense to buy in blocks of less than 100.

---

136. The number of contracts to hold would be -0.524 and -1.049 respectively. Both round to -1.
137. Doubling price volatility, all other things being equal, halves position size. The number of contracts to hold would be -1.049 and -0.524 respectively. Both round to -1.
138. Actually what you're trading here is the E-mini S&P 500 contract. There is an even larger full size future.

To find out where you could have minimum size problems you need to work through the calculations in earlier chapters, assuming the maximum combined forecast. This will give you the highest possible position for an instrument given the current level of volatility. My recommended maximum absolute forecast of 20 will give you a maximum position of 2 × **volatility scalar** × **instrument weight** × **instrument diversification multiplier**.

Staunch systems traders will need to check this for every instrument they are trading. **Semi-automatic traders** should do the same calculation for any instruments they are planning to place bets on. **Asset allocating investors**, whose forecast is always a constant +10, should use half of the usual figure to get their maximum position: 1 × **volatility scalar** × **instrument weight** × **instrument diversification multiplier.**

Let's check the result for the example we're using. In table 31 (page 172), the volatility scalar for the S&P 500 was 7.43. This was calculated with a €100,000 cash volatility target, so with a €20,000 volatility target it will be one-fifth the size. Hence the volatility scalar with a lower account size is one-fifth of 7.43, or 1.49. From table 32 the instrument weight is still 25%, and the diversification multiplier 1.41, so the maximum possible position then is 2 × 1.49 × 25% × 1.41 = 1.05. This is clearly too low. No matter what happens the position will be long or short one contract (or none).

It is a matter of judgment as to what kind of maximum position you'd find acceptable. My recommendation is to be satisfied with a maximum possible position of four or more instrument blocks. If you can't get to this level you will need to consider taking one of the following steps.[139]

Increase weight to instrument (only in moderation)	If instead of 25% you put 100% of the example portfolio into the S&P 500 then your maximum position would be a slightly more reasonable 3 contracts.* However any increase in weight will have to come from other instruments hence moving **instrument weights** away from their optimum, unless you also take the next option.
Reduce overall portfolio size	It's better to increase the **instrument weight** by reducing the number of instruments you have, but still using the correct **bootstrapped** or **handcrafted** weights. However this still reduces diversification. I'll go into more detail about determining the ideal portfolio size in the next section.
Remove instrument	If the instrument size is unreasonably large, and you will need to significantly reduce the total number of assets in your portfolio to accommodate it, then you should exclude it.

139. Another option which is theoretically possible but isn't shown is to trade with a higher **volatility target** by increasing the **trading capital** or the **percentage volatility target**. The former isn't usually viable and the latter is almost always extremely dangerous.

Live with it	You might have a large portfolio with just a few instruments where size is a problem. For example half a dozen of the futures contracts in my own portfolio of more than 40 have maximum positions of less than four contracts.
	On average my portfolio risk and return is about right, even if it is lumpier than I would prefer on individual instruments. However I still require that maximum positions are at least one instrument block, or there is clearly no point including the relevant asset.

---

* The instrument weight goes from 25% to 100% and the instrument diversification multiplier falls from 1.41 to 1, as there's only one instrument. The former increases the maximum position, the latter reduces it but by less. The new maximum position calculation is 2 x 1.49 x 100% x 1.0 = 2.98.

Determining overall portfolio size

Asset Allocating Investor

Staunch Systems Trader

Given that small account sizes present problems, how would an **asset allocating investor** with a few thousand euros decide how many of the thousands of **exchange traded funds** to hold? How does a **staunch systems trader** without millions of dollars in **trading capital** work out which of the 200 or so liquid futures contracts they should trade?

The principle you should follow is to hold the most diversified portfolio possible without running into any problems with maximum positions. Ideally you want at least one instrument from each major **asset class**. For each asset class you should choose instruments that don't give you a maximum position that is too small; as I said above my recommendation would be to avoid anything with a maximum of less than four instrument blocks.

You then only add additional instruments to an asset class if this doesn't cause a small maximum position problem to appear either in the new instrument or in an existing one. You should also consider costs and the other characteristics which I discussed in chapter six, 'Instruments'. You'll see examples of constructing these portfolios in the relevant example chapters fourteen and sixteen, in part four.

Semi-automatic Trader

Semi-automatic traders generally have smaller portfolios, and these are of an ad-hoc group of instruments, rather than the fixed set used by others. But you should still check you have no issues with low maximum positions on anything you're likely to trade, for example by using my recommendation to have at least a four block maximum position.

Remember from chapter eleven, 'Portfolios', (page 169) that your portfolio weights are 100% divided equally by the maximum number of bets you're likely to make, so adjusting **instrument weights** is not an option for dealing with size problems. So if you have problems you should consider reducing the size of your portfolio by lowering the maximum number of bets, or not trading that instrument.

Summary of tailoring systems for costs and capital

Standardised cost estimate

Cost to trade one block	**Execution costs**: Half the bid-offer spread except for those with large account sizes, dealing in illiquid markets or with very fast trading.
	Fixed fees per ticket.
	Fixed fees per position unit traded.
	Percentage value fees and taxes.
	The total cost to trade an **instrument block** should be calculated in the same currency as the instrument's value.
Instrument currency volatility	The expected daily **standard deviation** of the value of one **instrument block** in the currency of the instrument, as calculated in chapter ten, 'Position Sizing', (page 158).
Standardised cost	Annualised cost in **Sharpe ratio (SR)** per round trip (buy and sell):
	Twice the cost to trade one block divided by annualised instrument currency volatility (daily instrument currency volatility multiplied by 16).

Calculating cost of trading rules and trading subsystems

Approximate turnover from a back-test	To calculate the standardised **turnover** in round trips (buys and sells) per year: (Number of **instrument blocks** traded per year) ÷ (2 × average absolute number of blocks held)
Turnover for systematic trading rules	Calculated from **back-test** or implied from rules of thumb. Rules of thumb for my suggested trading rules explained in chapter seven, 'Forecasts', are available in the relevant example in chapter fifteen.
Cost of trading rule for instrument	**Turnover** for trading rule, in round trips per year, multiplied by **standardised cost** for instrument.
Turnover from forecast changes	**Staunch systems traders**: Can get this from back-test, or by taking a weighted average, using **forecast weights** of **trading rule** turnovers, multiplied by **forecast diversification multiplier**. The turnover of the 'no-rule' rule used by **asset allocating investors** is zero. **Semi-automatic traders** should use the turnover implied by the holding period which is determined by their stop loss, from table 34. More detail is given in chapter thirteen.
Turnover for trading subsystem	The **turnover from forecast changes** is corrected for the look-back used to estimate **price volatility** and **position inertia**, using table 36.
Cost of trading subsystem	**Turnover** for **trading subsystem** multiplied by **standardised cost** for instrument.

Taking action to cope with costs

Speed limit	I recommend that the costs of an instrument's **trading subsystem** should be at most one-third of a conservative estimate of the pre-cost **Sharpe ratio (SR)**. **Staunch systems traders** should assume a maximum pre-cost SR of 0.40 and others an SR of 0.25. This implies that **staunch systems traders** should not pay more than 0.13 Sharpe ratio per year in costs, and **semi-automatic traders** and **asset allocators** no more than 0.08 SR.

Which instruments to trade	For a given type of trader there is a minimum level of **turnover** in round trips per year. Given a limit on how much you are prepared to pay in costs a year, and this minimum level of turnover, you will get a maximum feasible **standardised cost**. This implies that certain instruments will be too expensive to trade.
	Asset allocators can get down to an annual turnover of 0.40, so using my recommended maximum of spending 0.08 **Sharpe ratio (SR)** units on costs would exclude all instruments with costs greater than 0.20 SR.
	For **semi-automatic traders**, who I also suggest shouldn't pay more than 0.08 SR on costs, the lowest achievable turnover with a very loose stop loss is 1.8 round trips per year, so instruments with standardised costs greater than 0.044 SR can't be used.
	For **staunch systems traders** using my suggested set of trading rules the minimum turnover would be 12.5 round trips per year, which with my recommended limit of 0.13 SR a year on costs, implies that you shouldn't use instruments with costs greater than 0.01 SR.
Deciding average holding period	If you're a **semi-automatic trader** then I recommend that you should set your stop loss rule to give an average holding period so that **turnover** multiplied by **standardised cost** of your most expensive **instrument** is at most 0.08 Sharpe ratio units a year.
Selecting trading rules	You should exclude trading rules which are unaffordable for a given instrument given my recommended maximum for **staunch systems traders** of spending no more than 0.13 Sharpe ratio units a year on costs. This can be calculated for each instrument individually, or using the highest and most conservative instrument cost.
Forecast weights for trading rules	**Bootstrap** the weights with cost adjustment or if using **handcrafting** I recommend assuming the same pre-cost **Sharpe ratio (SR)**.
	This means adjusting handcrafted weights depending on the SR cost versus average across **trading rules**, using 'with certainty' column A of table 13 (page 89).
Finding Sharpe ratio to set risk percentage	If you're **back-testing** the system yourself then you must deduct costs. You don't need to do anything further if using the default post-cost expectations that I use in the example chapters of part four.
Slowing down estimation of price volatility	**Asset allocating investors** and **staunch systems traders** should see table 36 for the effect on turnover of changing the look-back on volatility estimation. You should then check to see if slowing down your estimation will significantly reduce costs.
	Semi-automatic traders who need to lower costs should not adjust their eyeballed estimate of **instrument currency volatility** unless it has changed by more than 25%.
Instrument weights for trading subsystems	**Bootstrap** the weights with cost adjustment, or if **handcrafting** I recommend assuming the same after cost **Sharpe ratio**, implying no adjustment to instrument weights.

Too much capital

When simple cost calculations aren't enough	If you can't always trade for half the spread, due to trades larger than the typical size at the top of the order book, then you need to use more complex cost models to account for **execution costs**.

Too little capital

Calculate maximum possible position	**Staunch systems traders** and **semi-automatic traders** should assume the maximum **combined forecast** of +20, which implies a maximum possible position of:
	2 × **volatility scalar** × **instrument weight** × **instrument diversification multiplier**
	For **asset allocating investors** there is a constant forecast of +10, which implies a maximum possible position of:
	1 × **volatility scalar** × **instrument weight** × **instrument diversification multiplier**
Very low rounded maximum possible position	I recommend taking action if the maximum possible position is less than four **instrument blocks**.
	Consider dropping the instrument, increasing the portfolio weight and/ or reducing the number of instruments traded overall.
Sufficiently high rounded maximum possible position	No action required.
	I would personally be happy if the maximum possible position was at least four **instrument blocks**.

Determining portfolio size and make-up

Asset allocating investors and Staunch Systems Traders	You should hold the most diversified portfolio possible, consistent with avoiding issues with maximum positions that are too small. I recommend having a maximum possible position of at least four **instrument blocks** in any **instrument**.
Semi-automatic traders	Portfolio size is determined by the maximum number of bets. Check you won't have an issue with low maximum positions with any **instrument** before trading.

This is the end of part three. Part four will delve further into customising the framework as we look at three examples in detail: the **semi-automatic trader**, the **asset allocating investor** and the **staunch systems trader**.

PART FOUR.

Practice

·

Chapter Thirteen. Semi-automatic Trader

IN THIS FINAL PART OF THE BOOK I'LL SHOW YOU HOW TO PUT THE framework into action for three specific examples. This first chapter is for **semi-automatic traders,** who make their own discretionary **forecasts** about price movements, but then use my systematic **framework** to manage their capital and position risk.

Chapter overview

Who are you?	Introducing the semi-automatic trader.
Using the framework	How you will use the systematic framework as a semi-automatic trader.
Process	The process you need to follow each morning and as you are trading throughout the day.
Trading diary	A diary showing how you could have traded the markets as a semi-automatic trader in late 2014.

Who are you?

As a semi-automatic trader you want to make your own calls on the market, but within a systematic **framework**. With stop losses, risk targeting and position sizing taken care of you can focus on getting the buy or sell decision correct. This will give you the best of both worlds – your human ability to interpret and process information, combined with a system giving the correct amount of risk.

It will not be easy sticking to the framework. The system may force you to trade, or prevent you from trading, when you would rather do otherwise. However there are significant benefits in sticking to a consistent strategy. I strongly recommend that you design a system you're comfortable with and then do not deviate from it.

In the specific example discussed in this chapter we'll assume you're going to be trading spread bets on equity indices and FX, as reasonable sized amateur investors with a notional **trading capital** of £100,000. You could be trading full-time, or on a part-time basis for perhaps an hour each morning. However you can apply this framework to any market where leverage is possible and to any account size.

As a semi-automatic trader you'll be trading sporadically as opportunities arise. This presents some challenges in using my systematic framework, which normally requires a series of calculations to be performed each time you trade.

To reduce the workload you'll first do some daily housekeeping on your current portfolio: closing out any positions that have hit stop losses, adjusting estimates of **trading capital** and **price volatility**, and doing any trades on existing positions that are now required. You'll then put on any new trades which look promising based on overnight moves.

If you're trading part-time you will leave stop loss orders with your broker and go to your day job. However if you're trading full-time you'll continue to watch the markets, potentially putting further trades on, and closing positions that hit stop losses. You won't however repeat the more time-consuming housekeeping tasks until the next morning.

Using the framework

Instrument choice: size and costs

As **semi-automatic traders** you don't trade a fixed set of instruments. At any given time you will have a small number of positions, or 'bets', open. Those positions are drawn from a larger pool of **instruments** that you've formed opinions on.

You'll be using quarterly spread bets, with all bets in multiples of £1 per point. For example if you go long the FTSE at £2 per point, and it goes from 6500 to 6501, then you'd earn £2.[140] The bet size will be determined by the broker's minimum bet size, usually between £1 and £10 depending on the instrument. In line with the advice in chapter twelve, 'Speed and Size', (page 200) you should check that any position you're putting on would be at least four instrument blocks with a maximum forecast of 20.

You should also check that the **standardised costs** of trading any potential instrument will be 0.01 **Sharpe ratio** units or less, for reasons explained in detail below. Finally you should avoid very low volatility instruments, for the numerous reasons enumerated throughout part three.

---

140. There are several other important aspects of spread betting that I don't have space to discuss here. I assume that if you intend to actually trade the system shown here you are already familiar with spread betting. If not you should consult the books I've recommended in appendix A, or similar resources.

Forecasts and stop losses

As I discussed in chapter seven, 'Forecasts', (page 115) you'll need to have a graduated opinion on likely price movements whenever you decide to open a new position or 'bet'. These need to be translated into quantifiable **forecasts**, as in table 37. Note if you weren't using spread bets or other derivatives, and couldn't **short sell** assets, you'd need to limit yourself to making positive forecasts.

TABLE 37: TRANSLATING OPINIONS INTO A QUANTIFIED FORECAST[141]

Very strong sell	Strong Sell	Sell	Weak sell	Neutral	Weak buy	Buy	Strong buy	Very strong buy
-20	-15	-10	-5	0	5	10	15	20

I strongly recommend that you do not change your forecast once a bet is open. Otherwise you might be tempted to take profits too early, or double up on losses. You can sometimes add new bets on top of an existing position, of which more later. But you will be using a systematic trailing stop loss rule to close all your positions – no other exit rules are permitted.

The stop loss rule is loosely related to the 'early loss taker' system I've used for examples in previous chapters. It uses stops set at a multiple of the current value of the daily **standard deviation** of prices.

Parameter X	You should set a parameter X which will be related to how long you want to hold positions for and your trading costs.* I recommend X = 4, for reasons I explain below.
Volatility units	The expected **standard deviation** of daily price changes, in price points. Note we use volatility in price points, not percentage points as normal. The volatility in price points is equal to the percentage point volatility (price volatility as defined in chapter ten, 'Position sizing', on '"Price volatility" on page 155), multiplied by the current price. In this chapter you'll find this by eyeballing a one month chart of recent price changes (as discussed in chapter ten, page 155), since you're probably going to be using charts to decide on your entries. You need to update this estimate throughout the life of the trade and adjust the stop accordingly. (As suggested in chapter twelve, you don't need to update your volatility estimate unless it has changed by more than 25% from the previous value.)
	For example as I write this the standard deviation of oil prices is $1.5 per day.

---

141. This is identical to table 16 and is repeated here for ease of reference.

Trailing stop loss when long	If the price of the instrument falls by more than **X** volatility units from the high achieved since entry then you should close your position. As an example suppose the high of crude was $70, so with X = 4 and volatility units of $1.5, that implies a stop loss of $70 - (4 × $1.5) = $64
Trailing stop loss when short	You will generate a closing trade when a price rises by more than **X** volatility units from the low reached after entry. So again for crude if the recent low was $30, then that implies a stop loss of $30 + (4 × $1.5) = $46

* 'X' is equivalent to the 'B' parameter in the generic 'A and B' system which I describe in appendix B.

What value of X should you use? It depends on whether you have a short or long-term forecasting horizon, and on the costs of your instruments. So with a shorter forecasting horizon you'll cut more quickly, hold positions for less time, and it will be more expensive to trade. It's important to match the forecasting horizon and the tightness of your stop loss. There is no point making a forecast of prices for the next six months if you're likely to be stopped out by next Tuesday. Table 38 shows the average holding period for a given value of X.[142]

TABLE 38: HOW DOES THE X PARAMETER IN YOUR STOP LOSS RULE DETERMINE YOUR AVERAGE HOLDING PERIOD? SMALLER VALUES OF X MEAN TIGHTER STOP LOSSES AND SHORTER HORIZONS, BUT REQUIRE CHEAPER INSTRUMENTS

Value of X	Average holding period	Turnover, round trips per year	Maximum cost SR
1	4 days	64	0.0013
2	9 days	29	0.0027
3	17 days	15	0.0053
4	6.5 weeks	8	0.01
8	13 weeks	4.0	0.02
10	26 weeks	2.0	0.04

The table shows for each value of X (rows): the average holding period, in business days or weeks; the implied turnover in round trips per year; and the maximum instrument cost if

---

142. I produced this table using both artificial and real market data drawn from a number of **asset classes**. Because we obviously can't simulate a discretionary rule I used a random entry rule. Interestingly this is actually profitable in real data, because even with a random entry we can still capitalise on trends by using the stop loss exit rule.

we pay no more than 0.08 Sharpe ratio units per year. The turnover includes the additional trading we get from changes in price volatility and also assumes we don't trade position changes of less than 10% (position inertia).

As you saw in chapter twelve, 'Speed and Size', you need to adjust X given the cost of the **instruments** you're trading. The final column of table 38 shows a suggested maximum feasible **standardised cost**, in **Sharpe ratio (SR)** units per year, for a given value of X. This is calculated using my recommended **speed limit** of spending 0.08 SR units per year on costs, from chapter twelve.

Also in chapter twelve (page 183) I suggested you use a costs figure of 0.01 SR units as the standardised cost for all of your spread bets. The table shows you could safely use an X of 4 or higher with spread bets, although if you're trading cheap futures contracts you could go quicker.

I don't advise using different stop loss systems for different instruments as this complicates life and can lead to mistakes. So the value of X should be set conservatively using the cost of the most expensive instrument you're likely to trade.

In this chapter we are going to use an X of 4, which means I assume you're predicting trends that last for just over six weeks.

Note that unlike in the original 'early loss taker' system you won't be using a profit target. Why not? My own research shows no evidence that systematic profit targets work consistently.[143] This is because most markets exhibit trending behaviour, and a profit target will get you out of trends too early.

To summarise you mustn't close your trade until you hit a stop loss; then you must close it. Sticking to this rule will be difficult, but will mean that your risk is controlled and that your returns will have the favourable positive **skew** of **trend following** traders.

Volatility targeting

I've already set the initial **trading capital** of this example at £100,000. But how aggressive should you be with this money – what should your **percentage volatility target** be? You need to refer back to chapter nine, 'Volatility Targeting'. In this example I am going to assume that your **Sharpe ratio (SR)** will be at least 0.30 after costs, which I calculate below as 0.08 SR units. This is comfortably under my recommended maximum expectation of 0.50 (from page 46). Referring to column D of table 26 (page 148) an SR of 0.30 gives a risk percentage of 15%, and I'm assuming you can cope with the pain that implies.

---

143. There are some situations where closing trades before a stop loss is hit makes sense, such as **relative value** or **mean reverting** strategies, but in my opinion it is better to build the closing rule into a fully systematic trading rule.

This implies you'll have an annual **volatility target** of £100,000 × 15% = £15,000 and a daily target of £15,000 ÷ 16 = £937.50.[144] Because you're using spread bets there is no concern about hitting a relatively modest risk percentage of 15%. As always you should avoid low volatility assets where the required leverage will be too high.

You'll be measuring your account value daily, recalculating **trading capital**, and adjusting your **volatility target** accordingly. This might trigger trades on existing positions and the new volatility target will be used to size any new bets you make.

Position sizing

You can now think about 'Position sizing', as discussed in chapter ten. First you need to measure the recent percentage **standard deviation** of returns (**price volatility**) in each market to determine the expected daily variation in the value of one **instrument block** (the **instrument currency volatility**).

I'd suggest you use the eyeball technique described in chapter ten (page 155), which you're already using to calculate the volatility estimate needed for stop loss levels. This should be done daily on any instruments where you have positions, and ideally on anything you might place bets on today.[145] Changes in price volatility for your existing positions might trigger trades.

From table 38 (page 212) with the suggested X of 4 you would expect to get a turnover of 8 after accounting for the effects of sizing your position. With **standardised costs** of 0.01 SR units for spread bets this gives us an annual cost of 8 × 0.01 = 0.08 **Sharpe ratio (SR)** units, which just squeaks in at the maximum level of 0.08 SR that I recommended in chapter twelve, 'Speed and Size'.

With 15% annualised volatility that equates to a performance drag from costs of 0.08 × 15% = 1.2% a year. This is more than most **passive ETFs**, but significantly cheaper than a hedge fund. You'd also have to pay perhaps 0.6% for rolling your quarterly bets.[146]

You can save on costs by following the advice in the chapter twelve, 'Speed and Size', and not adjusting your estimate of **instrument currency volatility** if the previous level looks about right, say within 25% of the current value.

As you're spread betting, the value of a 1% move (the **block value**) depends on the bet size in pounds per point, so you won't need to use exchange rates even when betting on non-UK markets. So for example with crude oil at $65, a 1% move of $0.65 or 0.65 points, at a broker's minimum of £10 a point, will have a value of £6.50.

---

144. As before to go from annual to daily volatility you need to divide by the 'square root of time', which assuming 256 business days in a year is 16.

145. Working out the instrument currency volatility for a potential trade in advance makes the process more efficient but might not always be possible, in which case you will need to do your estimation just before you trade.

146. Assuming the full spread is charged on rolls.

With this information you can use your **volatility target** to work out the **volatility scalars** every morning to use for both existing and potential trades.

Portfolios

To size your bets you need to determine your preferred *maximum* and *average* number of concurrent bets, as I explained in chapter eleven, 'Portfolios'. These terms are self explanatory: the maximum number of bets is the most positions you will have on at any given time, and the average is what you expect to have on a typical day. As I said in chapter eleven, the **instrument weight** you use to size each of your positions will be 100% divided by the maximum number of bets.

The **instrument diversification multiplier** will be the maximum number of bets divided by the average. This multiplier ensures the total average absolute forecast will be 10 with the average number of bets on, which ensures your forecasting is consistent with the rest of the systematic **framework**. I recommended that the multiplier shouldn't be greater than 2.5, which limits the value of the maximum relative to the average.

If you already have your maximum number of bets on, and you desperately need to make a new bet, then sorry: you can't. Wait until one of your existing bets has stopped out. If they all continue to be profitable then perhaps your new bet wasn't necessary after all. Although this may seem rigid, sticking to this ensures that you have the correct risk on for each bet and it will stop you from putting on dangerous numbers of simultaneous bets. Make sure you set your maximum high enough when designing your system to cover your likely appetite for extra bets.

Earlier I said you shouldn't change the forecast on an existing bet. However you can add to positions by placing a new, separate, bet on an instrument which you're already holding. This allows pyramiding positions, such as buying into a strengthening trend. The new bet is completely distinct, will have its own stop loss, and could be closed at a different time. A new bet on an existing position counts towards your maximum number of bets.

This can't be used as a loophole to close positions; you can't put on a new bet which will make your existing position smaller or reverse it. Finally, to avoid concentrating your risk too heavily I strongly recommend that you don't have a total of more than 40 forecast units bet on any asset at once, added up over all the bets on that instrument. So a forecast of +10 on your first bet, followed by +25 on your second for the same instrument would be acceptable. But you couldn't place a third bet of more than +5.

In this chapter I am going to assume you have a maximum of four positions, with an average of three. So each position will have an instrument weight of 100% ÷ 4 = 25%, and the diversification multiplier is 4 ÷ 3 = 1.33.

As you saw in chapter nine, 'Volatility targeting', (page 150) the use of systematic stop losses allows you to compare my framework with traditional money management systems, where you put a fixed percentage of your capital at risk. Each bet you make puts at risk a percentage of capital equal to:

(X × forecast × **percentage volatility target**) ÷ (10 × 16 × average number of bets)

In this example with an X of 4, the average forecast of 10, a 15% volatility target and an average of three positions you are putting (4 × 10 × 15%) ÷ (10 × 16 × 3) = 1.25% of your capital at risk on average per bet. With the maximum forecast of 20 you'd be risking twice that, 2.5%. This is relatively large, but remember that you expect to be holding these positions for around six weeks.

Trading in practice

You should first check to see if any stop losses on existing positions have been hit, and trade on those immediately if you didn't leave stop losses with your broker.[147] Then you can look at potential new entries and come up with a numeric forecast for them. On every new trade you'll need to calculate a stop loss based on the value of X, the **price volatility** and the entry price.

Stop losses on existing positions will also need to be adjusted if price volatility changes. They also need to be moved up if prices reach new highs (for longs), and down for new lows (on shorts).

Part-time daily traders should then update the stop loss limits they have left with their brokers and go to work at their real jobs. If you're still trading intra-day you will continue to monitor the market for new entries and to see if stops have been hit. You could also update stop loss levels intra-day if significant new levels are reached, but with the relatively large value of X I've suggested for this chapter this probably isn't necessary.

Process

Here is the process to follow when running this system. The trading diary in the next section illustrates in more detail how the calculations are done.

---

147. I'm mostly agnostic about whether stop loss orders should be left with brokers, or entered only when prices hit the relevant level. However, unless you are watching the markets all day it is safer to leave stop loss orders in place. Pre-entered orders also prevent you from ignoring an exit and staying in the trade.

Daily housekeeping

Check stops	If not using stop orders left with brokers check to see if any stop levels have been hit on existing positions, and if necessary do closing trades.
Get account value	Get today's account value and calculate your current **trading capital**. Your **annualised cash volatility target** is current capital × **percentage volatility target** (In this chapter we use 15%).
Daily cash volatility target	Daily cash volatility target equals one-sixteenth of **annualised cash volatility target**. (As usual this is the 'square root of time' rule; with around 256 business days in a year you should divide by 16 to go from annual to daily risk.)
Get latest prices	Get charts for all instruments you have positions on and ideally anything you might wish to trade today.
Calculate daily price volatility	Using a one month chart eyeball the **price volatility** of each instrument you own, or might trade today. With FX rate of 1 and relevant **block values** convert this to **instrument value volatility**.
	For *existing* positions if the volatility level you used yesterday is not within 25% of today's level then update your estimate; otherwise stick with yesterday's estimate. For *potential* positions you should always use the most up-to-date estimate.
Recalculate stops	Update stops on existing instruments so they trail new highs (for longs) or new lows (for shorts), and account for the latest value of **price volatility**.
Volatility scalar	This is equal to the **daily cash volatility target** divided by instrument value volatility for each instrument.
Desired subsystem position on an existing bet	Original **forecast** multiplied by **volatility scalar,** divided by 10.
Desired portfolio instrument position on an existing bet	Desired subsystem position multiplied by instrument weight and by instrument diversification multiplier.
	With the maximum of four bets used in the example, and an average of 3 bets, you should use an instrument weight of 25% and a multiplier of 1.33.
Desired target position on an existing bet	**Portfolio instrument position** rounded to nearest whole block.
Issue trades on existing positions	Compare current position to target position. If out by more than 10% then issue adjusting orders (**position inertia**).
Check setups	Check charts and news for potential new bets. If any exist go to instructions for new position opening.

Further intra-day process (for full-time traders only)

Check stop losses	Check to see if any stop losses have been triggered. If not using broker stops then issue closing trades.
Check setups	Check charts and news for potential trade setups. If any exist go to instructions for new position opening.

New position opening

Calculate forecast	Use table 37 (page 211) to calculate your forecast for the instrument.
Is it allowed?	Do you already have the maximum number of bets on? (For the example system this is four.)
	Is the bet on an instrument with an existing position? If so it must not reduce or reverse the position, or put the total absolute forecast across all bets for this instrument over 40.
Calculate instrument value volatility	If not pre-calculated in the morning, using a one month chart eyeball the **price volatility** of each instrument. With FX rate of 1 and relevant **block values** convert this to **instrument value volatility**.
Calculate stop loss	Use X multiplied by the daily **price volatility** in price points to find where to set the stop loss relative to the entry price. In this chapter I've used an X of 4.
Volatility scalar	This morning's **daily cash volatility target** divided by instrument value volatility for the instrument.
Subsystem position	**Forecast** multiplied by **volatility scalar**, divided by 10.
Portfolio instrument position	Subsystem position multiplied by instrument weight (25% in the example) and then multiplied by instrument diversification multiplier (1.33 in the example).
Rounded target position	Portfolio instrument position rounded to nearest block.
Trade	You should now put on the trade and once completed calculate the initial stop loss relative to the entry price. With judicious use of spreadsheets the above steps can be completed in a few moments.

Trading diary

Here is some paper trading I did using the semi-automatic trading system. All the calculations here have been done with a spreadsheet, which is available from my website. Prices and other values are rounded to make the example clearer.

15 October 2014

Typical minimum spread bets are £10 a point on crude, £5 on US S&P 500 equities and £1 on the European Euro Stoxx equity index. These and the price determine the **block value.** Note that the block values are all in British pounds, the same currency as my account, even though the prices are quoted in other currencies, as we're betting in £1 per point. So the FX rates are all 1. Starting **trading capital** is £100,000; annual **volatility target** at 15% is £15,000 and starting daily volatility target is one sixteenth of that, £937.50.

	Crude	S&P 500	Euro Stoxx
Daily volatility target (A)	£937.50	£937.50	£937.50
Price (B)	83	1880	2900
Bet size, per point (C)	£10	£5	£1
FX (D)	1	1	1
Block value (E)	£8.30	£94	£29
C × B ÷ 100			
Price volatility, points (F)	1	20	50
Price volatility, % (G)	1.20	1.06	1.72
F ÷ B			
Instrument currency volatility (H)	£10	£100	£50
G × E			
Instrument value volatility (I)	£10	£100	£50
H × D			
Volatility scalar (J)	93.75	9.375	18.75
A ÷ I			

For my forecasts I'm feeling very bullish on US equities, bullish on crude and bearish on European equities.

	Crude	S&P 500	Euro Stoxx
Forecast (K)	10	15	-10
Subsystem position, blocks (L)	93.75	14.06	-18.75
K × J ÷ 10			
Instrument weight (M)	25%	25%	25%
Instrument diversification multiplier (N)	1.33	1.33	1.33
Portfolio instrument position, blocks (O)	31.25	4.687	-6.2
L × M × N			
Rounded target position, blocks (P = round O)	31	5	-6
Entry price (Q)	83	1880	2900
Stop loss offset (R)	4	80	200
F × X with X = 4			
Stop loss (S)	79	1800	3100
Q plus or minus R			

So I go long crude at 31 × £10 = £310 a point with a $79 stop loss, long S&P 500 at 5 × £5 = £25 per point with an 1800 stop loss, and short Euro Stoxx at 6 × £1 = £6 per point with a 3100 stop loss.

29 October 2014

	Crude	S&P 500	Euro Stoxx
Forecast	10	15	-10
Entry price	83	1880	2900
Current price	81	1980	3020
High (Low) since entry (T)	83	1980	(2900)
Stop loss (S = T plus or minus R)	79	1900	3100
Current position, blocks	31	5	-6
Gain (Loss)	(£620)	£2,500	(£720)
Portfolio instrument position, blocks (O)	31.5	4.73	-6.3
Rounded target position, blocks (P)	32	5	-6

No stops triggered and the trailing stop loss for S&P 500 has been moved up. The net profit in my account is £1,160, so current capital is £101,160 and the daily volatility target is £948. The **price volatility** and **instrument value volatility** hasn't changed on any instrument by more than 25%, so I haven't adjusted these. Current positions are still within 10% of the target; there is no need to buy one more **instrument block** of crude to get to a rounded position of 32.

I feel very strongly about the S&P bet now and I'm going to add to my position. So I will bet a separate +25 forecast, taking me up to the maximum of +40 for all S&P 500 bets. It will also help hedge my Euro Stoxx short, which is doing very badly though hasn't yet hit it's stop. I now have four bets on, two of which are in S&P 500, so I can't place any more.

S&P 500 (2)		S&P 500 (2)	
Daily volatility target (A)	£948	Forecast (K)	25
Price (B)	1980	Subsystem position (L)	23.7
		K × J ÷ 10	
Bet size, per point (C)	£5	Instrument weight (M)	25%
FX (D)	1	Instrument diversification multiplier (N)	1.33
Block value (E)	£99	Portfolio instrument position (O)	7.88
C × B ÷ 100		L × M × N	
Price volatility, points (F)	20	Rounded target position, and trade (P = round O)	8
Price volatility, % (G)	1.01	Entry price (Q)	1980
F ÷ B			
Instrument currency volatility (H)	£100	Stop loss offset (R)	80
		F × X with X = 4	
G × E			
Instrument value volatility (I)	£100	Stop loss (S)	1900
H × D		Q plus or minus R	
Volatility scalar (J)	9.46		
A ÷ I			

I go long another eight £5 a point blocks of S&P 500. Because we're trading at a recent high this has the same stop level as my existing bet.

4 November 2014

Sadly my long in crude is now closed.

	Crude	S&P 500 (1)	S&P 500 (2)	Euro Stoxx
Forecast	10	15	25	-10
Entry price	83	1880	1980	2900
Current price	78.7	2018	2018	3034
High (Low) since entry (T)	83	2018	2018	(2900)
Stop loss (S = T plus or minus R)	79	1938	1938	3100
Current Position, blocks	31	5	8	-6
Gain (Loss)	(£1,333)	£3,450	£1,520	(£804)
Portfolio instrument position, blocks (O)	0.0 (Hit stop loss)	4.81	8.01	-6.43
Rounded target position, blocks (P)	0	5	8	-6

The net gain is £2,833, so trading capital is up to £102,833 and daily volatility target is £964. Again **price volatility** hasn't changed significantly on any instrument. Apart from closing crude there are no adjustment trades needed. I'm tempted to take profits on my only profitable trade, the S&P 500 longs, but I can't because it isn't part of the system!

13 November 2014

I decide, belatedly, to short crude at $75 with a forecast of -10 which corresponds to a position of short 32 blocks with a stop of $79.

21 November 2014

Ouch! Euro Stoxx has also bitten the dust.

	Crude (2)	S&P 500 (1)	S&P 500 (2)	Euro Stoxx
Forecast	-10	15	25	-10
Entry price	75	1880	1980	2900
Current price	76	2063	2063	3130
High (Low) since entry (T)	(75)	2063	2063	(2900)
Stop loss (S = T plus or minus R)	79	1983	1983	3100
Position	-32	5	8	-6

Gain (Loss)	(£320)	£4,575	£3,320	(£1,380)
Portfolio instrument position, blocks (O)	-32.8	4.9	8.2	0.0 Hit stop
Rounded target position, blocks (P)	-33	5	8	0

My accumulated profit is £4,862. If I wasn't trading systematically I'd also be tempted to cut my oil short, as I don't seem to be calling crude very well.

28 November 2014

My crude oil is finally paying off – crude drops $5 in one day! The current **price volatility** of $1 per day for crude now looks too low, so I'm going to double it to $2. I'm up £7,682 in accumulated profits, so the daily **volatility target** is £1,010.

	Crude (2)	S&P 500 (1)	S&P 500 (2)
Daily volatility target (A)	£1,010	£1,010	£1,010
Forecast	-10	15	25
Entry price	75	1880	1980
Current price	68	2067	2067
Price volatility, points (F)	2	20	20
Stop loss offset (R)	8	80	80
F × X with X=4			
High (Low) since entry (T)	(68)	2067	2067
Stop loss (S)	76	1987	1987
T plus or minus R			
Position, blocks	-32	5	8
Gain / Loss £	£2,240	£4,675	£3,480
Instrument value volatility (I)	£20	£100	£100
Volatility scalar (J)	50.5	10.1	10.1
A ÷ I			
Portfolio instrument position, blocks (O)	-16.8	5.05	8.41
Rounded target position, blocks (P)	-17	5	8
Trade	Buy 15	No	No

I have to reduce my crude bet and buy 15 blocks of crude to get to my target position. Primarily because of the change in **price volatility** the current position was more than 10% away from the desired rounded **portfolio instrument position**. Note the stop loss gap in crude is also doubled to 4 × $2 = $8, which is added to the new low of $68 to give a stop level of $76, but my position is virtually halved so I have the same amount of capital at risk on this bet.

Although this looks like taking profits it is not; the system is trading automatically to keep the amount of capital at risk constant. If I hadn't adjusted the stop then the expected holding period of my bet would have shortened. Because I've adjusted the stop I also need to cut the position, or I'll have increased the risk on the trade.

This feels like a good place to stop this diary as I've shown most of the system's most interesting features. Notice how the system went against my natural instincts when I wanted to close trades too early, or let losses run. Hopefully this should show you the benefits of rigorously sticking to a position management **framework** once you've designed it.

Chapter Fourteen. Asset Allocating Investor

THIS CHAPTER IS FOR **ASSET ALLOCATING INVESTORS** WHO MOSTLY don't believe that assets' prices can be forecasted, and use the 'no-rule' trading rule within a systematic **framework** to allocate **trading capital** between different assets.

Chapter overview

Who are you?	Introducing the asset allocating investor.
Using the framework	How you will use the systematic framework for asset allocation.
Weekly process	The weekly process that asset allocators should use.
Trading diary	A diary showing how you could have invested over a few hectic weeks of 2008.

Who are you?

If you're an **asset allocating investor** you believe the best returns can be obtained by investing in a diversified portfolio of assets without trying to predict relative risk adjusted returns. The systematic **framework** in this book will allow you to do that, using the 'no rule' rule I introduced in chapter seven, 'Forecasts'. This rule has a constant forecast of +10, implying you think all assets will have the same **Sharpe ratio**.

To get access to different **asset classes** I assume you'll be using **exchange traded funds (ETFs)**, which are relatively cheap **collective funds**. These will allow you to access a wide range of asset classes whilst only holding positions in a relatively small number of instruments. I am assuming that you're not comfortable, or unable, to use leverage or to do **short selling**.[148] In the example of this chapter I use a notional **trading capital** of €10,000,000, the size of a small pension fund, although everything in this chapter is relevant to those with much larger and smaller portfolios.

Your imaginary pension fund trustees have specified some constraints on the portfolio. You can only invest in bonds and equities, and no more than 40% of your capital can be allocated to bonds. Within the equity portfolio no more than 30% can be put into emerging markets. In bonds you can't put more than 25% into emerging markets and no more than 25% into inflation linked bonds. All constraints are expressed in risk adjusted proportions.

An extension to the basic example will be to adjust **instrument weights** according to some expectations about asset **Sharpe ratios**. These aren't produced by a systematic **trading rule**, but this setup is common in institutional investing when allocations need to be adjusted to reflect in-house or consultants' strategic views.

Using the framework

Instrument choice: diversification, costs, volatility and size

You have quite a large account size, so in theory you could have an allocation to a large number of ETFs without having any difficulties with the minimum size problem I discussed in chapter twelve, 'Speed and Size' (page 200). However to make this example more tractable I am going to limit your portfolio to just ten **instruments**.

In selecting ETFs I've generally gone for those with the lowest total expense ratio (this is an annual holding cost you pay regardless of how often you trade). Additionally, because you can't use leverage there would be issues hitting the desired **percentage volatility target** if your portfolio contains very low **volatility** assets, as you'll see below.

In particular you should be concerned about bond ETFs that could have a **sigma** below 5% per year. To avoid this problem I've generally suggested longer maturity bond funds on which the volatility will be higher. Low risk instruments have other problems of course, which I've discussed earlier in the book, including generally higher **standardised costs**.

I'll assume, as I did in chapter twelve, 'Speed and Size', that you trade in 100 share blocks as this is more economical. Using this size you could implement this strategy with just €100,000 of **trading capital** and no issues of minimum size.[149]

---

148. This doesn't preclude buying short ETFs or those with leverage baked in, although I won't be using them in this example.
149. The smallest position you'd expect to get is seven blocks or 700 shares, which is above the minimum of four blocks I recommended in chapter twelve, 'Speed and Size'. Less trading capital would mean trading in odd lots, with potentially higher costs.

The costs of ETFs will vary depending on their volatility, so we'll conservatively use the standardised cost for the lowest risk ETF (IGIL: global inflation linked bonds) for all instruments. The relevant cost of 0.08 **Sharpe ratio** units was calculated in chapter twelve, 'Speed and Size'.

There are several other considerations when choosing ETFs and you should consult one of the books mentioned in appendix A to understand these. Finally, this selection does not constitute an endorsement for these specific products, and the information I've used to choose them will almost certainly change in the future.

Table 39 shows the final set of instruments. In the example you're constrained in your portfolio allocations by an outside investor. You have limits on how much you can allocate to bonds and equities, and to emerging markets and inflation linked bonds. This is reflected in the asset grouping I've chosen in the table. You need the grouping to allocate the **instrument weights** in your portfolio, which I'll do below using the **handcrafting** method.

TABLE 39: WHAT ETFS ARE YOU TRADING AND HOW SHOULD THEY BE GROUPED?

1. Asset class	2. Region/sub-class	3. ETFs (Ticker)
Bonds	Developed	$ US Bonds (IDTL)
		€ Euro bonds (EXHK)
		£ UK bonds (VGOV)
	Emerging	$ EM government bonds (SEMB)
	Inflation linked	$ Global inflation (IGIL)
Equities	Developed	€ Euro Stoxx 50 (EXW1)
		$ S&P 500 ETF (VUSD)
		£ UK equities (ISF)
		€ Japan equities, € hedged (EXX7)
	Emerging	$ MSCI EM ETF (VDEM)

The table shows the structure of the Asset Allocating Investor example portfolio. The grouping is driven by allocation constraints and the correlations in table 40.

The no-rule trading rule, position sizing and costs

Because you're going to use the 'no-rule' trading rule I introduced in chapter seven your **forecast** will always be +10. To scale positions you'll need to estimate the standard deviation of instrument returns, the **price volatility**. As suggested in chapter ten, 'Position Sizing', you'll estimate this with a moving average of daily returns. However you need to think about what look-back to use for the moving average.

Because ETFs are quite expensive you should follow the advice in chapter twelve, 'Speed and Size' (page 196), and use a relatively slow 20 week (100 business day) look-back to estimate price volatility.[150] In the earlier chapter I calculated that assuming conservative costs for trading ETFs the longer look-back would cost you 0.032 **Sharpe ratio (SR)** units annually, compared to 0.13 SR units for the default look-back of five weeks, which is a considerable saving.

With a 20 week look-back the **turnover** of your trades, in round trips per year, will be 0.4 times a year. If you use the **speed limit** I recommended in chapter twelve, and do not spend more than 0.08 SR each year on costs, then a turnover of 0.4 round trips per year implies any instrument you trade needs to have a maximum standardised cost of 0.08 ÷ 0.4 = 0.20 SR units per year. Fortunately by avoiding low volatility bonds all of your instruments are significantly cheaper than this, with the inflation linked bond ETF IGIL the most expensive with a standardised cost of 0.08 SR units.

Volatility target calculation

I've set your **trading capital** at €10,000,000, but how do you follow the advice in chapter nine to set your **percentage volatility target**? In this example it's most likely to be constrained by your lack of leverage, rather than a tolerance for losses or Sharpe ratio expectations.

Working out the achievable **volatility target** given limited **leverage** is a two step process. The first step involves making an initial guess as to what the target should be. You then work out if that is higher or lower than you could achieve given the amount of leverage you have available. The initial guess is then adjusted.

---

150. Alternatively using an **exponentially weighted moving average** estimate with a look-back of 144 days is equivalent to a 100 day simple **moving average**.

Desired leverage factor	I define the **leverage factor** as the size of your portfolio, divided by the value of your **trading capital**. So the factor would be 50% if you've invested half your trading capital and kept the rest in cash, 100% if you are using all your cash with no leverage, 200% if you've borrowed to invest twice your trading capital, and so on.
	First work out what your desired leverage factor would be. You should set this just below the maximum you can achieve. It should be less than the maximum because if **price volatility** falls you'll want to buy more assets, so it's worth keeping some cash in reserve.
	I recommend a desired leverage factor of 90% for investors who don't use leverage.
Annualised percentage volatility	For each instrument multiply the daily percentage **price volatility** by 16 to get an annualised version. (As usual to annualise a daily volatility you multiply by the 'square root of time', which with around 256 business days in a year is 16.)
	Annualised price volatility for the ETFs I've selected ranges from 6.88% for inflation linked bonds, up to 22.4% for emerging market equities.
Initial guess	Your initial guess of the correct **percentage volatility target** is equal to the lowest annualised price volatility of any instrument. This is 6.88% for the IGIL inflation linked bond.
Work out starting positions	You should now run the usual calculations from chapters ten and eleven: first work out the **volatility scalar**, and then given each instrument has a fixed forecast of 10 you can calculate the **subsystem position**. You also use the **instrument weights** and the **instrument diversification multiplier** that are calculated later in the chapter, to get the rounded **portfolio instrument position** for each instrument.
Value of each position	For each instrument you need to work out the value of the starting position. This is equal to the rounded **portfolio instrument position** in blocks, multiplied by 100 times the **block value** (since each block value represents 1% of the value of one block of the instrument), and the usual exchange rate you use to calculate the **volatility scalar**.
	For example with your initial guess of a 6.88% volatility target the portfolio instrument position for the UK equity ETF is 721 blocks, each of 100 shares. The value is: position 721 multiplied by block value £7.00, by 100, and the exchange rate (GBP/EUR) 1.2 is €605,640.
Total value	You add up the value of all your initial positions. In this case it comes in at around €8,262,000.
Calculate realised leverage factor	Your realised leverage will be the total value of your positions, divided by the **trading capital**. Here it's €8,262,00 divided by €10,000,000 equals 0.826, or 82.6%. This is less than one, indicating you aren't using any leverage and have some excess cash.

Adjust percentage volatility target for desired leverage	You can now adjust your initial guess of percentage volatility target according to whether your guess is overshooting or undershooting the leverage that you want to achieve.
	In this case you can increase your volatility target. Your desired leverage was 90%, but with the initial guess you got 82.6%. The initial volatility target can be multiplied by 90% ÷ 82.6% = 1.089
	So the achievable percentage volatility target is equal to the initial guess 6.88%, multiplied by 1.089, equals 7.5%.

This implies your **annualised cash volatility target** should be 7.5% multiplied by your **trading capital**, or €750,000. This shouldn't present problems to anybody's risk appetite; and if you assume the volatility target is at the correct **Half-Kelly** level then the required **Sharpe ratio (SR)** of 0.15 should be easily achievable.

It also implies you should have very modest expectations for account growth. For asset allocating investors I'd conservatively expect a maximum after cost SR of 0.4 (see page 46) which equates to returns of just 0.4 × 7.5% = 3.0% a year, plus the risk free interest rate (around 0.5% in Europe as I write this), which you should include as you're not using derivatives. To improve this you'd either have to use leverage, or reduce diversification and Sharpe ratio by lowering the **instrument weight on** low volatility instruments like bonds (or exclude them entirely).[151]

How much would you be paying in costs? I worked out above that you should expect to have a **turnover** of 0.4 round trips per year and **standardised costs** of 0.08 SR, implying an expected cost of 0.4 × 0.08 = 0.032 SR annually. With 7.5% annualised volatility that equates to a modest annual performance drag of 0.032 × 7.5% = 0.24%. In practice you should pay less since I used the most expensive instrument to work out the standardised cost.

On top of this would be the annual holding costs for ETFs – currently these range from about 0.05% for the cheapest S&P 500 tracker up to 0.55% for emerging market equities.

Portfolios: The basics

As I discussed in chapter eleven, a trading system consists of a portfolio of **trading subsystems**, one per instrument. You need to determine the **instrument weights** to allocate across this portfolio. Because you're using a **static** trading rule determining these weights is a key decision.

I introduced two methods for portfolio allocation in chapter four. **Bootstrapping** would be an excellent way of doing this, but I'll stick to the simpler **handcrafting** method in this example, using rule of thumb rather than **back-tested correlations**.

---

151. You can also use ETFs with internal leverage to help solve this problem, although you should first understand the complexities of their daily regearing.

Remember from chapter eleven that as asset allocating investors with a static, rather than **dynamic**, trading strategy you can use the unadjusted correlation of instrument returns as a proxy for **trading subsystem** returns. Table 40 shows some indicative correlations, based mainly on the tables of indicative asset return correlations in appendix C, without any adjustment.

As I discussed at the beginning of the chapter, you also have some constraints on your allocations. I'll explain in the optimisation where these affect your weights.

TABLE 40: WHAT ARE THE CORRELATIONS OF THE ETF PORTFOLIO?

	UK Bo.	US Bo.	EU Bo.	EM Bo.	Inf Bo.	EU Eq.	US Eq.	UK Eq.	JP Eq.	EM Eq.
UK bond	1									
US bond	0.75	1								
EU bond	0.75	0.75	1							
EM bond	0.35	0.35	0.35	1						
Infl. bond	0.3	0.3	0.3	0.25	1					
Euro Eq.	0.1	0.1	0.1	0.1	0.1	1				
US equity	0.1	0.1	0.1	0.1	0.1	0.75	1			
UK equity	0.1	0.1	0.1	0.1	0.1	0.75	0.75	1		
JP equity	0.1	0.1	0.1	0.1	0.1	0.75	0.75	0.75	1	
EM equity	0.1	0.1	0.1	0.1	0.1	0.5	0.5	0.5	0.5	1

This table shows the correlation matrix of instrument returns for the asset allocating example. Figures from tables 50 to 54, and my own estimates. We don't need to adjust instrument returns when calculating instrument weights, since we're trading a static portfolio.

Here is how I handcrafted the portfolio weights. Row numbers given refer to table 8 (page 79).

First level grouping **Within region/sub class**	Developed bonds: 33.3% to each of US, UK, Europe. Row 3.
	Developed equities: 25% to each of US, UK, Europe, Japan. Row 3.
	All other groups have a single asset, with 100% allocation. Row 1.
Second level grouping **Within asset class**	Bonds: 25% to emerging markets (constrained) and 25% to inflation linked (constrained); leaves 50% left over for developed markets.
	Equities: 30% to emerging markets (constrained), leaves 70% to developed markets.
Top level grouping **Across asset classes**	40% in bonds (constrained), leaves 60% in equities.

You can see the final weights in table 41. Using these weights, the correlations and the formula on page 297, I get an **instrument diversification multiplier** of 1.61.

TABLE 41: WHAT INSTRUMENT WEIGHTS SHOULD YOU USE FOR THE ETF PORTFOLIO?

	Within region/sub class	Within asset class	Across asset classes	Final weight
US bonds	33.3%	50%	**40%**	6.67%
Euro bonds	33.3%	50%	**40%**	6.67%
UK bonds	33.3%	50%	**40%**	6.67%
EM bonds	100%	**25%**	**40%**	10%
Inflation bonds	100%	**25%**	**40%**	10%
Euro Stoxx 50	25%	70%	60%	10.5%
S&P 500	25%	70%	60%	10.5%
UK equities	25%	70%	60%	10.5%
Japan equities	25%	70%	60%	10.5%
EM equities	100%	**30%**	60%	18%

The table shows the handcrafted instrument weights for the asset allocating investor. Final weights are the product of group weights at each stage. Weights in bold are constrained by the institutional mandate. Borders show groups.

Portfolios: Using predictions of performance

Sometimes you might want to incorporate views about asset returns into investment portfolios. In an institutional setting you'll often have internal or external opinions on asset returns like "The Euro Stoxx will hit 3,000 in 12 months time." To use these figures, they first need to be translated into annualised **Sharpe ratios (SR)** using your current estimate of **price volatility**. A 3,000 Euro Stoxx target is about an 8% rise from the price as I write this. With annualised price volatility of 16% (derived from the daily value of 1%), this equates to an annualised Sharpe ratio of 8% ÷ 16% = 0.50.

You could do this within the framework by using discretionary forecasts, which would make this example look more like the **semi-automatic trader** of the previous chapter. However, you'd end up trading a lot more, which doesn't fit well with your objectives as a long run asset allocating investor. Instead I would recommend changing the handcrafted **instrument weights** within the portfolio using the SR weight adjustments from table 12 in chapter four (page 86), according to any opinions you have about performance.

You should use column B 'Without certainty' in the table, which reflects the difficulty in guessing how assets will perform. As an example, if the average SR across your instruments was 0.20, and you expected the Euro Stoxx SR to be 0.5, then with an expected 0.3 SR outperformance you'd increase your Euro Stoxx instrument weight by 17%.

Don't forget to renormalise the weights to add up to 100% after adjustment. Please note that you don't need to change your **instrument diversification multiplier** when adjusting instrument weights, as this is designed to get your long run risk target correct. Finally, these adjustments should ideally be small and infrequent, since they are a source of additional trading and so will increase costs.

Weekly process

I've suggested a weekly rebalancing process here which given the low **volatility target**, lack of leverage and slow **turnover** should be fine. In practice rebalancing could be done more frequently for large funds or in times of market stress, others may choose to rebalance quarterly after meetings of investment committees, and amateur investors might be happy with annual rebalancing at the end of each tax year.

Detailed calculations are shown in the trading diary section which follows.

Get account value	Get today's account value and work out **current capital**.
Cash volatility target	Your **annualised cash volatility target** equals the **percentage volatility target** × current capital. In this example we're using a 7.5% percentage volatility target.
	Divide the annualised target by 16 for **daily cash volatility target**.
Get latest prices	Get prices for all instruments.
Get latest FX rates	Update FX rates. For this example you only need GBP/EUR and USD/EUR.
Calculate instrument value volatility	Using the recommended 20 week moving average look-back work out the **price volatility** of each instrument. With the FX rates and **block value** convert this to **instrument value volatility**.
Instrument subsystem position	Because you have a constant forecast of +10 this is equal to the **volatility scalar: daily cash volatility target** divided by **instrument value volatility**.
Optional: Get predictions for performance	Translate predictions into annualised **Sharpe ratios** using your estimate of price volatility.
Optional: Adjust instrument weights	Using Sharpe ratio predictions table 12 (page 86), column B 'Without certainty'.

Portfolio instrument position	**Subsystem position** multiplied by **instrument weight** (from table 41 for the example), with Sharpe ratio adjustments if required, and by **instrument diversification multiplier** (1.61 in the example).
Rounded target position	**Portfolio instrument position** rounded to nearest instrument block (in the example, 100 shares).
Issue trades	Compare current position to final desired position; if out by more than 10% then trade (**position inertia**).

Trading diary

This is a hypothetical and contrived example which I've constructed to show the main features of a system that could have been trading during the great crash of 2008.[152] Since many of the ETFs being traded did not exist at the time I am using today's prices, although the subsequent price changes and volatility levels are in line with what you would have seen in the past. As they are not a key part of the example I'm also using arbitrary fixed exchange rates. Spreadsheets detailing all the calculations are available on the website for this book, www.systematictrading.org.

1 July 2008

You begin with trading capital of €10,000,000, which with your 7.5% volatility target gives a daily volatility target of one sixteenth of €750,000, or €46,875. You haven't yet got any discretionary forecasts for asset prices, so you can keep the default unadjusted instrument weights.

BOND CALCULATIONS PART ONE

	$ US bonds	€ Euro bonds	£ UK bonds	$ EM bonds	$ Inflation bonds
Daily volatility target (A)	€46,875	€46,875	€46,875	€46,875	€46,875
Price (B)	$5	€150	£22	$75	$145
Number of shares per block (C)	100	100	100	100	100
FX (D)	0.9	1	1.2	0.9	0.9

---

152. Although I do run a similar portfolio to this I have only done so since 2011. Most of the time very little happens in a portfolio like this, so I've decided to set this example in a more interesting historical period.

Block value (E) C × B ÷ 100	$5	€150	£22	$75	$145
Price volatility, % (G)*	0.90	0.60	0.55	0.70	0.43
Instrument currency volatility (H) G × E	$4.5	€90	£12.1	$52.5	$62.35
Instrument value volatility (I) H × D	€4.05	€90.00	€14.52	€47.25	€56.12
Volatility scalar (J) A ÷ I	11,574	521	3228	992	835

* I've kept the row identifiers the same in all three example chapters so that comparisons can easily be made. Row F has been omitted as you don't require volatility in points per day here.

BOND CALCULATIONS PART TWO

	$ US bonds	€ Euro bonds	£ UK bonds	$ EM bonds	$ Inflation bonds
Forecast (K)	+10	+10	+10	+10	+10
Subsystem position, blocks (L) K × J ÷ 10	11574	521	3228	992	835
Instrument weight (M)	6.67%	6.67%	6.67%	10.00%	10.00%
Instrument Diversification Multiplier (N)	1.61	1.61	1.61	1.61	1.61
Portfolio instrument position, blocks (O) L × M × N	1242.3	55.9	346.5	159.7	134.5
Rounded target position, blocks (P = round O)	1242	56	347	160	135

So with 100 share blocks you buy 1242 × 100 = 124,200 shares of the US bond ETF and so on.

EQUITY CALCULATIONS PART ONE

	€ Euro equities	$ US equities	£ UK equities	€ Japan equities	$ EM equities
Daily volatility target (A)	€46,875	€46,875	€46,875	€46,875	€46,875
Price (B)	€37	$40	£7	€15	$54
Number of shares per block (C)	100	100	100	100	100
FX (D)	1	0.9	1.2	1	0.9
Block value (E) C × B ÷ 100	€37	$40	£7	€15	$54
Price volatility, % (G)	1.10	1.10	1.20	1.00	1.40
Instrument currency volatility (H) G × E	€40.7	$44	£8.4	€15	$75.6
Instrument value volatility (I) H × D	€40.70	€39.60	€10.08	€15.00	€68.04
Volatility scalar (J) A ÷ I	1152	1184	4650	3125	689

EQUITY CALCULATIONS PART TWO

	€ Euro equities	$ US equities	£ UK equities	? Japan equities	$ EM equities
Forecast (K)	+10	+10	+10	+10	+10
Subsystem position, blocks (L) K × J ÷ 10	1152	1184	4650	3125	689
Instrument weight (M)	10.50%	10.50%	10.50%	10.50%	18.00%
Instrument Diversification Multiplier (N)	1.61	1.61	1.61	1.61	1.61
Portfolio instrument position, blocks (O) L × M × N	194.7	200.1	786.1	528.3	199.7
Rounded target position, and trade (P = round O)	195	200	786	528	200

An interesting statistic is that 57% of the cash value of this portfolio is in bonds, despite them accounting for only 40% of the **instrument weight**. You need more in bonds because they are lower risk; this reflects the **risk parity** nature of the portfolio.

1 October 2008

The world is getting riskier but despite the Lehman's bankruptcy a couple of weeks ago the portfolio hasn't yet seen significant losses so your current capital is almost unchanged at €9,705,000. Your economic strategists feel the fear is overblown and are (a) insanely bullish on equities with an expected **Sharpe ratio (SR)** of 0.6 and (b) expecting all bonds to make exactly nothing; an SR of zero.

Using these predictions you can use table 12 (page 86), column B 'Without certainty', to calculate which Sharpe ratio adjustments to make. Since there is no performance differential within **handcrafted** groups we can do the adjustments in one go, treating the entire portfolio as a single group. The simple average of portfolio performance is the average of 0 (for bonds) and 0.6 (for equities), or an SR of 0.3.

BOND INSTRUMENT WEIGHT ADJUSTMENTS

	US bonds	Euro bonds	UK bonds	EM bonds	Inflation bonds
Instrument weight	6.67%	6.67%	6.67%	10.00%	10.00%
Expected Sharpe ratio	0.0	0.0	0.0	0.0	0.0
Average Sharpe ratio	0.3	0.3	0.3	0.3	0.3
Outperformance	-0.3	-0.3	-0.3	-0.3	-0.3
Sharpe ratio adjustment*	0.83	0.83	0.83	0.83	0.83
Renormalised instrument weight**	5.35%	5.35%	5.35%	8.03%	8.03%

* From table 12 (page 86) column B.
** After adjustment, weights add up to 103.4%. So we need to divide all adjusted weights by 1.034 to ensure they sum to 100%.

EQUITY INSTRUMENT WEIGHT ADJUSTMENTS

	Euro equities	US equities	UK equities	Japan equities	EM equities
Instrument weight	10.50%	10.50%	10.50%	10.50%	18.00%
Expected Sharpe ratio	0.6	0.6	0.6	0.6	0.6
Average Sharpe ratio	0.3	0.3	0.3	0.3	0.3
Outperformance	0.3	0.3	0.3	0.3	0.3

Sharpe ratio adjustment	1.17	1.17	1.17	1.17	1.17
Renormalised instrument weight	11.88%	11.88%	11.88%	11.88%	20.37%

BOND CALCULATIONS PART ONE

	$ US bonds	€ Euro bonds	£ UK bonds	$ EM bonds	$ Inflation bonds
Daily volatility target (A)	€45,492	€45,492	€45,492	€45,492	€45,492
Price (B)	$5.10	€160	£22.15	$72	$140
Number of shares per block (C)	100	100	100	100	100
FX (D)	0.9	1	1.2	0.9	0.9
Block value (E) C × B ÷ 100	$5.10	€160	£22.15	$72	$140
Price volatility, % (G)*	1.00	0.65	0.55	1.00	0.46
Instrument currency volatility (H) G × E	$5.1	€104	£12.1825	$72	$64.4
Instrument value volatility (I) H × D	€4.59	€104.00	€14.62	€64.80	€57.96
Volatility scalar (J) A ÷ I	9911	437	3112	702	785

* I've kept the row identifiers the same in all three example chapters so that comparisons can easily be made. Row F has been omitted as you don't require volatility in points per day here.

BOND CALCULATIONS PART TWO

	$ US bonds	€ Euro bonds	£ UK bonds	$ EM bonds	$ Inflation bonds
Forecast (K)	+10	+10	+10	+10	+10
Subsystem position, blocks (L) K × J ÷ 10	9911	437	3112	702	785
Instrument weight (M)	5.35%	5.35%	5.35%	8.03%	8.03%

Instrument Diversification Multiplier (N)	1.61	1.61	1.61	1.61	1.61
Portfolio instrument position, blocks (O)	853.9	37.7	268.1	90.7	101.4
L × M × N					
Rounded target position, blocks (P = round O)	854	38	268	91	101
Current position, blocks	1242	56	347	160	134
Trade, blocks	Sell 388	Sell 18	Sell 79	Sell 69	Sell 33

EQUITY CALCULATIONS PART ONE

	€ Euro equities	$ US equities	£ UK equities	¥ Japan equities	$ EM equities
Daily volatility target (A)	€45,492	€45,492	€45,492	€45,492	€45,492
Price (B)	€35	$37	£6.5	€14	$50
Number of shares per block (C)	100	100	100	100	100
FX (D)	1	0.9	1.2	1	0.9
Block value (E)	€35	$37	£6.5	€14	$50
C × B ÷ 100					
Price volatility, % (G)	1.20	1.30	1.30	1.10	1.60
Instrument currency volatility (H)	€42	$48.1	£8.45	€15.4	$80
G × E					
Instrument value volatility	€42	€43.29	€10.14	€15.4	€72
H × D					
Volatility scalar (J)	1083	1051	4486	2954	632
A ÷ I					

EQUITY CALCULATIONS PART TWO

	€ Euro equities	$ US equities	£ UK equities	¥ Japan equities	$ EM equities
Forecast (K)	+10	+10	+10	+10	+10
Subsystem position, blocks (L)	1083	1051	4486	2954	632
K × J ÷ 10					
Instrument weight (M)	11.88%	11.88%	11.88%	11.88%	20.37%
Instrument Diversification Multiplier (N)	1.61	1.61	1.61	1.61	1.61
Portfolio instrument position, blocks (O)	207.2	201.0	858.2	565.1	207.2
L × M × N					
Rounded target position, blocks (P = round O)	207	201	858	565	207
Current position, blocks	195	200	786	528	200
Trade, blocks	No	No	No	No	No

You wouldn't trade any equity markets as all positions are within 10% of their desired value. This is because the increase in equity price volatility, which would otherwise reduce positions, has mostly been compensated for by the increase in instrument weights.

10 October 2008

The equity markets fell off a cliff last week so you've come in on Saturday to assess the damage. Fortunately your portfolio is diversified enough that your losses are limited, even with the stupid equity overweight. You increased your equity allocation only modestly, from 60% to 68%, which reflects the uncertainty involved in forecasting returns. This means you just tilted the portfolio towards equities, rather than completely reallocating.

But there has been some pain – your current capital is now down to €9,126,500. Even with your long look-back, **price volatility** has exploded, especially in equities. The economic strategists have belatedly decided that bonds are now the way to go and they have shifted to underweight in all equities. Your previous **Sharpe ratio** adjustments are now inverted.

BOND INSTRUMENT WEIGHT ADJUSTMENTS

	US bonds	Euro bonds	UK bonds	EM bonds	Inflation bonds
Instrument weight	6.67%	6.67%	6.67%	10.00%	10.00%
Expected Sharpe ratio	0.6	0.6	0.6	0.6	0.6
Average Sharpe ratio	0.3	0.3	0.3	0.3	0.3
Outperformance	0.3	0.3	0.3	0.3	0.3
Sharpe ratio adjustment*	1.17	1.17	1.17	1.17	1.17
Renormalised instrument weight**	8.07%	8.07%	8.07%	12.11%	12.11%

* From table 12 (page 86) column B.
** After adjustment weights add up to 96.6%. So you need to divide all adjusted weights by 0.966 to ensure they sum to 100%.

EQUITY INSTRUMENT WEIGHT ADJUSTMENTS

	Euro equities	US equities	UK equities	Japan equities	EM equities
Instrument weight	10.5%	10.5%	10.5%	10.5%	18%
Expected Sharpe ratio	0.0	0.0	0.0	0.0	0.0
Average Sharpe ratio	0.3	0.3	0.3	0.3	0.3
Outperformance	-0.3	-0.3	-0.3	-0.3	-0.3
Sharpe ratio adjustment	0.83	0.83	0.83	0.83	0.83
Renormalised instrument weight	9.02%	9.02%	9.02%	9.02%	15.47%

BOND CALCULATIONS PART ONE

	$ US bonds	€ Euro bonds	£ UK bonds	$ EM bonds	$ Inflation bonds
Daily volatility target (A)	€42,780.47	€42,780.47	€42,780.47	€42,780.47	€42,780.47
Price (B)	£5.8	€170	£23.8	$70	$135
Number of shares per block (C)	100	100	100	100	100

FX (D)	0.9	1	1.2	0.9	0.9
Block value (E)	$5.8	€170	£23.8	$70	$135
C × B ÷ 100					
Price volatility, % (G)*	1%	0.65%	0.6%	1.1%	0.6%
Instrument currency volatility (H)	$5.8	€110.5	£14.28	$77	$81
G × E					
Instrument value volatility (I)	€5.22	€110.5	€17.14	€69.3	€72.9
H × D					
Volatility scalar (J)	8195	387	2497	617	587
A ÷ I					

* I've kept the row identifiers the same in all three example chapters so that comparisons can easily be made. Row F has been omitted as you don't require volatility in points per day here.

BOND CALCULATIONS PART TWO

	$ US bonds	€ Euro bonds	£ UK bonds	$ EM bonds	$ Inflation bonds
Forecast (K)	+10	+10	+10	+10	+10
Subsystem position, blocks (L)	8195	387	2497	617	587
K × J ÷ 10					
Instrument weight (M)	8.07%	8.07%	8.07%	12.11%	12.11%
Instrument Diversification Multiplier (N)	1.61	1.61	1.61	1.61	1.61
Portfolio instrument position, blocks (O)	1065.4	50.3	324.5	120.4	114.4
L × M × N					
Rounded target position, blocks (P = round O)	1065	50	325	120	114
Current position, blocks	854	38	268	91	101
Trade, blocks	Buy 211	Buy 12	Buy 57	Buy 29	Buy 13

EQUITY CALCULATIONS PART ONE

	€ Euro equities	$ US equities	£ UK equities	Japan equities	$ EM equities
Daily volatility target (A)	€42,780.47	€42,780.47	€42,780.47	€42,780.47	€42,780.47
Price (B)	€27	$30	£5	€13	$38
Number of shares per block (C)	100	100	100	100	100
FX (D)	1	0.9	1.2	1	0.9
Block value (E) $C \times B \div 100$	€27	$30	£5	€13	$38
Price volatility, % (G)	1.90	2.00	2.00	1.70	2.50
Instrument currency volatility (H) $G \times E$	€51.3	$60	£10	€22.1	$95
Instrument value volatility (I) $H \times D$	€51.3	€54	€12	€22.1	€85.5
Volatility scalar (J) $A \div I$	834	792	3565	1936	500

EQUITY CALCULATIONS PART TWO

	€ Euro equities	$ US equities	£ UK equities	Japan equities	$ EM equities
Forecast (K)	+10	+10	+10	+10	+10
Subsystem position, blocks (L) $K \times J \div 10$	834	792	3565	1936	500
Instrument weight (M)	9.02%	9.02%	9.02%	9.02%	15.47%
Instrument Diversification Multiplier (N)	1.61	1.61	1.61	1.61	1.61
Portfolio instrument position, blocks (O) $L \times M \times N$	121.1	115.1	517.8	281.2	124.6
Rounded target position, blocks (P = round O)	121	115	518	281	125
Current position, blocks	195	200	786	528	200
Trade, blocks	Sell 74	Sell 85	Sell 268	Sell 247	Sell 75

Notice how most of the equity selling is caused by increases in **price volatility**, rather than the changes to **instrument weights**. That draws this example to an end as you've now seen most of the significant trading action, although it's tempting to continue and let the bond overweight come good.

Chapter Fifteen. Staunch Systems Trader

THE LAST TWO CHAPTERS HAVE BEEN FOR THOSE WHO DON'T really believe that simple **trading rules** work, but are happy to use the systematic **framework**. However this chapter is for the **staunch systems trader** who wants to use both the framework and multiple systematic **trading rules** for predicting asset prices.

Chapter overview

Who are you?	Introducing the staunch systems trader.
Using the framework	How you will use the systematic trading rules and framework.
Daily process	The daily process you need to follow to run your system.
Trading diary	A diary showing how the example system traded the market in late 2014.

Who are you?

The specific example in this chapter will cover futures trading, but in principle any leveraged **instruments** could be operated in a similar way. Trading futures is a complex task and I'm not covering a lot of the mechanics around practicalities like getting data, execution and optimal rolling.[153] I will assume that you have $250,000 of initial **trading capital**. The example will focus on building a system suitable for part-time traders which trades daily and for which data can be obtained for free.

---

153. Appendix A provides pointers to where you can find further help and advice, including the website for this book: www.systematictrading.org

Using the framework

Instrument choice: Size, diversification and costs

Unless you have many millions of dollars, choosing which futures to trade is mostly a balance between getting reasonable diversification and running into the issues with large minimum **instrument block** sizes discussed in chapter twelve, 'Speed and Size'. These issues are common with an account of this size given that you can't trade less than one futures contract, and many contracts are quite large.[154] You should also avoid **instruments** that are very expensive to trade and as always those with low **volatility**.

In my opinion the set shown in table 42 is a good selection for this account size.[155] It is highly diversified since it contains one future from each major **asset class**.[156] You wouldn't have any maximum positions of less than the four contracts threshold suggested in chapter twelve, although Euro Stoxx is close. It might seem strange that a US investor would prefer the European stock market (Euro Stoxx) and **equity volatility index** (V2TX), but these are the only liquid futures in these categories where you can avoid maximum positions that are too small.

TABLE 42: WHAT INSTRUMENTS SHOULD YOU USE FOR THE STAUNCH SYSTEMS TRADER EXAMPLE?

	Standard cost SR	Currency	Maximum position
Eurodollar	0.008	USD	8
US 5 year note	0.004	USD	5
Euro Stoxx	0.002	EUR	4
V2TX	0.009	EUR	11
MXP/USD	0.007	USD	15
Corn	0.005	USD	9

The table shows my selected instruments (rows), standardised costs (using the method in chapter twelve), traded currency and maximum possible positions (calculated with a forecast of +20 using the formula on page 201).

---

154. This issue was discussed in chapter twelve from 'Trading with relatively little capital' on page 200 onwards.

155. These instruments also have the advantage that long histories of daily prices can be obtained for free from the sources listed in appendix A, and live data is relatively cheap through most brokers.

156. In an ideal world I'd add a metal like gold, and an energy future like WTI Crude. However all the contracts in these **asset classes** have relatively large minimum sizes.

As well as the maximum expected position, the **volatility standardised** costs and currency for each future are also shown in table 42.[157] All of these instruments have costs that are less than the maximum of 0.01 Sharpe ratio units which I recommended for staunch systems traders in chapter twelve, 'Speed and Size'.

In chapter six, 'Instruments', I said you should also consider **skew** and volatility when choosing instruments. With a short position the European equity volatility index future (V2TX) is a markedly negative skew instrument (as discussed in the skew concept box, page 32), but as you'll see later you'll only allocate 10% of your portfolio to it. None of the instruments have especially low volatility as I write this chapter, as long as you avoid trading the closest Eurodollar delivery months (where volatility is very low due to zero interest rate policies). For this reason I recommend trading Eurodollar around three years out; much beyond that and the liquidity starts to drop off.

Selecting trading rules

You will use both of the trading rules introduced in chapter six: the **trend following EWMAC** rule and the **carry** rule. Your trend following rules and measures of **price volatility** will be based on a series of stitched futures prices using the 'Panama method'.[158] For carry, as appendix B explains, the optimal calculation requires that you're not trading the nearest contract, but one further in the future. This is achievable for volatility (V2TX), Eurodollar and corn.[159] However for the bond, equity and FX future you'll need to trade the nearest futures contract, as the subsequent deliveries aren't liquid enough.

In table 43 I've shown the **back-tested turnover** in round trips per year for the trading rule variations you'll be using. You can also see the maximum standardised cost at which you could use each rule, if you stick to my recommended **speed limit** from chapter twelve of spending no more than 0.13 **Sharpe ratio (SR)** units on costs each year. Only the very cheapest futures instruments can use the fastest EWMAC variations.

I strongly recommend that you use at least three of the EWMAC variations for trend following, as there is insufficient evidence to say that one or two of these variations would

---

157. Costs are based on **average price volatility** and bid-offer spreads during 2014. Maximum position depends on the current level of price volatility and is correct as of December 2014.

158. Very briefly, the Panama method involves first taking the price series of the currently traded future. You then take the price series of the future you traded before the last roll. The prices of the previous future are shifted up or down in parallel, until the adjusted price of the previous future aligns with the actual price of the current future on the day when you would have rolled from one contract to the next. You then repeat this for all the futures contracts you could have traded in the past. Other methods of stitching are also available, and as long as they do not leave a discontinuous jump in the price when a roll occurs, they will give roughly similar results. There's much more detail about stitching methods available on my blog, which can be accessed from the book's website (www.systematictrading.org).

159. I trade three years out in Eurodollar. For V2X I trade the second contract. For corn I always trade the December contract to avoid different seasonal effects influencing the price, and I usually roll to the following year by summer. There's a much longer discussion about optimal rolling available on my blog.

be better than the others. So the slowest portfolio you can construct will contain the carry rule and the three slower variations of EWMAC (fast look-backs of 16, 32 and 64).

TABLE 43: CAN YOU USE ALL OF THE TRADING RULE VARIATIONS FOR EVERY INSTRUMENT? ONLY CHEAP INSTRUMENTS CAN TRADE VERY QUICK RULES

	Raw turnover	Maximum standardised cost
EWMAC 2,8	54	0.0024
EWMAC 4,16	28	0.0046
EWMAC 8,32	16	0.0081
EWMAC 16,64	11	0.012
EWMAC 32,128	8.5	0.015
EWMAC 64,256	7.5	0.017
Carry	10	0.013

The table shows for each trading rule variation (rows) the turnover in round trips per year, and the maximum possible standardised cost to use the trading rule variation (assuming you stick to my recommended limit of spending no more than 0.13 Sharpe ratio units on costs).

Looking back at table 42 you could use the three slowest EWMAC variations for all of your instruments without having issues with costs. But EWMAC 2,8 would be limited to Euro Stoxx, EWMAC 4,16 to Euro Stoxx and the US 5 year note, and EWMAC 8,32 is too quick for the European volatility future (V2TX).

For simplicity in this example chapter let's drop the fast variations and use the three slowest (EWMAC 16, 32 and 64), all of which are acceptable even with the most expensive instrument. Along with carry that makes a total of four trading rule variations.[160]

Forecast weights and trading speed

Now you need to blend your trading rule **forecasts** into a **combined forecast**, as in chapter eight. I'll show you how to determine the necessary **forecast weights** using the **handcrafting** method that I explained in chapter four, although you could also use the **bootstrapping** procedure. To use the handcrafting method I'll need **correlations** and some way of grouping the trading rule variations. Table 44 shows I first group variations

---

160. Of course it would be equally valid to have different variations for the cheaper instruments, and this is the approach I use myself.

within the same rule and then *across* rules. I'll use rule of thumb correlations as shown in table 45, which have come from appendix B.

TABLE 44: GROUPING FOR TRADING RULE VARIATIONS

Rule and variation	1st level	2nd level
EWMAC 16,64		
EWMAC 32,128	EWMAC	
EWMAC 64,256		Across rules
Carry	Carry rule	

In line with the advice in chapter twelve, 'Speed and Size', I will assume all variations have the same pre-cost **Sharpe ratio (SR)**, since consistent evidence of statistical outperformance by one rule or another is difficult to find. This implies that instruments with different costs, and so varying after-cost SR, would have different forecast weights once I'd adjusted the original handcrafted weights.

But for brevity I've calculated a single set of weights using the cost of the most expensive instrument – V2TX futures. The turnover in round trips per year of each trading rule and the resulting annual cost in SR units using the V2X **standardised cost** of 0.009 SR units is shown in table 45. Since the largest difference in costs is only 0.031 SR units, the resulting SR adjustments will be extremely small and I haven't made any Sharpe ratio adjustments in this example.

TABLE 45: WHAT IS THE EXPECTED ANNUAL COST FOR EACH TRADING RULE?

	Turnover	Annual cost; SR units	Forecast weight
EWMAC 16,64	11	0.099	21%
EWMAC 32,128	8.5	0.077	8%
EWMAC 64,256	7.5	0.068	21%
Carry	10	0.09	50%

The table shows for each trading rule variation (rows) the turnover in round trips per year, and resulting annual costs in Sharpe ratio (SR) units for most expensive instrument V2TX (European volatility futures) with standardised cost of 0.009 SR per round trip. It also shows the handcrafted forecast weights.

This set of rules is identical to those I looked at in chapter eight, in the section from page 126 onwards. This means you can use the forecast weights and **forecast diversification multiplier** that I'd already worked out in that earlier chapter. To save you referring back I've repeated the weights in table 45 and the multiplier is 1.31. Notice again that the EWMAC 32 variation has a lower weight because it is more highly correlated with the 16 and 64 variations, than they are with each other.

Volatility target calculation

With predetermined **trading capital** of $250,000 you need to determine how much of that you are willing to put at risk; your **percentage volatility target**. As I said in chapter nine, 'Volatility targeting', this is a matter of determining your achievable performance, inferring from that a safe level of risk to take, and checking you are comfortable with the likely levels of losses.

You'll be running a reasonably diversified system, with two trading rules drawn from different styles, and six instruments from different **asset classes**. When I **back-tested** this system using **out of sample bootstrapping** to ensure a conservative result, I got a **Sharpe ratio (SR)** after costs of 0.53. Using table 14 (page 90) suggests that about 75% of this is achievable, for an SR of 0.40.

There is a mixture of positive and negative skew trading rules and 90% of the portfolio is in relatively benign assets, with only 10% in the potentially negative skew V2TX volatility future. I'm happy to assume this is a slightly positive zero skew system, which the back-test confirms. From the achievable Sharpe ratio 0.4 row, column A, of table 25 (page 147), you would get a 20% volatility target and hence an **annualised cash volatility target** of $250,000 × 0.20 = $50,000.

This is slightly lower than the level I run my own system at; I assume you're also comfortable with the potential pain of a 20% target, and with leveraged futures achieving the risk won't be an issue. With this relatively high volatility target you'll be checking your account value, and adjusting your risk, every day.

Position sizing and measuring price volatility

Now you need to come up with a method for position sizing, which means calculating the **instrument value volatility**. This in turn depends on the value of each **instrument block** in USD (to match your hypothetical account), for which you need exchange rates, an estimate of **price volatility** and the **block value**, all of which were discussed in chapter ten, 'Position sizing'.

Currencies for each instrument are shown in table 42 and you'll update FX rates daily. You will be using a moving average of recent daily returns to find the **price volatility** of each **instrument**. However we need to determine what look-back to use for your moving averages.

As I discussed in chapter twelve, 'Speed and Size', we need to compare the cost of the default look-back of five weeks versus a slower look-back. I'll do this conservatively using the costs of your most expensive instrument, the European volatility index future V2TX. Let's refer back to table 36 (page 197) in chapter twelve. First of all I need to find the turnover of your trading rules. With your portfolio of the **carry** rule and three EWMAC variations, and the relevant **forecast weights** from table 45, the weighted average turnover comes in at around 9.57 round trips per year.[161]

Once I've multiplied this by the **forecast diversification multiplier** (1.31) the turnover of your **combined forecast** will be 9.57 × 1.31 = 12.5. From the relevant row in table 36, the final turnover will be 12.6 using the recommended default look-back of five weeks (or equivalent for **exponentially weighted moving average**), or 11.7 with a look-back of 20 weeks.

Using the most expensive instrument (VT2X) with standardised costs of 0.009 **Sharpe ratio (SR)** units, the costs will be 12.6 × 0.009 = 0.113 SR units per year with the default look-back and 11.7 × 0.009 = 0.105 SR with the slower one.

It isn't worth slowing down the estimation of price volatility for a saving of 0.008 SR in costs, so I recommend you stick to the default look-back of 25 days. Also I suggest using an **exponentially weighted moving average (EWMA)** of daily squared returns, for which a look-back of 36 business days is the equivalent of 25 days.

With your 20% **volatility target** a cost level of 0.113 SR equates to an annual performance drag of 20% × 0.113 = 2.3% on V2TX, and less on the cheaper instruments. There will also be a small additional cost for rolling open futures positions into new delivery months.

It's also worth noting that 0.113 SR comes in safely under the maximum **speed limit** that I recommended in chapter twelve of 0.13 SR spent on costs each year.

Portfolio of trading subsystems

You've now got a set of six **trading subsystems**, one for each instrument, which you need to put together into a portfolio by setting **instrument weights** as I discussed in chapter eleven. Again this is a job for **handcrafting**, so we need to think about how to group instruments. The **correlation** matrix of subsystem returns in table 46 implies some obvious groupings, which I've put into table 47.

Additionally you are constrained by the minimum contract size problems which I discussed in chapter twelve, 'Speed and Size'. In particular the Euro Stoxx future needs to have an instrument weight of at least 20%. Less than this and even with the maximum possible position, at a **combined forecast** of 20, you wouldn't get the minimum of four instrument blocks that I recommended in chapter twelve.

---

161. Weights are 50% to carry, 21% to EWMAC16, 8% to EWMAC 32, and 21% to EWMAC 64. With trading rule turnovers from table 43 we get a weighted average of ([0.5 × 10] + [0.21 × 11] + [0.08 × 8.5] + [0.21 × 7.5]) = 9.57.

To avoid distorting the instrument weights too much, I propose putting 30% of the portfolio into the equities top level group, rather than the 25% that handcrafting would otherwise suggest. I then suggest that you put two-thirds of that 30% into Euro Stoxx, which gets it to the minimum 20%. The remaining 10% can go into VT2X **equity volatility index** futures.

I'm comfortable with this adjustment, since the alternative is not to trade equities at all, but a larger shift in weights would concern me.

TABLE 46: WHAT ARE THE CORRELATIONS OF THE TRADING SUBSYSTEMS IN THIS EXAMPLE?

	Euro$	T-note	Estxx	V2X	MXP	Corn
Eurodollar	1					
US T-note	0.35	1				
Euro Stoxx	0.07	0.07	1			
V2X	0.07	0.07	0.42	1		
MXP/USD	0.07	0.07	0.07	0.14	1	
Corn	0.07	0.07	0.07	0.07	0.18	1

The table shows the correlation of trading subsystem returns in the example system. These are derived from instrument returns correlations in table 49 in appendix C, which were then multiplied by 0.7 because we have a dynamic trading system (as recommended in chapter 11).

TABLE 47: HOW DO WE GROUP FUTURES CONTRACTS FOR HANDCRAFTING INSTRUMENT WEIGHTS?

1: Asset group	2: Asset class	Name of future
Interest rates	STIR	Eurodollar
	Bonds	5 year T-note
Equities	Equity indices	Euro Stoxx
	Volatility	V2X
Foreign exchange		MXP/USD
Commodities	Agricultural	Corn

The table shows the grouping of instruments in the staunch systems trader example. STIR = short term interest rate futures.

The **handcrafting** allocation process is shown below. Row numbers refer to table 8 (page 79). As I recommended in chapter twelve, I haven't adjusted these weights for different instrument costs, since there is no evidence that post-cost returns vary between instruments.

First level grouping Within asset groups	Interest rates: 50% to US 5 year T-note, 50% to Eurodollar. Row 2.
	Equities: 66.6% to Euro Stoxx (constrained), 33.3 % to V2X European volatility future.
	FX: 100% to MXPUSD. Row 1.
	Commodities: 100% to Corn. Row 1.
Top level grouping Across asset groups	Inter-asset correlations are between 0.07 and 0.18, all of which round to zero. In the absence of constraints, row 4 would apply and we'd have equal weighting.
	However we need at least 30% in the equities group as discussed above. This leaves 70% shared between three remaining groups, or with equal weighting 23.3% each.

You can see the final weights in table 48. Using the weights, the correlations in table 46 and the formula on page 297 I get an **instrument diversification multiplier** of 1.89.

TABLE 48: WHAT ARE THE FINAL INSTRUMENT WEIGHTS?

	Within asset group	Across asset groups	Final weight
Eurodollar	50%	23.3%	11.7%
US T-note	50%	23.3%	11.7%
Euro Stoxx	**66.6%**	**30%**	20%
V2X	**33.3%**	**30%**	9.8%
MXPUSD	100%	23.3%	23.3%
Corn	100%	23.3%	23.3%

*This table shows handcrafted instrument weights for the staunch systems trader example. Numbers in **bold** have been adjusted because of Euro Stoxx minimum size issues.*

Daily process

This process can be done using spreadsheets, or entirely automated if desired. Detailed calculations are shown in the trading diary below.

Get account value	Get today's account value to calculate **trading capital**.
Volatility target	Annualised cash volatility target equals **percentage volatility target** × **trading capital**. In this example we're using a 20% volatility target. Divide by 16 for **daily cash volatility target.***
Get latest prices	Get price for all **instruments**.
Get latest FX rates	Update FX rates (only USD/EUR needed in this example).
Calculate price volatility	Using a 35 day look-back **exponentially weighted moving average** as in appendix D (page 298), work out the **price volatility** of each instrument. With the FX rates and **block values** convert this to **instrument value volatility** using the formulas in chapter ten.
Calculate forecasts	Calculate **forecasts** for each **trading rule variation** and **instrument**. Apply the recommended cap of 20 to each forecast.
Combined forecast	Using forecast weights (such as those in table 48), and **forecast diversification multiplier** (1.3 in this example), calculate combined forecast for each instrument. Apply the recommended cap of 20.
Volatility scalar	**Daily cash volatility target** divided by instrument value volatility for each instrument.
Subsystem position	For each instrument the **combined forecast** multiplied by **volatility scalar,** divided by 10.
Portfolio instrument position	Subsystem position multiplied by instrument weight (as in table 48), and by instrument diversification multiplier (in this example 1.89).
Rounded target position	**Portfolio instrument position** rounded to nearest instrument block (whole futures contract).
Issue trades	Compare current position to rounded target position. If out by more than 10% then trade to get to target (**position inertia**).

* As usual to go from annual to daily volatility you divide by 'the square root of time', assuming around 256 business days in a year this is 16.

Trading diary

This diary is very close to reality, since I run a very similar system to this, albeit with many more instruments and a few extra trading rules. Spreadsheets detailing all the calculations are available on the website for this book, www.systematictrading.org.

15 October 2014

I've chosen today as the nominal starting date, to match the **semi-automatic trader** example earlier.

	Euro$	T-note	Estxx	V2TX	MXP	Corn
Daily volatility target (A)	$3,125	$3,125	$3,125	$3,125	$3,125	$3,125
Price (B)	97.35	118.9	2760	18.9	0.0726	399
Each point is worth (C)	$2,500	$1000	€10	€100	$500,000	$50
FX (D)	1	1	1.1	1.1	1	1
Block value (E) C × B ÷ 100	$2433.8	$1189	€276	€18.9	$363	$199.5
Price volatility, % (G)* F ÷ B	0.07	0.24	1.8	5.13	0.51	1.48
Instrument currency volatility (H) G × E	$170.4	$285.4	€496.8	€97.0	$185.1	$295.3
Instrument value volatility (I) H × D	$170.4	$285.4	$546.5	$106.7	$185.1	$295.3
Volatility scalar (J) A ÷ I	18.3	11.0	5.7	29.3	16.9	10.6

* I've kept the row identifiers the same in all three example chapters so that comparisons can easily be made. Row F has been omitted as you don't require volatility in points per day here.

	Euro$	T-note	Estxx	V2TX	MXP	Corn
Combined forecast (K)	15.8	20	-2.1	-11.7	2	-11.6
Subsystem position, contracts (L) K × J ÷ 10	29.0	21.9	-1.2	-34.3	3.4	-12.3
Instrument weight (M)	11.7%	11.7%	20%	10%	23.3%	23.3%

Instrument Diversification Multiplier (N)	1.89	1.89	1.89	1.89	1.89	1.89
Portfolio instrument position, contracts (O) L × M × N	6.40	4.83	-0.45	-6.45	1.49	-5.42
Rounded target position contracts (P = round O)	6	5	0	-6	1	-5

Notable positions are a large long in US treasury notes, which had been rallying strongly for a month giving positive **momentum**, and also had a **carry** forecast of over 19. The V2X also had a substantial short carry forecast of -20, and although volatility spiked substantially over the last two weeks, the very slowest **EWMAC** rules were still short after the steady fall in implied volatility for most of 2014.

1 December 2014

Let's move forward to 1 December. The system has made cumulative profits of around $10,000 so your **trading capital** is $260,000 and **annualised cash volatility target** is $52,000. There has now been a pronounced rally in the equity markets so we're now modestly long Euro Stoxx, with volatility easing and V2X falling in price. Interestingly the V2X forecast hasn't strengthened as much as you might expect, primarily because the **carry** forecast has weakened.

	Euro$	T-note	Estxx	V2TX	MXP	Corn
Daily volatility target (A)	$3,250	$3,250	$3,250	$3,250	$3,250	$3,250
Price (B)	97.41	119.1	3170	17.9	0.0707	415
Each point is worth (C)	$2,500	$1000	€10	€100	$500,000	$50
FX (D)	1	1	1.1	1.1	1	1
Block value (E) C × B ÷ 100	$2435	$1191	€317	€17.9	$354	$208
Price volatility, % (G)* F ÷ B	0.045	0.22	1.18	3.46	0.47	1.25
Instrument currency volatility (H) G × E	$110	$262	€374	€62	$166	$259
Instrument value volatility (I) H × D	$110	$262	$412	$68.1	$166	$259
Volatility scalar (J) A ÷ I	29.7	12.4	7.9	47.7	19.6	12.5

* I've kept the row identifiers the same in all three example chapters so that comparisons can easily be made. Row F has been omitted as you don't require volatility in points per day here.

	Euro$	T-note	Estxx	V2TX	MXP	Corn
Combined forecast (K)	14.1	16.5	4.7	-12.7	-1.7	-8.8
Subsystem position, contracts (L)	41.8	20.5	3.7	-60.6	-3.3	-11.0
K × J ÷ 10						
Instrument weight (M)	11.7%	11.7%	20%	10%	23.3%	23.3%
Instrument Diversification Multiplier (N)	1.89	1.89	1.89	1.89	1.89	1.89
Portfolio instrument position, contracts (O)	9.2	4.5	1.4	-11.46	-1.47	-4.9
L × M × N						
Rounded target position, contracts (P = round O)	9	5	1	-11	-1	-5

I'm not showing trades because there would have been trading almost every day between these two snapshot dates. We'll leave the staunch systematic portfolio there.

Epilogue. What Makes a Good Systematic Trader?

To FINISH THE BOOK I'D LIKE TO SUMMARISE WHAT I THINK ARE the main qualities a good systematic trader or investor should have.

A systematic trader should be *humble*, and underestimate their intelligence, skill and luck. Assume your trading will go badly, be prepared for that eventuality, and be pleasantly surprised if it doesn't. Don't try anything too clever; it is probably unnecessary and it's more likely to go wrong.

Use simple trading rules that have not been **over-fitted** or even fitted at all; constant no-rule forecasts, or discretionary forecasts combined with a strict stop loss policy. The **handcrafting** method of portfolio optimisation is both simple and effective.

You should be *sceptical*. Do not trust anybody. Don't trust the broker encouraging you to trade more, the trainer peddling you an expensive course, or the author[162] with a trading system that apparently worked for them, but might not be right for you.

Be *pessimistic*. Do not trust **back-tests**, even if you haven't over-fitted them, and even if they've been done on a **rolling out of sample** basis. The future is unlikely to be quite as good as the past. In my opinion a highly diversified system of systematic **trading rules** is unlikely to beat a **Sharpe ratio (SR)** of 1.0. If you're a **semi-automatic trader** who can't back-test their system, or an **asset allocating investor** with a **static** portfolio, then you should be even more pessimistic and assume maximum Sharpes of 0.5 and 0.4 respectively. You may do better, but you shouldn't expect to.

If you're making, or expect to make, steady gains with very few losses then there is a good chance you have a negative **skew** trading style which hasn't yet blown up, but probably will eventually. Adjust your **percentage volatility target** accordingly.

A good systematic investor will be *thoughtful*. You should know why you might be making money and why you might not. Understand your markets and your trading rules.

---

162. This includes me.

Thriftiness is another virtue. Know your trading costs. Stick to **speed limits**: I recommend you set your **turnover** so you never spend more than a third of the pessimistic expected Sharpe ratio for each **trading subsystem** on trading costs. Don't make your broker, or market makers, any wealthier.

You should be *nervous*. Only commit **trading capital** you can afford to lose. Use **Half-Kelly**: your maximum percentage volatility target should be half what you pessimistically expect your Sharpe ratio to be. At some point some instruments or trading rules in your portfolio will go badly wrong. Limit your exposure to this by trading the most diversified set of instruments and rules that you can. Stay away from low volatility instruments – they're expensive to trade and dangerous.

The best systematic traders will be *diligent* when creating their systems, but *lazy* when running them. Put the hard work into designing a safe system that you are comfortable with and then do not change it. Make a commitment: don't be tempted to meddle, improve or risk manage. These time-consuming activities usually destroy performance.

Finally to make money you need to be *lucky*. Even if you do everything right you could still be unprofitable if the chance turns against you. You can't entirely eliminate risk from investing but you should quantify it, and make sure you can cope with the likely downside.

So it only remains for me to say: Good Luck!

Glossary

Active fund, Active management	A **collective fund** where securities are bought and sold actively to try and outperform the general market. Normally more expensive than **passive funds**, as active fund managers think they can generate, and charge for, **alpha**. Hedge funds are an extreme example of active funds. As distinct from passive funds and **passive management**. See page 106.
Alpha	The returns of an **active manager** or trader can be split into **beta** and **alpha**. The beta are the returns you could get from investing in the general market, i.e. in a **passive index** fund. Any additional return due to the manager's skill is alpha.
Alternative beta	A kind of **beta**, but which requires active trading to achieve. So for example to earn the **equity value** premium, which is the return from being long low price:earnings (PE) and short high PE equities, you need to buy and sell the appropriate shares at the right time. Like **beta**, and unlike **alpha**, this kind of return does not require skill.
Annualised cash volatility target	See **volatility target**.
Asset allocating investor	An investor who usually does not forecast asset prices, but uses a systematic **framework** to create the best possible portfolio. See page ix and page 225.
Asset class	Name for a general kind of investable security, e.g. equities, bonds, commodity futures and commercial property are all asset classes.
Back-testing	A back-test is a historical simulation of what performance and behaviour would have been for a trading system, based on the data and prices that occurred in the past. See page 14.

Beta	Used as a shorthand for getting returns from being exposed to the market generally, without having any particular skill; as distinct from **alpha**. Owning a **passive index fund,** such as an ETF linked to the French CAC 30 stock market, will give you **beta** returns for the relevant market. See also **alternative beta**.
	Also: to what extent a particular asset is exposed to the overall market. Low beta assets have less exposure to the overall market, and are safer, than high beta assets.
Block value	The increase in value of one **instrument block** when it's price goes up by one percentage point. See page 154.
Bootstrapping	A method of **portfolio optimisation** which takes into account the uncertainty in historical data, unlike **single period optimisation**. See page 75.
Calibration	Fine tuning a **trading rule** by looking at the performance or behaviour of **variations** during **back-testing;** a kind of **fitting**. See page 52.
Carry	A trading strategy where you profit from the difference between yields and funding costs if prices remain unchanged. A recommended carry trading rule is discussed in chapter seven, on page 119 and in appendix B, from page 285.
	See also **FX Carry**.
Cash volatility target	See **volatility target**.
Cognitive bias	A psychological flaw in human thought processes which results in poor decisions being made. See page 12.
Collective fund	A kind of fund which buys you a share in a portfolio of securities. These can be **exchange traded funds,** mutual funds in the US, or in the UK investment trusts and unit trusts. Collective funds can be **active** or **passive**. See page 106.
Combined forecast	The forecast you get for a particular **instrument** after combining the individual forecasts from multiple **trading rules** and multiplying by the **forecast diversification multiplier**. See page 125.
Correlation, Correlated	A measure of how two things co-move. Normally used in relation to daily returns from assets or profits from **trading rules**.
	A correlation of -1 indicates two things always move in opposite directions, +1 indicates they always move in the same direction and 0 means there is no linear relationship (uncorrelated).
Daily cash volatility target	See **volatility target**.

Data first	A kind of **fitting** where you specify a very general trading rule or model of price movement with many parameters and then use a statistical method to find the best choice of parameters from the available data. Opposite to **ideas first**. See page 26.
Data mining	The process of **fitting** to historical data in such a way that you will always find at least one apparently profitable **trading rule**. For example, if you run thousands of **back-tests** for different rules over a particular historical period, at least one will look great. Because they are highly tuned to fit the past, data mined trading rules usually perform badly in a future that is never the same. Also see **over-fitting**.
Derivative	A way of benefiting from an asset going up or down in price without actually owning it. Futures, spread bets, options and contracts for difference are all examples of derivatives. Derivatives often provide more **leverage** than the underlying assets.
Diversification multiplier	A portfolio will have a lower **standard deviation** of returns than its individual assets, assuming they are not perfectly **correlated**. This assumes the assets all have the same **standard deviation** of returns.

The diversification multiplier multiplies portfolio returns to get them back to the same standard deviation as the underlying assets. It is always 1, for portfolios where all assets are perfectly correlated, or larger than 1. See **instrument diversification multiplier** and **forecast diversification multiplier.** See page 129. |
Dynamic	A strategy where we actively buy and sell assets to express opinions on risk adjusted asset returns. As opposed to **static**. See page 38.
Equity value	A type of **relative value** trading in the equity market where you buy 'cheap' stocks with low price earnings (PE), high divided yield or similar value characteristics, and sell 'expensive' stocks with high PE, low yield or similar.
Equity volatility index	A measure of how volatile an equity market is expected to be, derived from option prices. Sometimes called the 'fear index'. The key European index is the V2TX and in the US it's the VIX. Futures can be traded on each of these indices. See skew concept box, page 34.
Exchange traded fund (ETF)	Usually a type of **passive indexed**, **collective fund** which can be traded and owned like a normal equity, and has low fees. Some ETFs implement **dynamic** strategies and are more expensive.
Execution cost	Part of the cost of trading an **instrument**, equal to the difference between the mid-price and the traded price. Those who do not trade in large sizes can assume they will pay the bid (if selling) or offer (if buying), which implies it will cost them half the difference between the bid and the offer to trade. See page 179.

Expanding window	A way of doing **out of sample** testing. You pretend you are at a point in the past and then use data from the beginning of your price history up to that point to choose trading rules or portfolio weights. You then test those rules or weights on the data for a year after that point. Then you move forward a year to the next point and repeat. See page 56.
Exponentially weighted moving average (EWMA)	A kind of **moving average** where you weight more recent observations more heavily.
	If P_t is the most recent data point then the EWMA is:
	$(A \times P_t) + (A \times (1 - A) \times P_t - 1) + (A \times (1 - A)^2 \times P_t - 1) + ((A \times (1 - A)^3 \times P_t - 2) \dots$
	You can also calculate this recursively. If you have yesterday's EWMA E_{t-1} then today's EWMA is:
	$(A \times P_t) + (E_{t-1} \times (1 - A))$
	Used in the **EWMAC** trading rule and also in the estimation of **price volatility**.
Exponentially weighted moving average crossover (EWMAC)	A **trend following** trading rule where you take a fast **exponentially weighted moving average (EWMA)** of the price with a short look-back, and a slow EWMA with a longer look-back. If the fast EWMA is above the slow then prices have been rising and you buy, and vice versa.
	See page 117 and page 282 in appendix B.
Fitting	The process of picking the best **trading rule**. Usually this would involve running **back-tests** over historical data and finding the most profitable rule. See page 52. See also **ideas first** and **data first**, and **over-fitted**.
Forecast	An estimate of how much an **instrument**'s price will go up or down, translated into a numeric scale. The forecast can either be the discretionary forecast of a **semi-automatic trader** or the fixed forecast of the **asset allocating investor**; for **staunch systems traders** a single systematic **trading rule** or a **combined forecast** blending different trading rules. See page 110.
Forecast diversification multiplier	The **diversification multiplier** required so that the **combined forecast** for a particular instrument has the expected average absolute value (recommended value: 10). See page 129.
Forecast scalar	A value you multiply a **forecast** by to ensure it has the right average absolute value (recommended value: 10). See page 297.
Forecast weights	The weights used to combine forecasts from multiple **trading rules** into a single **combined forecast** for a particular **instrument**. See page 126.
Foreign exchange (FX) carry	A foreign exchange (FX) trading strategy where you borrow in low interest currencies, exchange the money for a high interest currency, put it into the bank, and earn the difference. This strategy will fail if the high interest currency depreciates by more than the gap in interest rates. See also **carry**.

Framework	The process I describe in this book to translate **forecasts** into actual investment decisions. The framework includes components for combining trading rules and **instruments, volatility targeting** and position sizing. Together with any trading rules the framework makes up the **trading system**. See page 95.
Fundamental data	Non-price data used for forecasting, e.g. earnings of a firm, inflation rates or weather forecasts. Opposite of **technical data**. See page 43.
Gaussian normal distribution	A statistical distribution which is shaped like a bell, often assumed for returns. If your returns are Gaussian normal then you will see returns one **sigma** or less around the average about 68% of the time, and returns two sigma or less about 95% of the time. See page 21.
Half-Kelly	See **Kelly criterion**.
Handcrafted optimisation	A method of **portfolio optimisation** where you set weights by hand, grouping assets together and using only estimates of **correlations** (and optionally, **Sharpe ratios**). See page 78.
Ideas first	A type of **fitting** where you conceive an idea, choose a specific trading rule and then **back-test** the rule on historical data. Opposite to **data first**. See page 26.
In sample	Using historical data to select trading rules or portfolio weights and then testing those rules on the same data, which means including future information. A bad thing. Opposite to **out of sample**. See page 54.
Index tracker	See **passive fund**.
Instrument	Something you trade or invest in, e.g. an equity like Apple stock, an oil futures contract or a spread bet on the EUR/USD FX rate. See page 101.
Instrument block	'One' of an **instrument** – the minimum discrete unit you can economically trade an instrument in, which might be 100 shares, one futures contract or £1 a point on a spread bet. See page 154.
Instrument currency volatility	The expected daily **standard deviation** of returns of owning one **instrument block**, measured in the currency of the instrument. Equal to **price volatility** multiplied by **block value**. See page 158.
Instrument diversification multiplier	A type of **diversification multiplier** that accounts for the diversification across the returns of **trading subsystems**. See page 169.
Instrument value volatility	The expected daily **standard deviation** of returns of owning one **instrument block**, measured in the same currency as the trader or investor's **trading capital**. Equal to **instrument currency volatility** multiplied by the relevant exchange rate. See page 158.

Instrument weights	In my **framework** the weights that different **trading subsystems,** each trading a single **instrument**, have in a portfolio of subsystems. See page 165.
Kelly criterion	A way of determining the **percentage volatility target** you should use, given your expectation of **Sharpe ratio (SR)**. A SR of 0.5 implies you should use a risk percentage of 50%. However it is safer to use **Half-Kelly** and set the risk to half what Kelly requires, i.e. for an SR of 0.5 set risk to 25%. See page 143.
Law of active management	An equation which states that the information ratio of a trading strategy is proportional to the square root of the number of independent bets made each year. See page 42.
Leverage	Borrowing to invest, either in an explicit way or by using a derivative such as a future or spread bet where your exposure is greater than your initial cash payment.
Liquidity	How easy it is to trade quickly in size without changing the price significantly. Shares in blue chip companies are liquid because you can usually sell $1 million worth within minutes at close to the prevailing price. A $1 million house cannot be sold in a single day without giving buyers a substantial discount from what it could achieve given more time. The blue chip shares are liquid; the house is not. See page 35.
Mean reversion	Any trading strategy where you assume asset prices will revert to an equilibrium or fair value. For example, you might think 1.70 is a fair value for the price of the GPB/USD FX rate. If the rate goes below 1.70 you'll buy pounds and sell dollars, and if it goes higher you'd sell pounds (and buy dollars). See also **relative value**.
Merger arbitrage	A trading strategy, where if a merger or takeover is occurring you buy the company to be acquired, and usually short sell the acquirer as a hedge. Normally this is done at a discount to the takeover price, the gap reflecting uncertainty about whether a deal will go ahead. Profits can be made by selecting deals where the gap is too large given the level of uncertainty. This is a negative **skew** style of trading, because occasional large losses are made when deals fall through.
Momentum	When asset prices go up after previous rises; or go down after falls. **Trend following** rules try and profit from momentum.
Moving average	A weighted average of a value over the last N points in time, where N is the look-back window. The weighting can either be a simple average, with all points equally weighted, or an **exponentially weighted moving average**, with more recent points given a higher weight. Used in the estimation of **price volatility**.
Open interest	The number of futures contracts outstanding for a particular **instrument**. A measure of how actively an instrument is traded.

Out of sample	Using historical data to select trading rules or portfolio weights without looking into the future. A good thing, in contrast to **in sample**. See page 54.
Over-fitted	When something is **fitted** in such a way that it matches the past data too well and is unlikely to perform well when actually traded. Sometimes referred to as curve fitting. Also see **data mining**. Refer to page 52.
Passive fund, Passive index, Passive management	A type of **collective fund** which is invested and managed passively in a portfolio of securities according to some predefined weights. Usually these funds are **index trackers** which follow indices such as the FTSE 100 or S&P 500. Passive funds are a cheap way to get broad market, or **beta**, exposure. As distinct from **active funds**. See page 106.
Percentage volatility target	The target expected annualised percentage risk your trading system is exposed to. When multiplied by **trading capital** we get the **annualised cash volatility target**. See also **volatility target** and page 138.
Portfolio optimisation	The process of finding the optimal (best) portfolio by deciding in which **portfolio weights** to hold your assets.
	Normally a portfolio consists of positions in various assets, e.g. stocks and bonds. In my **framework** portfolios can be of (a) multiple **trading rules** for which we find **forecast weights**, and for (b) **trading subsystems**, one per **instrument**, for which we optimise **instrument weights**.
	You should use **handcrafting** or **bootstrapping** to calculate portfolio weights; I do not recommend **single period optimisation**. See page 70.
Portfolio weighted position	The position you hold in an instrument at the trading system level. Because a trading system consists of a portfolio of **trading subsystems**, one for each instrument, this is equal to the instrument's **subsystem position** multiplied by the **instrument weight** and the **instrument diversification multiplier**. See page 173.
Portfolio weights	In general the weights that assets have in a portfolio. See **instrument weights** and **forecast weights**.
Position inertia	If the current position is less than 10% away from the **rounded target position** then to reduce costs you shouldn't trade. See page 174.
Predictable risk	The component of volatility in asset prices or portfolio returns which you can predict using estimates of **standard deviation** and **correlation**. See **unpredictable risk** and page 39.
Price volatility	The expected **standard deviation** of instrument price daily returns, in percentage points per day. See page 155.
Relative value	Any trading strategy where you buy something that is cheap, and sell something similar that is expensive as a hedge. For example, see **equity value**. Often a negative **skew** strategy, as we suffer occasional large losses.

Risk parity	A type of **passive fund** where assets are held in equal shares according to expected risk. See page 38.
Risk premium	The reward you get from investing in something that carries some risk. For example, equities are riskier than bonds so we should expect higher returns to compensate us. See page 31.
Rolling window	A method of **out of sample** testing. You pretend you are at a point in the past and then use data from the last N years (where N can be any value) up to that point to choose trading rules or portfolio weights. You then test those rules or weights on data for a year after that point. Then you move forward a year to the next point and repeat. See page 56.
Semi-Automatic Trader	A trader who makes their own forecasts about price movements in a discretionary fashion, but then incorporates them into a systematic **framework**. See page ix and page 209.
Sharpe ratio (SR)	A measure of how profitable a trading strategy is, with returns adjusted for risk. Formally it is the mean return over some time period divided by the **standard deviation** of returns over the same time period. In this book I normally use the annualised Sharpe ratio – annualised returns divided by annualised standard deviation.
	If we're not using derivatives the 'risk free' interest rate should be deducted from annualised returns before calculating the Sharpe ratio. See page 32.
Short selling	A way of benefiting from an asset's fall in price, usually used for equity trading. You would usually borrow the stock with a loan agreement before selling it. On closing the trade the stock is returned and you'll profit if the price has fallen since inception.
Sigma	Shorthand for one unit of **standard deviation**. See page 21.
Single period optimisation	The classic way of performing a **portfolio optimisation**: using a single average over historical data of asset return means, **standard deviations** and **correlations**; these estimates are then used to do a single optimisation.
Skew	A measure of how symmetric the returns from an asset or **trading rule** are. Positive skew means you get more losses and fewer gains. But the average loss is smaller than the average gain. Negative skew means you get more gains and fewer losses, and average losses are larger than average gains. See page 32.
Speed limit	A limit on how quickly you should trade an **instrument**. The speed limit will depend on the **standardised cost** of the instrument, and how much you are prepared to pay in **Sharpe ratio (SR)** units per year in costs. I recommend paying no more than 0.13 SR units if you are a **staunch systems trader** and 0.08 SR units for **semi-automatic traders** and **asset-allocating investors**. See page 187.

Standard deviation	A measure of how dispersed some data is around its average value. If your data points are $x_1, x_2, \dots x_n$ then the average $x^* = (x_1 + x_2 + \dots x_n) \div n$. The standard deviation is $\sqrt{\{(1 \div n)[(x_1 - x^*)^2 + (x_2 - x^*)^2 + \dots (x_n - x^*)^2]\}}$
	Often applied to daily returns in prices or trading system profits. An approximate way to calculate an annualised standard deviation of returns is to multiply the daily standard deviation by 16 (the square root of 256, approximately the number of trading days in one year). See page 21.
Standardised cost	A **volatility standardised** method of measuring costs which is comparable across **instruments**. To calculate, add up all the costs of trading C, including **execution costs**, fees and taxes. Then double to get the cost of a 'round trip' (a buy and sell), and divide by the annualised **instrument cash volatility** (*ICV*) of the instrument. The formula is $2 \times C \div (16 \times ICV)$. See page 181.
Static	A strategy where you do not actively trade the assets you are investing in because of changes in expected risk adjusted returns. As opposed to **dynamic**. See page 38.
Staunch Systems Trader	A trader who uses one or more systematic trading rules and incorporates them into a systematic **framework**. See page x and page 245.
Subsystem position	The position nominally held by a single instrument's **trading subsystem**, trading only one instrument with the entire **trading capital**, given a **forecast** of returns. Equal to the **volatility scalar** multiplied by forecast, divided by 10. See page 159.
Survivorship bias	A problem where assets that disappeared are missing from historic data sets, such as shares in firms which went bankrupt. Because we don't see the losses from these **instruments** we are likely to overestimate how profitable investing really was in the past.
Technical	A kind of **trading rule** that uses only price data to predict prices, such as **trend following**; no **fundamental** data is used. See page 43.
Trading capital	The amount of capital at risk in your **trading system**. Also see **volatility target**. See page 138.
Trading rules	A systematic rule used to predict whether the price of an **instrument** will go up or down, and by how much. When one or more trading rules are put into a **framework** they form a complete **trading system** for trading systematically. See page 109.
Trading subsystem	A **trading subsystem** is a notional part of a larger **trading system** which trades a single **instrument**. See page 103.

Trading system	A set of one or more **trading rules** within a **framework** creates a complete **trading system**; it makes forecasts about **instrument** price movements and translates these into positions and hence trades suitable for a particular level of **trading capital**.
	For **asset allocating investors** and **staunch systems traders** the **trading system** is made up of a portfolio of **trading subsystems**, one per instrument, for a fixed set of instruments and trading rules (although asset allocating investors use only one rule with a constant forecast).
	For **semi-automatic traders** the system is made up of discretionary forecasts for an ad hoc group of instruments, so the make-up of the group of trading subsystems will vary over time. See page 97.
Trend following	A **technical** trading strategy which tries to capture **momentum** in price; you buy things going up and sell things that have fallen in price. Tends to have positive **skew**.
Turnover	A way of measuring trading speed. Turnover is measured in round trips per year, where a round trip consists of a buy and a sell of an average sized position. So a **trading system** with a turnover of 10 units is expected to do ten buys and ten sells in a year. See page 184.
Unpredictable risk	The component of volatility in asset prices or portfolio returns which you didn't or couldn't predict in advance. This could be because **standard deviations** or **correlations** changed, or because your risk model was wrong. See **predictable risk** and page 39.
Variation	A variation on a **trading rule** has different parameter value(s) but is otherwise the same. For example 'buy in the range 1.5 to 2.0' is a variation of the general rule of 'buy in the range X to Y'. See page 53.
Volatility	A shorthand term for **standard deviation**.
Volatility look-back period	Period of recent time used to calculate a **standard deviation** of returns. Used to calculate the **price volatility** and in trading rules like **EWMAC**.
Volatility scalar	A parameter which accounts for the difference in the risk you want for your portfolio (**volatility target**) relative to the risk of an **instrument**. It's the number of **instrument blocks** you would hold if you invested your entire **trading capital** into one instrument, with a forecast of +10. Equal to **daily cash volatility target** divided by **instrument value volatility**. See page 159.
Volatility standardisation	Adjusting returns or costs so they have the same expected risk. See page 40.

Volatility target	The target expected **standard deviation** of returns for the entire **trading system**.
	Can be expressed in cash terms, in the same currency as **trading capital**, either as the **annualised cash volatility target** or **daily cash volatility target**. The **daily cash volatility target** is the **annualised cash volatility target** divided by 'the square root of time', which assuming a 256 business day year is 16.
	It can also be expressed as a **percentage volatility target**, as a percentage of **trading capital**. The cash targets are equal to trading capital multiplied by the percentage volatility target. See page 137.

APPENDICES

Appendix A. Resources

Further reading

The flawed human brain

Thinking, Fast and Slow, Daniel Kahneman, 2011, Penguin

   Excellent book on **cognitive bias.** A must read.

Beyond Greed and Fear, Hersh Shefrin, 2007, OUP USA

   Relatively short book on **cognitive bias** in finance specifically. Worth reading if you don't have time for *Thinking, Fast and Slow*.

The Education of a Speculator, Victor Niederhoffer, 1998, Wiley

   Fascinating and esoteric book by a famous partly systematic, negative skew, hedge fund manager. Part autobiography, part book on the philosophy of trading. Optional reading.

Systematic trading rules

More Money than God, Sebastian Mallaby, 2011, Penguin

   A history of hedge funds, but also a very readable guide to different strategies. Compulsory reading.

Expected Returns, Antti Ilmanen, 2011, Wiley Finance

   Comprehensive guide to the sources of returns and risk premia. Read after Mallaby, if you can cope with the sometimes technical treatment.

When Genius Failed: The Rise and Fall of Long-Term Capital Management, Roger Lowenstein, 2001, Random House

A **negative skew** disaster and a real-life example of the disadvantage of leveraging up too much on low volatility positions. Probably the most useful market history in this list and should be compulsory reading for anyone contemplating negative skew trading.

Rogue Trader, Nick Leeson, 1999, Sphere

Very famous example of when negative skew goes wrong; amongst other things Nick lost much of his money selling option straddles. Optional reading.

The Greatest Trade Ever, Gregory Zuckerman, 2010, Penguin

A great story about a positive skew trade that worked: John Paulson's bearish bet on mortgage backed securities. Optional reading.

The Black Swan, Nassim Taleb, 2008, Penguin

A book about unknown unknowns. Taleb's usual mixture of unique philosophy and market folklore. Interesting, but optional reading.

Trading rule fitting

Fooled by Randomness, Nassim Taleb, 2001, Penguin

A very interesting book on uncertainty in general. Compulsory for anyone who thinks back-testing is worthwhile.

Trading rules and forecasts

Trading Systems and Methods, 5th Edition, Perry J. Kaufman, 2013, John Wiley & Sons

The bible of trading strategies. Great resource for trading rule ideas if you need them.

Technical Analysis, Jack Schwager, 1995, John Wiley & Sons

This, and the next book, are the best in a large crop of similar books. Compulsory if you want ideas for new technical trading rules.

Fundamental Analysis, Jack Schwager, 1997, John Wiley & Sons

See above. Compulsory if you want to trade fundamentals.

Hedge Fund Market Wizards, Jack Schwager, 2012, John Wiley & Sons

Interviews with many successful hedge fund managers. There are many useful nuggets of information in here. The chapter on Michael Platt is the most relevant to systematic traders. Optional reading.

Volatility targeting

Fortune's Formula, William Poundstone, 2005, Hill & Wang

Highly readable story about the **Kelly criterion**, and the history of finance in general. Compulsory reading.

Semi-automatic trader

How to Win at Financial Spread Betting, Charles Vincent, 2002, FT Prentice Hall

This is one of several books which provide a good introduction to the mechanics of spread betting in its first half. I don't advise using the strategies in the second half, but then I would say that!

Asset allocating investor

FT Guide to Exchange Traded Funds and Index Funds, David Stevenson, 2012, Financial Times

UK book about ETFs.

The ETF Book, Richard Ferri, 2009, Wiley

US book about ETFs.

Staunch systems trader

Trading Commodities and Financial Futures, George Kleinman, 2013, Prentice Hall

One of many books that give a good introduction to futures trading. There are also some ideas for trading rules. A fine alternative would be any of the Schwager books mentioned above.

Sources of free data

For professional investors sourcing data is usually straightforward, but it can be harder for amateurs, especially those not wishing to pay. Sources of historical data that I've used are listed below. Website links are correct at the time of writing, but are subject to change.

Many brokers and exchanges provide access to live prices, usually with a 15 minute delay. This delay is not problematic unless you are trading on a high frequency basis or using execution algorithms.

www.quandl.com	Source of numerous kinds of price and **fundamental** data, both free and subscription. Has a powerful API to automate data collection, available for multiple languages.
	For my own trading I currently use a combination of data from my broker and quandl.
finance.yahoo.com	Source of equity and index data. Has an API to automate data collection.
www.bloomberg.com/markets/chart/data/1D/AAPL:US	One of the main providers of costly data for professional investors.
	As the link shows you can get a certain amount of free historic data from Bloomberg, if you know the reference code.
www.eoddata.com	Free/subscription source of equity data.
www.ivolatility.com	Source of option prices.
www.oanda.com/currency/historical-rates	Source of historic FX rates.
stats.oecd.org	Official source of macroeconomic data.
mba.tuck.dartmouth.edu/pages/faculty/ken.french/data_library.html	Academic source of **equity value** data.

Brokers and platforms

If you are not running a fully automated trading system, I hesitate to recommend a specific broker. A key selection criteria is price. Estimate the expected annual total fee from how often you're trading, in what size, and with what total account value. Then use this for comparison purposes.

Equally important is whether you can trade the products you want and with leverage if needed. Customer service should be a factor, but it is hard to evaluate in advance. Generally all other features are of secondary importance; although brokers seem to love jazzing up their platforms a flash website won't make you any more money.

For those running an automated system there is only one broker accessible to amateur clients that I can recommend at the time of writing and that is Interactive Brokers (which I use myself). This is because it offers a flexible API which can be used to fully automate your trading and although it is not easy to get it working there is some help on my website: www.systematicmoney.org/systematic-trading

There are online platforms that offer to implement your automated strategies for you, as distinct from software that runs on your desktop, which I discuss below. I haven't tested any of these but they look intriguing. Just be very careful, as you are handing over your money to someone else's software!

There are also now 'social trading' online platforms that allow you to put your money into other amateurs' systematic trading strategies. I would strongly advise against this.

Automation and coding

It is perfectly possible to run non-automated strategies using only simple spreadsheets. There are three avenues for implementing fully automated trading strategies. Firstly it is possible to use Excel to perform automated trading with Interactive Brokers, though this requires some knowledge of Visual Basic.

Secondly you can use commercially available software, of which probably the most ubiquitous are NinjaTrader, TradeStation and MetaTrader, as well as broker specific packages. I haven't used, and so can't recommend, any particular product. The obvious advantage of these is that they allow you to create an automated strategy without having to write software.

When deciding which to use, the most important criterion is the ability to implement your **trading rules** within the right **framework**. **Back-testing** technology is an added bonus, but make sure it is **expanding out of sample** or equivalently **walk forward**. Also it should allow you to fit across multiple **instruments** and include conservative cost estimates.

Finally you can code up your own trading strategy. In the short term this is far more work, although it's also the most flexible and powerful option. The Interactive Brokers API allows you to use several languages, and there are third-party wrappers available which widen this choice further. For example I use Python to run my strategy via a library which is wrapped around the broker's C++ API. I include some snippets of python code on my website to show you how to implement various parts of the framework.

Appendix B. Trading Rules

The A and B system: Early profit taker and early loss taker

I USE TWO SIMPLE TRADING RULES IN EXAMPLES THROUGHOUT THE book – the early profit taker and the early loss taker. These are both variations of a more general rule: the 'A and B' system. For the profit taker I use A = 5 and B = 20. The loss taker has these values reversed, A = 20 and B = 5. I don't recommend using the A and B system for actual trading, but I've included the specification here to satisfy the curious.

Specification

Parameters A and B	For a given **variation** you need two parameters, **A** and **B**.
Standard position size	A **standard position size** is $100,000, divided by the **instrument value volatility** (as defined on '"What's that in real money?" on page 158) measured in dollars at the time you take on your position.
Initial position	You go long one standard position size.
Deviation	A deviation is one daily **standard deviation** of returns, as measured at your last entry point. Note we use volatility in price points, not percentage points as normal. The volatility in price points is equal to the percentage point volatility (price volatility as defined in chapter ten, 'Position sizing', on page 155), multiplied by the current price.
Profit target when long	If the price rises by more than **A** deviations from your last entry price, then you should sell out and go short one standard position size (reverse your position). You are always long or short.
Trailing stop loss when long	If the price of the instrument falls by more than **B** deviations from its high since you entered, then sell and go short one standard position size.

On reversal	When you reverse your position re-measure the **deviation** level to set your stop loss and profit target levels, and to determine the new standard position size.
Profit target when short	When currently short you would generate a profit taking trade when the price falls by more than **A** deviations from your last entry price; and then go long.
Stop loss when short	You will generate a stop loss trade when a price rises by more than **B** deviations from its low, and then reverse your position by going long.

Notice that this is a complete **trading system**, not just a **trading rule**, since it tells you exactly what size positions to take. If you've read part three of the book you can probably see that the system does position sizing correctly, but for an arbitrary **volatility target** on a single **instrument**.

Here are some interesting characteristics of the A and B system.

If A is larger than B	The system will tend to hit stop losses more frequently, but when trends occur it will exploit them. This is the case for the early loss taker.
If B is larger than A	The system will take profits frequently but suffer losses on large adverse movements. This will be profitable if prices remain range bound. This is how the early profit taker behaves.
Larger values of B	Will mean that slower trends will be more profitable than faster ones.
Smaller values of B	The system will exploit faster trends better.

The stop loss rule defined for **semi-automatic traders** in part four of the book is based on the stop loss component of the A and B system.

The exponentially weighted moving average crossover (EWMAC) rule

The **EWMAC** trading rule was briefly introduced in chapter seven. The forecast is the difference, or crossover, between two **exponentially weighted moving averages (EWMA)** of the price, one fast and one slow. The difference is then standardised by the recent **standard deviation** of prices, and a **forecast scalar** applied to ensure we get an average absolute value of 10 for our forecasts.

In this version of the rule I assume you are working with daily prices for the relevant instrument, with no weekends in the price series. It is possible to work with intra-day prices, but this is slightly more involved.

Look-back windows, fast and slow	To pick up trends over different time periods you're going to want EWMAC variations which work over different horizons. For each variation you need to specify two look-back windows, in days: a shorter window for the fast EWMA L_{fast}, and a larger one L_{slow} for the slow EWMA.
	L_{fast} should be larger than 1, or you will only have one price in your average.
	For reasons I discuss below, I use the following pairs of look-back values for L_{fast} and L_{slow} 2:8, 4:16, 8:32, 16:64, 32: 128 and 64:256.
Decay parameters, fast and slow	The EWMA formula uses a decay parameter, A, which is between 0 and 1. This is equal to $2 \div (L+1)$ where L is the look-back window.* So you will have A_{fast} and A_{slow}.
	A short look-back and a high value of A means you are giving more weight to more recent prices, so the EWMA adjusts faster; and vice versa.
	* I use a look-back window to calculate the decay rather than specifying the latter directly, because it's more natural to think in terms of windows. If you're interested this formulation comes from the Python language's 'Pandas' package specification for an **EWMA**, which uses the term span rather than look-back window.
EWMA formula	If Pt is the most recent price of the **instrument** then the EWMA is:
	$(A \times P_t) + (A \times (1-A) \times P_{t-1}) + (A \times (1-A)^2 \times P_{t-1}) + ((A \times (1-A)^3 \times P_{t-2})...$
	You can also calculate this recursively. With yesterday's EWMA E_{t-1} then today's EWMA is:
	$(A \times P_t) + (E_{t-1} \times (1-A))$
	Note that if A = 1 then you are using only the current price in your EWMA, hence why I require L to be 2 or more.
Slow EWMA	The slow EWMA E_{slow} will be an EWMA using A_{slow} based on the price history.
Fast EWMA	The fast EWMA E_{fast} will be an EWMA using A_{fast} based on the price history.
Raw EWMA crossover	E_{fast} minus E_{slow} is the raw EWMA crossover.
	If this is positive then there has been a recent price uptrend, if it's negative then prices are trending down. Since both the EWMAs are measurements of price, the crossover tells you by how much prices have changed recently.
Standard deviation adjustment	This is the **standard deviation** of returns in price points, not percentage points as normal. The volatility in price points is equal to the percentage point volatility (**price volatility** as defined in chapter ten, 'Position sizing', on page 155), multiplied by the current price.

Volatility adjusted EWMA crossover	You should divide the raw EWMA crossover by the standard deviation of daily price changes (in price terms, not percentage points). As I pointed out in chapter seven, you usually need forecasts to be adjusted for return standard deviation.
Forecast scalar	The forecast scalar depends on the look-back window and is shown in table 49.
Forecast	The **forecast** is the **forecast scalar** multiplied by the **volatility adjusted EWMA crossover.** It should have an average absolute value of around 10.
Capped forecast	This is the forecast with capping of values above +20 and below -20.

What ratio of fast and slow look-backs to use?

To reduce the set of parameters to consider for evaluation, I first fixed the ratio of fast and slow look-backs. As this requires looking at performance to avoid over-fitting I initially used artificial data which contained trends of various lengths plus an element of noise. There was not much difference in performance over look-backs between 2 and 6, so I selected a ratio of 4. A subsequent check on real data confirmed this was reasonable.

This reduces the set of possible look-backs to 2:8, 3:12, 4:16, 5:20 and so on.

Which pairs of look-backs to use?

Different look-back pairs will capture different length trends. Since we don't know what length trends will occur in reality, I advise using a reasonable number of pairs. However it turns out that using the series of look-backs 2:8, 4:16, 8:32... gives enough coverage. As table 57 in appendix C (page 295) shows, the adjacent look-backs in this set have **correlations** of 0.90. Any intervening values that are added would have correlations above the cutoff of 0.95 which I recommend using to prune trading rule variations in chapter six, 'Forecasts'.

Beyond the pair 64:256 **turnover** the holding period gets excessively long, and as the **law of active management** suggests performance will be poor, it isn't worth adding any more pairs beyond this.

Which forecast scalars to use?

I use the technique in appendix D on page 297 with data from a large number of futures markets, which isn't likely to lead to **over-fitting** as I'm not looking at performance. This gives the forecast scalars shown in table 49.

TABLE 49: FORECAST SCALARS FOR DIFFERENT EWMAC LOOK-BACK PAIRS

	Forecast scalar
EWMAC 2,8	10.6
EWMAC 4, 16	7.5
EWMAC 8, 32	5.3
EWMAC 16, 64	3.75
EWMAC 32, 128	2.65
EWMAC 64, 256	1.87

The carry trading rule

I introduced the **carry** rule in chapter seven. The rule calculates an annualised **volatility standardised** expected return for the asset, assuming nothing happens to prices.

Because the carry rule is slightly different for various **asset classes**, the definition here is in two parts. The first part calculates the annualised *net expected return* in price points for different assets. Then in the second part, which applies to all assets, this is converted to a forecast.

Equities, bought with cash or on margin

Dividend yield, %	The expected dividend yield per year during the holding period, or for simplicity the historic dividend divided by current price.
Funding cost, %	Either:
	On a cash purchase the interest you could have received on your money if you had not invested it.
	If borrowing on margin your cost of funding.
Net expected return, %	Dividend yield minus funding cost.
Net expected return in price units	Net expected return % points, multiplied by the current price.

Equities, contracts for difference (CFD)

Dividend yield, %	The expected dividend yield per year during the holding period, or for simplicity just the historic dividend divided by current price.
Funding cost, %	The average of the interest you pay to fund a long position and what you receive on short positions.
Net expected return, %	Dividend yield minus funding cost.
Net expected return in price units	Net expected return % points, multiplied by the current price.

Foreign exchange, cash

Interest, %	The interest you get in the foreign currency.
Funding cost, %	The interest you pay to borrow the domestic currency.
Net expected return, %	Interest minus funding cost.
Net expected return in price units	Net expected return % multiplied by current price.

Spread bet, e.g. on FX or equities

Spread bet level	The level of the spread bet (mid-price). (I assume that the financing cost is wrapped up in the relationship between the spot and spread bet price.)
Spot level	The level of the spot price of the relevant instrument at the same time.
Net expected return over bet period	Spot level minus spread bet level.
Time to maturity	Time to expiry of the bet, in years. So a quarterly three-month bet would be 0.25.
Net expected return in price units	Net expected return over bet period divided by time to maturity.

Futures: If not trading nearest contract (preferred)

Current contract price	The price of the contract you are trading.
Nearer contract price	The price of the next closest contract. So if you are trading June 2017 Eurodollar it would be March 2017.
Price differential	Nearer contract price minus current contract price.
Distance between contracts	The time in years between the two contracts (current and nearer). For adjacent quarterly expiries it is 0.25 and for monthly 0.083.
Net expected return in price units	You need to annualise the price differential by dividing by the distance between contracts.

If you are already trading the nearest contract you obviously can't use this method.[163] Instead there is an approximation below, which assumes you get the same amount of expected return for the first two available contracts.

Futures: If trading nearest contract (approximation)

Current contract price	The price of the contract you are trading.
Next contract price	The price of the contract with the next expiry. So if you had June 2017 Treasury bonds it would be September 2017.
Price differential	Current contract price minus next contract price.
Distance between contracts	The time in years between the two contracts (current and next). For adjacent quarterly expiries it would be 0.25, for monthly 0.083 and so on.
Net expected return in price units	You need to annualise the price differential by dividing by the distance between contracts.

Now let us turn to the actual forecast calculation, which is the same for all assets.

---

163. Ideally you'd use the spot price relative to the future, but this isn't easily available except for equity indices.

Forecast calculation

Net expected return in price units	From relevant information above. Note this is an annualised measure.
Standard deviation of returns	This is the **standard deviation** of returns in price points, not percentage points as normal. The volatility in price points is equal to the percentage point volatility (**price volatility** as defined in chapter ten, 'Position sizing', on page 155), multiplied by the current price.
Annualised standard deviation of returns	Multiply the standard deviation of returns by the 'square root of time' to annualise it. Assuming 256 business days in a year you should multiply by 16.
Raw carry: Volatility standardised expected return	As I pointed out in chapter seven, you want forecasts to be adjusted for return standard deviation. So this is the net expected return in price units divided by the annualised standard deviation of returns.
Forecast scalar	The forecast scalar is 30. I explain below where the multiplier comes from.
Forecast	The forecast will be the forecast scalar times the raw carry.
Capped forecast	This is the forecast with values outside the range -20, +20 capped.

Which forecast scalar to use?

The raw carry measure is effectively an annualised **Sharpe ratio (SR)**, an expected return divided by standard deviation. I used the technique in appendix D and data from a large number of markets across different **asset classes** to work out the right forecast scalar. This gives a forecast scalar of around 30.

What is the turnover of carry?

It's hard to generalise about the **turnover** (round trips per year) of carry since it depends on the asset class and how often you update the value of the forecast. I suggest checking the forecast weekly to avoid spurious noise which can otherwise be a problem. If you do this then it is reasonable to use a rule of thumb value of 10 for the turnover of the carry rule.

Appendix C. Portfolio Optimisation

More details on bootstrapping

Bootstrapping 101

BRIEFLY, YOU SHOULD TAKE THE FOLLOWING STEPS, ASSUMING returns have already been **volatility normalised** and have the same expected standard deviation:[164]

1. Choose a random subset of past returns (either from all history or a recent period depending on whether an expanding or rolling window is being used).

2. Calculate the correlation and average returns implied by that subset of returns.

3. Run your normal optimisation using the correlation and mean returns of the subset.

4. Record the resulting instrument weights.

5. Repeat step 1 a number of times.

6. For each asset take all the instrument weights from past optimisations and average them out.[165]

In practice then there are a few options which you need to consider.

How should you select return periods?

In the simple example in chapter four I drew individual daily returns at random; 30 August 2002 could easily have been followed by 1 February 2000 in a particular subset. This makes life easier and is usually a reasonable approximation to reality. But sometimes this arbitrary selection might not make sense. Poor returns in one asset might often

---

164. Technically what we are using here is a non-parametric bootstrap which I believe was first proposed by David Jobson and Bob Korkie in the early 1980s.

165. I am assuming that all weights are constrained to add up to 100%. If this isn't the case then some renormalisation would have to be done here.

be followed by good returns in another. This time series correlation will be lost unless adjacent days are kept together.

In this case you need to do 'block' bootstrapping. Each subset will consist of an appropriate number of *consecutive* returns. The only randomness is in the choice of the starting date for the block. The length of the block needs to be long enough to capture any time dependence.

How long should each period be?

How many returns should be in each sample? A month of daily returns, a year or longer? Shorter periods mean that each optimisation will be more extreme. Their distribution will be wider and confidence intervals larger. With longer periods the results will be more sensible, but that doesn't mean the average will perform better.

This subject has been examined in some depth by academic researchers. My own analysis suggests that there is a small benefit from using longer periods; perhaps a 0.05 **Sharpe ratio** improvement from using multiple years versus only a month, assuming a couple of decades' worth of data in total.

A good rule of thumb is to use samples of returns equal in length to 10% of the period of history available. So if you had 30 years of data then you should use three year-long samples for each optimisation.

How many times to repeat?

Here the choice is clearer; more iterations always produces better results but with decreasing benefits. So there will be almost no value in doing 200 rather than 100 iterations unless your block size is very small relative to your history.

Does bootstrapping work?

Again academic research has focused on this subject in great detail. For me personally bootstrapping definitely wins over **single period optimisation** and equal weights. My own research using artificial data shows that single period can perform a little better when there is a lot of structure in the data, so that the underlying **Sharpe ratio (SR)** and **correlations** are quite different. Obviously equal weights are better when the underlying SR and correlations are very similar. However you will never know in advance or with certainty which of these situations you are in!

Overall bootstrapping is the most consistent method, with less variability in performance over different kinds of data sets. If anything these kinds of study probably understate the benefits of bootstrapping. This is because the random data generated isn't as noisy as real data.

Personally I also find bootstrapping to be as good or better than other, relatively complex, methods.[166]

Rule of thumb correlations

The following are approximate and should be used with caution. Remember **correlations** vary considerably over time, and can be much higher or lower than shown here. First I look at the correlation of instrument price returns across different 'super' **asset classes**. 'Volatility' refers to positions in **equity volatility indices**, such as holding a position in VIX or V2TX futures. To avoid showing negative correlations this is displayed as if you had a short position, i.e. you want volatility to fall.

TABLE 50: CORRELATIONS OF INSTRUMENT RETURNS, ACROSS SUPER-ASSET CLASSES

	Bonds	Equities	FX	Commodities	Volatility
Rates	1				
Equities	0.1	1			
FX	0.1	0.1	1		
Commodities	0.1	0.1	0.25	1	
Volatility	0.1	0.6	0.2	0.1	1

The table shows correlations given long positions in all assets except volatility – shown as if selling option risk or short VIX futures. Rates are interest rate sensitive assets, e.g. Bonds and STIR futures.

Next I break down the instrument returns for the asset classes that form the commodity and interest rate super classes (the other super classes do not have any decomposition).

---

166. Many solutions to the optimisation problem revolve around shrinkage – making the inputs of the calculation more like a 'prior' by shrinking towards them. I have used these techniques in the past and they do have some advantages. However two main difficulties are involved – the first being how much to shrink, the second where your prior comes from without itself containing forward looking information. Getting these right is tricky and an entire book would be needed to explain how to do it right. In contrast bootstrapping is very easy and needs no calibration.

TABLE 51: CORRELATION OF INSTRUMENT RETURNS, ACROSS ASSET CLASSES

	Bonds	STIR	Agricultural	Metal	Energy
Bonds (R)	1	0.5			
STIR (R)	0.5	1			
Agricultural (C)	-	-	1		
Metal (C)	-	-	0.2	1	
Energy (C)	-	-	0.25	0.35	1

The table shows the correlation of returns within commodity (C) and Rates (R) super classes.

In the next table I dig further into the agricultural, metal and energy asset classes.

TABLE 52: CORRELATION OF INSTRUMENT RETURNS, BY SUB ASSET CLASS, WITHIN COMMODITY ASSET CLASSES

	Grain	Softs	Livestock	Oil	Gas	Precious metals	Base
Grains (A)	1						
Softs (A)	0.4	1					
Livestock (A)	0.25	0.15	1				
Crude oil & products (E)	-	-	-	1			
Natural gas (E)	-	-	-	0.25	1		
Precious metals (M)	-	-	-	-	-	1	
Base metals (M)	-	-	-	-	-	0.5	1

The table shows the correlations for instruments in the sub asset classes within Agricultural (A), Energy (E) and Metal (M) asset classes.

Within the financial (bond, equity, FX) asset classes, the main distinction is regional, between emerging and developed markets.

TABLE 53: CORRELATION OF INSTRUMENT RETURNS FOR REGIONS WITHIN FINANCIAL ASSET CLASSES

Emerging and developed market bonds	0.35
Emerging and developed market STIR	0.35
Emerging and developed market equities	0.50
Emerging and developed market volatility	0.50
Emerging and developed FX rates	0.15

The next table gives typical values within regions and commodity sub asset classes.

TABLE 54: CORRELATION OF INSTRUMENT RETURNS, WITHIN REGIONS AND SUB ASSET CLASSES

For bonds in same region, different countries	0.75
For equities in same region, different countries	0.75
For FX rates in same region, different rates against USD	0.75
For volatility in same region, different countries	0.75
For commodities in same sub asset class, different products	0.70
For equities in same country, different industry	0.70
For equities in same industry, different firms	0.80

The final table of instrument return correlations covers bonds within the same country.

TABLE 55: CORRELATION OF INSTRUMENT RETURNS, FOR BONDS OR BOND FUTURES OF DIFFERENT DURATION IN SAME COUNTRY

	2 year	5 year	10 year	20 year	30 year
2 year	1				
5 year	0.80	1			
10 year	0.65	0.85	1		
20 year	0.50	0.80	0.85	1	
30 year	0.50	0.75	0.80	0.90	1

In my **framework** you will be optimising the weights of **trading subsystems**, each taking positions in one **instrument**, rather than looking at portfolios of positions in instruments. Because **asset allocating investors** have **static** portfolios they can use the correlation of the underlying instrument returns from tables 50 to 55 without any adjustment.

For **staunch systems traders** with **dynamic** forecasts a good rule of thumb is that the correlation between instrument subsystem returns will be around 0.70 multiplied by the correlation of instrument price returns.

We now turn to the correlations of different **trading rules** applied to the same instrument, which are used to find **forecast weights**. Let's begin with the correlation between different trading rules, rather than **variations** on a single rule.

TABLE 56: CORRELATION OF TRADING RULE RETURNS WITHIN AN INSTRUMENT

Between different styles, e.g. momentum and carry	0.25
Same style, different rules, e.g. EWMAC and other trend following rules	0.5

Correlations of variations of the same rule will obviously depend on the precise rule. Table 57 provides the correlations between returns of **EWMAC** variations.

TABLE 57: CORRELATION OF TRADING RULE RETURNS WITHIN AN INSTRUMENT, VARIATIONS ON EWMAC RULE

	EW 2	EW 4	EW 8	EW 16	EW 32	EW 64
EWMAC 2, 8	1					
EWMAC 4, 16	0.90	1				
EWMAC 8, 32	0.60	0.90	1			
EWMAC 16,64	0.35	0.60	0.90	1		
EWMAC 32, 128	0.20	0.40	0.65	0.90	1	
EWMAC 64, 256	0.15	0.20	0.45	0.70	0.90	1

Numbers shown are the fast and slow look-back respectively, in days.

Appendix D. Framework Details

Rescaling forecasts

IF YOU'RE GOING TO CREATE YOUR OWN TRADING RULES YOU NEED to rescale them, so that the average absolute value of the forecast is around 10. To do this you need to run a **back-test** of the trading strategy, although you only require forecast values and you don't need to check performance. You should also average across as many **instruments** as possible.

From the back-test you should measure the average absolute value of forecast values from a back-test, or at least eyeball them to estimate the average absolute forecast. These values should be roughly similar across instruments and long periods of time, otherwise your trading rule could be badly specified and not properly **volatility normalised**.

Once you have the average absolute value then you should divide it into 10. The result is the trading rule's **forecast scalar**. So for example if the average absolute value was 0.3 then the scalar would be $10 \div 0.3 = 33.33$.

Calculation of diversification multiplier

Forecast diversification multiplier

Given N **trading rule variations** with a **correlation** matrix of forecast values H and **forecast weights** W summing to 1, the diversification multiplier will be $1 \div [\sqrt{(W \times H \times W^{T})}]$.[167]

Any negative correlations should be floored at zero before the calculation is done, to avoid dangerously inflating the multiplier.

---

167. 'T' is the transposition operator.

Instrument diversification multiplier

Given N **trading subsystems** with a correlation matrix of returns H and **instrument weights** W summing to 1, the diversification multiplier will be $1 \div [\sqrt{(W \times H \times W^T)}]$.[168]

Any negative correlations should be floored at zero before the calculation is done, to avoid dangerously inflating the multiplier.

Spreadsheet example (for either application)

For a three asset portfolio, if the correlation matrix is in cells A1:C3 and the relevant weights are in cells F1:F3, then the diversification multiplier will be:

```
1/SQRT(MMULT(TRANSPOSE(F1:F3), MMULT(A1:C3,F1:F3)))
```

Calculating price volatility from historic data

In a spreadsheet package, assuming that the column A contains daily prices, then you first populate column B with percentage returns:

```
B2 = (A2 - A1) / A1, B3 = (A3 - A2) / A2, ...
```

You can then calculate the price volatility from row 26 onwards, using the default of a 25 day moving average:

```
C26=STDEV(B2:B26), C27=STDEV(B3:B27), ...
```

The alternative is to use an **exponentially weighted moving average (EWMA)** of volatility. In general for some variable X if you have yesterday's EWMA Et-1 then today's EWMA given a smoothing parameter A is:

```
(A × X_t) + [E_{t-1} (1-A)]
```

First of all you need to calculate the A parameter, based on your **volatility look-back**, using the formula A = 2 ÷ (1 + L). For my suggested default look-back of 36 days, equivalent to a simple moving average of 25 days, we get A = 0.054.[169]

Assuming you've put 0.054 into cell AA1, and the returns are in column B, in column C we get the squared returns:

```
C2 = B2 ^ 2, C3 = B3 ^ 2, ...
```

---

168. 'T' is the transposition operator.
169. This is set to give the same half-life as the default look-back of 25 days for a standard moving average.

You set your first estimate of the variance equal to the first square return:

```
D2 = C2
```

After that you set the estimate recursively based on your smoothing parameter:

```
D3 = C3 × AA1 + ((1 - AA1) × D2)

D4 = C4 × AA1 + ((1 - AA1) × D3) ...
```

Finally the actual volatility is the square root:

```
E2 = SQRT(D2), E3 = SQRT(D3), ...
```

Acknowledgements

This book only exists because I spent seven years at AHL learning the craft of systematic trading, although there are no corporate secrets revealed here (as their lawyers will be pleased to know). I wouldn't have been able to write this without spending most of a decade immersed amongst a group of people who almost uniquely in the finance industry managed to be incredibly clever and successful, whilst still being fantastically nice and interesting people to work with.

There are many people I'd like to thank individually who worked, or still work, at AHL, their parent company the Man Group, and their research centre the Oxford Man Institute; but it would take another book to do it. You know who you are.

I'd like to thank my friend Pietro Parodi for his feedback on early drafts of the theoretical chapters where his outside expert viewpoint was invaluable. One former AHL colleague I will mention by name is Thomas Smith. Whilst launching his own hedge fund, Thomas still found the time to spend dozens of unpaid hours reviewing drafts of my work, and behaved exactly like he did when we worked together; he was never afraid of telling me when I had written something that was unintelligible, meaningless, pointless or wrong (and sometimes all of those at the same time).

I'm very thankful to Stephen Eckett at Harriman House for discerning the seed of an interesting idea in amongst the turgid ramblings of my original proposal. My editor Craig Pearce has managed the difficult job of reassuring me that I've written a good book, whilst also politely suggesting how it could be improved.

Last, but certainly not least, I'd like to thank my family. One day they came home and found that their normal office working father and husband had been replaced with a stay at home writer. Worse still he was not creating something interesting like the next Harry Potter, but was instead writing "Some boring book about money". Despite that you have still been the most supportive and wonderful people I could ever ask for. Thank you for that, and for everything.

Index

THANKS
FOR READING!

Our readers mean everything to us at Harriman House. As a special thank you for buying this book, let us help you save as much as possible on your next read:

If you've never ordered from us before, get £5 off your first order at **harriman-house.com** with this code: st51

Already a customer? Get £5 off an order of £25 or more with this code: st25

Get 7 days' FREE access to hundreds of our books at **volow.co** – simply head to the website and sign up.

Thanks again!
from the team at

Codes can only be used once per customer and order. T&Cs apply.

www.ingramcontent.com/pod-product-compliance
Ingram Content Group UK Ltd.
Pitfield, Milton Keynes, MK11 3LW, UK
UKHW010835150125
453528UK00003B/21